Praise for

The Financial Services Marketing Handbook:
Tactics and Techniques That Produce Results
by Evelyn Ehrlich, Ph.D., and Duke Fanelli

"Marketers who understand the complex and rapidly changing financial services industry are rare and increasingly in demand. *The Financial Services Marketing Handbook* **is a unique and invaluable training tool for beginners that also offers new insights to veteran financial marketers**."

ANDREA TRACHTENBERG
Senior Vice President, Head of Global Marketing
Lehman Brothers Wealth & Asset Management

"Until now, financial marketing has lacked a standard reference work that encompasses what every practitioner should know. **Ehrlich and Fanelli are recognized industry veterans who have combined their own broad-ranging experience with fundamental principles of marketing.** This is a must-have book for every financial advertising and marketing professional."

BILL WREAKS
Publisher, *Journal of Financial Advertising & Marketing*
President, Financial Communications Society (2002–2004)

"Today's financial sales professionals face a range of new challenges that require strategic understanding and tactical planning ability. ***The Financial Services Marketing Handbook* gives sales professionals a road map to success, through real-world examples, practical how-to's, and a structured approach to market planning.**"

MARY RUDIE BARNEBY
First vice president and divisional sales manager at a major US brokerage firm
Past president, Financial Women's Association

"Combining a solid academic orientation with the insights of knowledgeable practitioners, *The Financial Services Marketing Handbook* should prove **an invaluable text in both undergraduate and graduate level business programs**."

PROFESSOR IRV SCHENKLER
Stern School of Business, New York University
Coauthor, *Guide to Media Relations*

"This is truly time well spent—**a practical, powerful, and engaging guide to all aspects of financial services marketing**. Timeless in scope, this is a guide you'll want to keep within easy reach for years to come."

CLIFF OBERLIN AND JILL POWERS
CEO and President of Oberlin Financial Corporation
Authors of *Building a High-End Financial Services Practice*

THE
FINANCIAL SERVICES
MARKETING
HANDBOOK

Also available from
BLOOMBERG PRESS

22 Keys to Sales Success:
How to Make It Big in Financial Services
by James M. Benson and Paul Karasik

Brands and Branding
by Rita Clifton and John Simmons, et. al.

Full Frontal PR:
Getting People Talking About You, Your Business, or Your Product
by Richard Laermer with Michael Prichinello

Building a High-End Financial Services Practice:
Proven Techniques for Planners, Wealth Managers, and Other Advisers
by Cliff Oberlin and Jill Powers

Getting Started as a Financial Planner
by Jeffrey H. Rattiner

A complete list of our titles is available at
www.bloomberg.com/books

THE
FINANCIAL SERVICES
MARKETING
HANDBOOK

Tactics and Techniques
That Produce Results

Evelyn Ehrlich, Ph.D., and Duke Fanelli

BLOOMBERG PRESS

PRINCETON

First edition published 2004

1 3 5 7 9 10 8 6 4 2

Library of Congress Cataloging-in-Publication Data

Ehrlich, Evelyn.
    The financial services marketing handbook : tactics and techniques that produce results / Evelyn Ehrlich, Duke Fanelli. – 1st ed.
        p. cm.
    Includes bibliographical references and index.
    ISBN 1-57660-156-0 (alk. paper)
1. Financial services industry–United States–Marketing. 2. Financial planners–Marketing. 3. Customer relations. 4. Financial services industry–Computer network resources. I. Fanelli, Duke. II. Title.

HG181.E38 2004
332.1'068'8–dc22   2004009637

Contents

Section One

Strategic Market Planning

S e c t i o n   T w o

Marketing Tactics

Figures and Tables

Acknowledgments

Many people helped us by giving their time and by sharing their knowledge and contacts. We would both like to thank the people who were instrumental in getting this project off the ground: Goldie Alfasi-Siffert, Sandy Anderson, and Jim Levine. Barb Seitz provided invaluable design and layout suggestions. We would also like to thank those at New York University's Center for Marketing for their help in developing our Financial Services Marketing course: Renée Harris and Debbie Saccochio. Bill Wreaks was enormously helpful, with everything from the NYU course to referrals from his own vast knowledge of financial advertising. And, of course, we would particularly like to thank our editor, Jared Kieling, for his support and thoughtful editing of the manuscript, along with his editorial colleague Tracy Tait and everyone we've been fortunate to work with at Bloomberg Press.

Evelyn Ehrlich would particularly like to thank the following for providing information and contacts: Stephanie Ackler, Wachovia Securities; Richard Alpert, TIAA-CREF; Mary Barneby, UBS; Pat Bertucci, *Institutional Investor;* Bob Burke, Mercer Consulting; Brian Carty; Anne Cawley, Neuberger Berman; Sheila Colucci, Guardian Life; William Craeger, Merrill Lynch; Charlie Fisher, Triad Securities; Seija Goldstein; Lenore Kantor, Bank of New York; Carolyn Kelly, Unisys; Leslie Klein, J. P. Morgan Chase; Wendy Leibowitz; David May, Goldman Sachs; Patti Norton, Bear Stearns; Jennifer Putney, Pentegra; Lynthia Romney; Irv Schenkler, Stern School of Business, NYU; Nancy Sellar, Financial Women's Association; Gregg Sibert, Silver Communications; Tom Tarrant, Jefferies & Co.; Andrea Trachtenberg, Lehman Asset Management; Jane Washburn; Betsy Werley, J. P. Morgan Chase.

Duke Fanelli cowrote this book from a desire to provide financial services marketers and practitioners with a tool to help them grow and prosper in this important and exciting profession. His contribution to this book would not be possible without his wife Donna's caring and unyielding support and enthusiasm for this book and all his endeavors; his children Michael, Carina, and Alicia's daily inspiration; his supportive parents, for always being there; his friends and colleagues at AXA Financial who provided encouragement, advice, and invaluable marketing insight; and the Association of National Advertisers for their readiness to provide background and research for this book.

THE
FINANCIAL SERVICES
MARKETING
HANDBOOK

The Unique Challenges of Marketing Financial Services

Marketing financial services used to be easier. Banks gave a toaster to a new depositor and had a customer for life. Stockbrokers rarely left their parent company to go to a competitor. Institutional financial services was a clubby business in which multimillion-dollar deals were negotiated on the golf course. No more. Today, competition in financial services is fierce; sales and market-share growth can hinge on a few basis points, a friendlier voice on the phone, or an easier-to-navigate website. Not only has competition become more intense, financial services have also changed structurally. Old customs and laws that isolated banks by geography and separated investment banks from commercial banks, and insurance companies from mutual fund companies, have disappeared.

Now, everyone is competing for hot business segments. Retirement services, for example, are offered by banks, brokerages, mutual funds, insurance companies, and independent advisers. And it's not just customers they're competing for. With mergers and acquisitions occurring all the time, financial companies are no longer lifelong employers to whom employees naturally feel loyalty. Today's financial marketplace is a free-for-all, where top sales producers act like pro basketball players, demanding signing bonuses and salaries that can far exceed the CEO's.

But even as the financial industry has undergone momentous structural change, financial services marketing has remained pretty much what it's always been: passive, conservative, and relatively undisciplined. The words are different now; marketing managers talk about "brand management" and "customer value" and "share of wallet." But with few exceptions, financial services marketers are using old and not always effective methods of acquiring and retaining customers and sales professionals. This is true both in consumer and institutional markets, in traditional brick-and-mortar businesses like banks, and in cutting-edge businesses like online brokerages.

Some financial companies have attempted to update their methods by applying lessons learned in more marketing-oriented disciplines, such as consumer products. And there are certainly lessons to be learned that way. One of the objectives of this book is to introduce and apply modern marketing principles to the practice of financial marketing.

But financial products are not consumer products. In fact, they're not products at all in the way product marketing is usually described. Nor are they altogether like services. The financial industry operates in a unique way, and its marketing tasks are correspondingly complex. Consider an example: Product marketers can target consumers and can position and brand their products with the confidence that all samples of their products are manufactured to be the same—every bottle of Stolichnaya vodka tastes the same, looks the same. But a marketing manager at a private bank can't make the same assumption. The experience that clients have

Advertising Is Not Marketing

We've run into a lot of people, often in sales, who think that the most essential thing you need in order to improve sales is advertising. Or conversely, we've run into other people, also often in sales, who don't believe in marketing because advertising doesn't work. So let's get this straight right away; advertising is only one tool in marketing, and it's not always a central one. Anyone who wants to increase business is going to look for the fastest and easiest way to do it, which usually means committing a lot of money. And yes, a good ad campaign can call attention to a new or under-recognized product, as Fallon Worldwide demonstrated with its brilliant campaign for Archipelago.

But marketing is a discipline that requires strategic thinking more than it requires a big budget. Careful planning means setting goals, choosing target market segments, determining or creating a product's differentiation and positioning, and selecting the tactics that will get the product noticed and bought by your targets. Successful marketing can mean playing golf with your best client's CEO, or it can mean opening new markets in Asia. What's important is not just what you do but why you do it.

These ads were featured in one of the most-talked-about campaigns on Wall Street in 2001–2. Archipelago was created in 1997 as one of four electronic communications networks (ECNs) to provide a system for traders to find buyers or sellers of Nasdaq stocks electronically. Whereas most business-to-business advertising in the financial services industry is staid to the point of boredom, Archipelago sought to quickly make its name recognized on Wall Street. Its edgy and often outrageous print campaign succeeded in generating "buzz"—and helping the company's salespeople get appointments with prospects.

of the bank's service will differ, depending on the particular private banker who serves them and on support staff throughout the organization.

If financial products don't act like products, neither do they act entirely like services. Consider that, in many cases, a "product" will be sold not by someone who works for the parent company but by someone who is independent—an insurance broker, pension fund adviser, or personal financial planner. Or they may work for the parent company but still act independently, as do many stockbrokers who can easily walk away to a new firm. Your job as a marketer is not only to make sure that sales professionals are sustaining your brand strategy but also to keep them selling your product. You've got a two-tiered marketing task: selling the customer and selling the salesperson.

But note that the ads, while certainly attention-getting, work on the level of matching the brand image with the firm's positioning strategy. The one-word headlines "Anonymity" and "Information" express some of the company's most important offerings. Other ads in the series, always using one-word headlines, included "Consistency" and "Liquidity." Thus, if

Not your typical financial services advertising. These ads not only produced buzz but also supported the marketer's message.

the targets only saw the photo and the headline, they would have a pretty good idea of what Archipelago could do for them. The point is that smart advertising is only one of the tactics that marketers can use to support their overall goals. See chapter 4 for a more detailed discussion of advertising and what makes it effective.

Note that in 2004, however, as Archipelago prepared to go public, it abandoned its cheeky humor for a more staid image designed to appeal to corporate chieftains.

And this only begins to describe the challenges for the financial services marketer. Even defining financial services is hard in an industry that encompasses everything from mass-marketing of consumer banking, insurance, and investments to one-on-one selling of institutional products and services that may cost millions of dollars.

This book is designed for anyone whose job it is to market or sell any financial product or service—consumer or institutional—through a multitude of sales channels. The following chapters provide the basic tools and techniques that every financial marketer needs to be familiar with, along with case studies of how these methods have been applied (some successfully, some less so). To begin, let's look more closely at how financial marketing is different.

Products or Services?

In order to apply general marketing principles to financial services, we first need to ask: are the goods being sold as products or as services? What difference does it make? For your bottom line, plenty. Let's say, for example, that you're in charge of a new credit card, called Topnotch, for the high-net-worth market. It offers lots of extras and has a hefty annual fee. One of your jobs, as a product marketer, would be to use focus groups, surveys, and other market research methods in order to help the product people determine which bells and whistles would be most valued by prospective customers and how much they would be willing to pay for them. You would then need to pinpoint your product's advantages over your competition and find a way to communicate these benefits to your target market segment. This is all classic product marketing.

You've done all this brilliantly, and your Topnotch card has taken off beyond your projections. But then you start noticing some disturbing numbers—customers are canceling their cards far beyond the levels you anticipated. And after a lot of interviews with current and former customers, you find out that the service provided on your card is uneven. Sometimes the customer service representatives are extremely helpful, but other times they leave the customer unsatisfied. And the reason is that even though they are trained to offer Topnotch service, the reps' compensation is tied to the number of customers they service rather than the satisfaction of each customer they service. As a result, the customers' experience with the card does not match the brand image of luxury and customization. Your mistake was to market a product (all Topnotch cards are the same), rather than a service (each experience of using the Topnotch card is different).

Financial Services as Products

As the example shows, financial services are neither products nor services, but have elements of each. Here are some ways in which financial services are like products:

Separability. Unlike many services, the production of many financial products can be separated from their consumption. A consumer does not have to be physically present in the bank to use a checking account. Like an athletic shoe, the checking account is "manufactured" in advance of its sale and subsequent use.

Lack of perishability. Unlike a dinner reservation, a credit card will be there when the customer wants one. It is not perishable. This makes it easier for the financial provider to manage supply and demand. Unlike the finite seating in a restaurant where every customer wants a table on Saturday at 8 p.m., the supply of credit cards can be adjusted to meet demand.

Mass production. Services are typically created and delivered one at a time, while products are usually mass-produced. Whereas many financial services are individualized, such as financial advice, others can be mass-produced and mass-marketed, like insurance policies, college savings accounts, or data analysis systems for bond traders. Mass production enables mass distribution and cost savings.

Financial Services as Services

A checking account may be "manufactured," but it is not tangible. Unlike a car, you can't touch it or examine its features with your eyes and hands. It has no physical presence. Despite the vocabulary often employed in the financial world, financial services "products" are not entirely products, because they are intangible. Intangibles have certain common qualities.

Low cost of entry. There is little or no cost to manufacture, inventory, or distribute a financial "product." Start-up costs are very low, which means that there are few barriers to creating—or copying—a financial product. Although there may be legal restrictions and expenses associated with marketing, the capital costs of creating a new product are negligible. Also, there are no warehousing or physical distribution costs.

Speed to market. A manufacturer of a new toy or airplane must develop blueprints, build models, test the integrity of the design, and often reengineer several prototypes before a product can even be test-marketed. But in financial services, the idea is the product. If an investment bank comes up with a new

Nearly Anyone Can Start a Hedge Fund

After the stock market crashed in early 2000, the new "hot" investing vehicle for institutions such as pension funds became the hedge fund. These lightly regulated investment funds are so named because of their ability to hedge their investments by buying options, futures, or otherwise protecting against downside risk—and oftentimes they far exceed the return of the stock market.

Starting a new hedge fund requires not much more than a telephone and a computer. Hedge fund managers are active traders, which makes them highly profitable to Wall Street trading and clearing firms. As a result, large firms such as Bear Stearns and Morgan Stanley, along with many smaller firms, have prime brokerage programs that attempt to woo new hedge fund managers with a range of services. These may include providing office space, technology services, marketing support, initial advice on legal and accounting issues, and even start-up money and introductions to the brokerage firm's own clients. Thus, the amount of capital a new hedge fund manager has to raise up front can be very small indeed.

Not surprisingly, given the ease of entry and potentially huge fees, the number of hedge funds has skyrocketed. In 1992, there were 2,000 hedge funds; by 2003, there were nearly 7,000.[1] But as new hedge funds enter the marketplace and more brokerage firms seek their business, profit margins are being squeezed. According to *Institutional Investor,* fees on hedge fund–related services fell by as much as 30 percent from 2001 to 2002.

way to securitize cash flow (say, by selling shares of the future royalties of a pop singer), the bank can start selling the securities almost as soon as the ink is dry on the offering plan.

Lack of exclusivity. A successful new manufactured product can usually enjoy a period of exclusivity, during which there is no competition. The product may be patented (like a drug) or trademarked (like software) to prevent competitors from using exactly the same formulation. Or the costs of building a competitive manufacturing facility (as for a new airplane model) are just too high to be feasible.

But in financial services, there are few protections, and the cost of entry is low. Merrill Lynch "invented" the first CMA (cash management account) in the late 1970s. It was the first time that a brokerage firm had offered an account that combined investments with checking. It was very successful and brought Merrill a lot of new business. But within a few years, every brokerage firm had one. Although Merrill trademarked the name, it could not protect the idea. Its first-mover advantage quickly dissipated.

Service Is What It's About

Because it's easy to copy a new financial idea, product differentiation is difficult. Whatever bells and whistles you come up with for your product, for example, affiliation credit cards or online bill paying, can be easily replicated by your competitors. Over time, additional value has to come from somewhere other than the product itself.

Where does added value come from? Service is almost always the most important differentiator. With products, you can control quality at the source—in the manufacturing process. With a service, quality is added (or not) by the people who sell to or manage the clients. This means that the quality of your product can vary because of the individual who is selling or providing it. All Hewlett-Packard color copiers Model 2210 are the same, but all financial advisers are not. Thus, one of the biggest challenges within organizations that are marketing financial services is controlling service quality. This is particularly difficult in those areas where third parties who are not employed by the service creator are responsible for servicing your product—such as investment advisers, independent insurance agents, or third-party administrators of pension plans.

Marketing Money Is Different

Key marketing issues differ from service to service—marketing a vacation resort, for example, will involve a different set of variables than marketing a law firm. So it is with financial services, which have their own unique service attributes.

Psychology of Money

Financial services are about money, and money carries a lot of psychological baggage. People's attitudes toward money are highly emotional. This may matter less at the institutional level, but for the consumer marketer, hitting the right emotional notes can be critical. One financial institution, for example, developed a typology that classified attitudes and behaviors toward financial matters

Financial Personalities

Are there identifiable financial personality types? Some researchers have attempted to apply conventional psychological measurement tools to financial behavior. One such study, conducted by Shoya Zichy, a psychologist specializing in financial behavior, has analyzed such data using the familiar Myers-Briggs personality typology. Zichy found, for example, that there are correlations between certain financial attitudes—such as risk tolerance, desire for financial planning assistance, and degree of interest in financial issues—to one's Myers-Briggs personality type. For example, "extroverted perceivers" had a higher tolerance for risk than other personality types, but "introverted judgers" were more likely to be successful investors, because they placed a high value on setting up and sticking to a well-defined asset-allocation strategy.[2]

into five categories, based on the following variables: degree of control over spending and saving, interest in and knowledge about money matters, desire to accumulate versus spend, and trust in or need for advice.

Other typologies have addressed investor psychology—for example, market-follower versus contrarian, degree of risk tolerated, or spending and saving behaviors. Spending and saving typologies go back to Freud, who described compulsive spenders and non-spenders, as well as subtypes, such as the pretended wealthy and the pretended poor. Modern psychologists have built on Freudian taxonomies, describing categories such as "fanatical shoppers," "passive buyers," and "esteem buyers." Marketers of debt products are particularly interested in the psychology of spending because they seek to identify targets who are likely to build up balances while continuing to pay them off steadily. There is a fine line between overspenders who default and those who do not.

Third-Party Relationships

Because money is so personal, relationships become very important in some areas of financial services—particularly investments, retirement planning, and insurance. In these areas, consumers don't necessarily buy a brand (Salomon Smith Barney) so much as they do an individual (my stockbroker). In fact, in some cases, the person who sells the product is also the creator of the product, for example, independent financial advisers.

For the marketer, the fact that the customer has a relationship with a financial intermediary is a double-edged sword. On the one hand, customer loyalty tends to be very high. On the other hand, today's Salomon Smith Barney sales executive may be tomorrow's Merrill Lynch sales executive—and his or her clients will follow along. Thus, the marketer's task is as much to sell to the intermediary as it is to sell to the end user.

Multiple Sales Channels

One of the reasons for the complexity of marketing financial services is that there are numerous ways to reach the end customer. In conventional product marketing, you generally have a sales chain: manufacturer to wholesaler or distributor, to retail store, to customer. The sales reps for a pharmaceutical company are talking to doctors; for a consumer products company, to retailers. The end user is seldom the manufacturer's customer.

In financial services, end users are reached directly and indirectly, sometimes in both ways at the same time. Each sales channel requires a different marketing strategy. Here are some of the possible avenues:

Direct-to-end user. Methods include direct mail (often used by credit card companies), telemarketing, and online sales (as for online brokerage services and some loans and insurance products).

Commissioned salespeople. This is the most common way institutional products are sold, via employees or dedicated representatives of the manufacturer. The model is prevalent in retail services as well, for example, stockbrokers or insurance agents who are compensated by the company that creates the products, such as Merrill Lynch or State Farm.

Independent commissioned sales agents. Third-party sales to consumers are commonplace in the investment and insurance industries. In this arrangement, the financial adviser or insurance agent represents numerous lines of business. When the agents sell a product (such as a mutual fund) to the end consumer, they receive a commission from that mutual fund management company.

Independent noncommissioned advisers. Some advisers—including investment advisers, pension consultants, and insurance brokers—are paid by their customers to provide advice that is not influenced by commissions. Their job is to investigate the entire universe of products and select those that are most suitable for their customers.

Retail. Banks traditionally have relied on brick-and-mortar branches as their primary sales channel. Other companies that have physical branches include brokerage firms, mutual fund companies, and stand-alone lenders (like the Money Store).

How End Users Select a Financial Services Provider

When buying a tangible product, consumers can choose which product to buy on a comparative basis. Savvy customers will consider technical specifications (which computer has the fastest processor), availability, reliability, warranties, and other items that can be assessed on an apples-to-apples basis. And, of course, they can compare prices. Financial services are rarely comparison-shopped this way. Although the Internet has made it easier to compare, say, mortgage rates or the price of term life policies, decisions about financial providers are often based on factors beyond the marketer's control. For example, convenience—the closest bank branch, the credit card solicitation that arrived today—will usually trump better features or prices.

As with most services, the most common selection factor is word-of-mouth referral. This is not surprising, since most people don't have an objective way of judging the quality of financial advice, insurance claims handling, or other types of services. When seeking the services of a stockbroker, pension adviser, private bank, or hedge fund manager, both institutional and consumer buyers seek the advice of their peers.

Cost Doesn't Matter Very Much

Because financial services decisions are often made without comparison shopping, the cost of a given service is often a less important consideration than convenience, reputation, or other factors. Most banks offer different tiers of pricing; consumers will generally decide on one tier or another, rather than comparing pricing within each tier at different institutions. Take, for example, a consumer looking for free checking. If a commercial bank branch is the closest and it offers free checking with a minimum of $2,500 in deposits, the consumer may choose to do business with that bank, at that tier of service, rather than walking an extra few blocks to a savings bank that offers free checking with no minimum. The convenience of the closest branch outweighs the cost of lost interest on the funds on deposit.

In some areas of financial services—notably, investments—consumers may focus on return and ignore costs, even though costs will affect return. In mutual

---

The Advantage of Being the Low-Cost Provider

John Bogle, former chairman of Vanguard Funds, has been a voice in the wilderness calling for a reduction in management fees for mutual funds. He has pointed out, quite sensibly, that fee structures should have some connection to assets under management: a fund with few assets may need to charge higher fees to cover its costs and generate a small profit. But even as assets doubled and tripled in some funds, the percentages charged for management fees stayed the same, thus doubling or tripling profits to the fund manager. Only in response to the mutual fund scandals of 2003–4 did regulators begin demanding more transparency in fund fees.

For the Vanguard Group, the failure of many consumers to pay attention to management fees has provided the money manager with a potent prod-

Vanguard Group is among the few financial marketers to differentiate based on price.

uct differentiation as an extremely low-cost provider. There are seemingly enough consumers who *are* fee-conscious to have made Vanguard the No. 2 mutual fund investment company in the United States, second only to Fidelity Investments.

---

funds, for example, management fees for the same type of fund can vary by more than a percentage point, as personal finance experts have been telling the public for years. But very few investors pay attention to management fees, 12b-1 fees, or even sales loads that can deduct 5 percent or more from the investment before the money is ever put to work. Even on the institutional side, returns trump fees. Top hedge funds may take as much as 50 percent off the top, but if returns are sufficiently high, investors are willing to share 50/50 the return on their own money.

"Stickiness" of Money Decisions

Online merchants refer to their sites as "sticky" if the visitors stick around for a while once they get there. Most financial services are "sticky" in the sense that once a purchase decision has been made, the buyer tends to stay with the

Learning Marketing Lessons from Schwab

Unlike many financial companies, Charles Schwab & Co. is a leader in marketing practice, both in product innovation and in marketing techniques. On the product side, Schwab was the first mutual fund company to differentiate itself in the marketplace when it created the mutual fund supermarket. Historically, mutual funds had been sold on the basis of performance. By offering investors a one-stop shop for multiple mutual fund brands, Schwab assured them of access to top-performing funds in each category. Schwab also took another clever tack in its positioning strategy by differentiating itself not against its direct no-load competitors but against the universe of brokerage funds. By offering fee-only financial advisers as a value-added service, Schwab branded itself as a source of unbiased investment advice.

Schwab was among the first firms to systematically use online methods to attract, retain, and cross-sell customers. Its sophisticated use of the Internet has been far ahead of most of its competitors. For example, many financial companies talk about "one-to-one" marketing online but send e-mail communications that are not customized. Schwab, on the other hand, offers individualized monthly comparative performance reports for each fund held by the shareholder.

product even when the reason for the initial decision is no longer valid. Thus, consumers who chose a bank that was nearby will continue to bank with the same company even after they have moved to another location that may be further from the nearest branch. Or an investor who chose a fund because it was a top performer will continue to hold the fund's shares even after it has become a performance also-ran.

For marketers, this customer loyalty (inertia is probably a more apt term) is a boon, since retention rates are generally far higher than in other industries. One British study showed defection rates of 3 percent annually for banks, compared with a 15 to 20 percent defection rate for business in general. U.S. bank attrition rates are estimated at 10 percent, still below most other industries.[3]

The reasons for the "stickiness" of financial services are not primarily marketing-driven, however. The reality is that for many consumers, it is simply too much trouble to change service providers. It's easy to switch toothpaste brands or to go to a different grocery store. It's much more of a hassle to move your money from one bank or broker to another. Or consider refinancing a mortgage; the costs and paperwork make doing so such a time-consuming and expensive proposition that few people bother to refinance unless rates have dropped significantly. This inertia is particularly evident in the institutional market. A corporation doesn't lightly change benefits providers or lenders, for example, because there is an enormous cost in doing so.

For marketers, this inertia presents many opportunities. First, the costs of acquiring a new customer can be amortized over many years. Thus, more money can be devoted to acquisition versus retention marketing. Because the financial marketer doesn't need to spend great sums of money to keep customers from defecting, there are numerous opportunities to gain greater "share of wallet" among this captive audience. These opportunities include relationship building to increase cross-sales, as well as opportunities for referrals.

Are financial marketers making the most of their advantages? Airlines have spent billions of dollars to build customer loyalty, something that financial services companies take for granted. Not only do financial services marketers have a near captive audience in their current customers, but they also have the opportunity to communicate with these customers on a regular basis—in the branches, through monthly statements, online, and through service calls. And consumers are likely to open a piece of mail or respond to a phone call from their financial institution.

What's more, financial services companies have an enormous marketing advantage in that they generally know a great deal about their customers. In fact, the credit card industry was among the first to segment its markets based on profitability analyses, because it readily had the data in hand to determine not only who was using the product, but also how often, how quickly they were paying off, and what they were spending their money on. Banks and brokerage firms have more information about their customers than most other types of marketers—information like value of their home, age, income, borrowing behavior, and much more. A savvy consumer marketer like Coca-Cola could turn such information to huge advantage.

But financial services companies have traditionally been among the least marketing-focused industries. Segmentation and target marketing in these industries is often at an unsophisticated level. Some insurance companies, for example, are only beginning to target such large market segments as women and minorities; very few attempt to "slice and dice" the kind of narrow demographic segments

---

Fitting "Small Print" into a Broadcast Spot

The regulations that govern the financial services industry often have a direct impact on marketing programs and their execution. In this highly regulated industry, allowing for required disclosure information can become a nightmare unless you plan ahead. You have to arrange for compliance and legal review of all material, and adequate time for these reviews must be factored into production schedules and launch dates. Furthermore, you must design disclosure language into your layout as well as allow for it in your broadcast advertising. Failing to do so will not only cost you time but also potentially thousands of dollars in new creative and production costs.

The disclosure information for one large financial services company was so extensive that it required fifteen seconds of a thirty-second radio commercial. The choice was to either reduce the amount of disclosure or buy more airtime. After much discussion, agreement was reached on a way to tighten the disclosure language—to ten seconds, leaving twenty seconds of the thirty-second spot for the sales message.

---

that consumer products marketers routinely pursue. Customer relationship management (CRM) is a big buzzword in the industry. In theory, it means using the information the company has about its customers to develop products, services, and communications to meet those customers' needs. In practice—well, it isn't much practiced. Because there are "silos" between credit and debit products or between competing sales forces, information is often not shared across an institution.

Similarly, financial institutions sometimes fail to exploit their ability to communicate regularly with customers. Although there are exceptions, few financial institutions have created compelling reasons for their customers to read their messages. The airlines, for example, have developed very successful online programs that provide alerts to bargain airfares. The weekly e-mail from airline to customer creates an opportunity for brand building and developing customer loyalty. Some online brokerage firms provide a similar service with investment alerts, and there have been other creative uses of the Internet, but the vast majority of financial institutions passively wait for their customers to contact them.

Legal and Regulatory Constraints

As if financial marketers didn't have it tough enough dealing with the structural issues of the industry, they must also answer to a higher authority. Financial services are among the most regulated of industries, at the federal, state, and industry-watchdog level. These regulatory constraints affect numerous marketing decisions. For example, the National Association of Securities Dealers must review all marketing materials created by investment companies. Not only does this govern what claims may be made in those materials but it also affects decisions about timing of materials (to allow for review) and even layout and design ("small print" is regulated as to size).

As another example of how regulatory constraints limit marketing decisions, consider that insurance products have to be approved on a state-by-state basis. If a product is not available in a particular state, this will complicate advertising strategy, since national advertising may not be cost-effective. Or the timing of bringing a new mutual fund to market will be dictated by Securities and Exchange Commission regulations, which mandate approval by the fund company's own shareholders before the product can be distributed.

Successful Financial Marketing

You don't have to be a genius to market financial services, but it couldn't hurt. Some institutional investment firms employ quantitative analysts who are referred to in the industry as "rocket scientists." These prodigies come up with complex formulas to predict or hedge market behavior. But once they create their Einsteinian product, someone has to market it. Understanding and communicating the work of geniuses is just one of the many challenges facing the financial marketer.

Whether it's applying the latest marketing tools or mastering clinical psychology, the task of the financial marketer is unlike that of any other professional. Unfortunately, there is no Nobel Prize for marketing, but there are quantifiable rewards for marketing success. The following chapters will help you better plan your marketing and sales strategy to achieve that success.

Getting the Most from This Book

This book is meant for three types of readers: (1) marketers and managers at financial services companies, (2) those who sell financial products or services, and (3) students and those who are looking for positions in financial services marketing and sales. The chapters that follow are organized into two sections. Section 1 addresses the strategic tools of financial marketing, including segmentation, targeting, positioning, branding, competitive analyses, SWOT analyses, market research, and market planning. Section 2 covers specific financial marketing tactics, including advertising, public relations, sponsorships, direct marketing, the Internet, personal selling, trade shows, and customer retention tactics.

The appendix, "Applying Marketing Principles to Sales Practice," is a bonus feature designed to help sales professionals visualize how the lessons outlined in the chapters can be applied in real-life situations.

Readers who are already marketing practitioners may be familiar with the strategic principles outlined in section 1. Although a review of these principles and the associated case studies will be valuable, such readers may wish to skip ahead to the tactical chapters. For those in sales or in training, strategy is often overlooked. Many product managers or sales executives, eager to fill their pipeline with prospects, jump over the planning process and start implementing tactics. "I need more prospects, so I'll advertise," the thinking often goes. But advertise where? With what offer? In expectation of what?

Implementing marketing tactics without a strategic plan is like building a home without a blueprint. It may work—or the edifice may collapse in the first strong wind. Consider the sales manager who spent tens of thousands of dollars to get prime space at a trade show only to find that the attendees were not his customers but his competitors.

Strategic marketing serves to prevent these kinds of mistakes. By identifying target segments, the marketer avoids wasting money on prospects who will never buy or on buyers who will never be profitable. Market research can help determine the characteristics of potentially profitable segments in order to reach them more effectively. Competitive analyses, environmental analyses, positioning, and branding strategies can help determine how a company or product is viewed in the marketplace and what opportunities exist to build greater market share. In other words, planning before making any promotional decisions helps maximize the return on investment of every marketing dollar. Strategic market-

---

Resources

Standard general marketing textbooks include Philip Kotler, *Marketing Management,* 11th ed. (Upper Saddle River, NJ: Prentice Hall, 2003) and *Principles of Marketing,* 10th ed. (Upper Saddle River, NJ: Prentice Hall, 2003). Another widely used textbook is William M. Pride and O. C. Ferrell, *Marketing Concepts and Strategies,* 12th ed. (Boston: Houghton Mifflin, 2003).

The American Marketing Association (http://www.marketingpower.com) is the umbrella organization for all aspects of marketing strategy, planning, and tactics. For more resources, as well as articles, case studies, and marketing exercises, see our related *Financial Services Marketing Handbook* website at http://www.fsmhandbook.com.

---

ing asks the questions "who," "what," "when," "where," and "why." Only after answering these questions can you successfully implement the tactical "how's" that are addressed in section 2.

CHAPTER NOTES

1. Data for 1992 are cited in Stephen Taub, "That's Rich," *Institutional Investor,* June 2002, 33. Data for 2003 are from Marietta Cauchi, "Hedge Funds Attract Record $60 Billion in 2003 vs. $16.3 Billion in 2002," *Dow Jones Business News,* January 26, 2004, www.biz.yahoo.com/djus/040126/1255001061_2.html.

2. Shoya Zichy, "A *Type* of Investment: Research Shows Link between Financial Choices and Preferences," *Bulletin of Psychological Type,* Spring 2002, 6–7; 32–36.

3. Tina Harrison, *Financial Services Marketing* (Edinburgh: Pearson, 2000). Harrison's source for the 15–20 percent attrition rate is a Bain and Company study, published by F. F. Reichheld and W. E. Sasser Jr., "Zero Defections: Quality Comes to Services, *Harvard Business Review,* September/October 1990, 105–111. For the 3 percent British bank attrition rate, she cites *Financial Times,* November 16, 1998. American data on bank attrition are from Jeffrey Kutler, "Bank Shot," *Institutional Investor,* September 2003, 149–152.

STRATEGIC
MARKET
PLANNING

CHAPTER ONE

Segmentation

1

The science of marketing is built on fact-based research, sophisticated statistical methods, the testing of hypotheses, and the analysis of results. The art of marketing comprises experience, imagination, and creativity. Both art and science must go into choosing target segments.

1

Segmentation is the most basic marketing strategy. Although all marketers segment to some degree (even if they aren't aware they are doing
so), many financial companies, particularly on the institutional side, do
not take full advantage of segmentation strategies to improve their marketing effectiveness. Most institutional sales executives work through personal
industry contacts and industry gatherings, thus segmenting on a de facto
basis by industry. For example, a bond salesperson will tend to know and
interact with others in the bond industry. In fact, some institutional markets
are so limited—to take a random example, defined-benefit pension plans
with over $250 million in assets—that salespeople can list every potential
client company by name.

Even within such narrow market segments, there is usually a benefit to segmenting further. A salesperson only has so much time and needs to prioritize.
Circumstances change; threats and opportunities arise. Segmenting means
answering questions such as these:

Which organizations do business with your company? Can they be further divided into those that are solid relationships and those that need to be
cultivated? Can they be segmented by current or potential future profitability, so
that the sales force spends more time with the 20 percent of clients that provide
80 percent of profitability? Can clients be analyzed by the types of products they
currently buy and others that they may need?

Which organizations do business with your competitors? Can these companies be further divided into those who are unlikely to change suppliers in the
near future and those that may be looking for a change? Can they be segmented

So Many Prospects, So Little Time

A group within a large institutional brokerage invented a new type of institutional cash fund, similar to a money market fund but offering some unique advantages. While it was successful among the sales force serving the middle market, the capital markets sales force ignored it. The inventors decided to set up their own business to market the product. As there were only three principals, their time was limited. A marketing plan devised by an outside consultant recommended the following segmentation strategies:

- Limit potential clients geographically, so that the principals would not have to travel extensively (geographic segmentation).
- Concentrate on the middle market, because it had already shown its viability and because it could be reached through marketing tactics other than direct sales, such as advertising, public relations, direct mail, and other means (demographic segmentation by size of business).
- Select larger institutions in a few key industries (such as local governments) to target for sales calls. The industries were selected based on benefits analysis, ease of reach, potential profitability, and other factors (demographic segmentation by industry).

However, the group did not act on this advice and continued to sell on an ad hoc basis through personal contacts, referrals, and "luck." As a result, the three were constantly chasing perceived opportunities, wasting a good deal of their time. Unfortunately, "luck" was not enough, and the business never met their expectations.

by profitability or revenues or other financial characteristics so that salespeople focus on the highest-value prospects?

Learning from the Consumer Side

On the consumer side, it is better understood that the market is no longer undifferentiated. Back in the 1950s, there was a mass market. There was one kind of Coke, and Coke sold it to everyone in the world in the same way. But those were also the days when television consisted of three networks and most people read mass-market magazines like *Life*.

One Hundred Thousand Market Segments at Capital One

How many segments are enough? As many as you need. One good reason to create ever-smaller "cells" is to test results of different variables in direct mail offers. Capital One, for example, runs more than 45,000 tests annually, on a global basis—everything from how much credit to offer to what color envelope to use. From these test results, Capital One has divided its market into one hundred thousand different segment or product combinations. Do the small differences in scores merit this much data handling? It has certainly paid off for Capital One. In eight years, it grew its customer base from 6 million to 46.6 million in the United States alone, and every day it adds another twenty-five thousand customers.[1]

Today, the "mass market" is made up of multiple niche segments that do not intersect. Girls ages 12 to 15 read different magazines, watch different television programs, go to different websites than do older or younger girls. Television has splintered into hundreds of cable channels, devoted to specific demographic market segments (women, Hispanics) or niche interests (golf, Wall Street). Very few magazines reach a heterogeneous audience—today magazines are targeted to ever-narrower niches (black entrepreneurs, retirees in Florida).

Very few companies can afford to be everything to everyone any more. Even companies with mass-market products (like basic checking accounts) segment their markets so that they can focus their limited marketing dollars on the most profitable segments. Mass advertising is often a waste of money. For example, a thirty-second spot on the Super Bowl can cost $2 million for airtime, plus a few more million in production costs. Advertising an online brokerage when only half the viewers transact their business online is wasting half one's marketing dollars—something many dot-coms didn't learn until too late.

Choosing Target Segments

Targeting is picking the actual market segments you want to go after. The benefits of targeting include the following:

- *Targeting helps you identify the media that best reach your target segments.* When you've identified a particular segment (for example, young professionals just starting out in practice), you can more easily determine the media that best

Targeting for Referrals

A financial adviser of Indian origin sold an investment plan to a relative, who was an Indian physician. The adviser began getting business from colleagues of this relative, who were also Indian physicians. Because the segment was potentially highly profitable and there was little competition seeking its business, the adviser decided to target this group more systematically. He offered seminars on financial planning for physicians at local hospitals that had a high percentage of Indian doctors. He sought an invitation to speak at a national conference of Indian physicians. He offered to write a regular column on financial planning for physicians in a magazine targeted to Indians in the United States. The success of these efforts was not surprising, since most people seek referrals from those they trust. Because this market segment was small and easily reached, the adviser soon did not need to actively market at all, as referrals from current clients enabled his business to prosper.

reach these markets (for example, law or medical school alumni magazines).

- *Targeting helps build referral business.* People tend to affiliate with people who are similar in interests or demographics. They are also likely to refer business to their friends and follow each other's purchasing patterns.
- *Targeting specific market segments increases the potential return of your marketing dollars.* It might seem obvious that when you buy a mailing list, you should limit your use of it to people who have the ability to buy your product. Yet, at least one bank, failing to cross-analyze its own customer list, sent a solicitation for renters' insurance to homeowners who had mortgages with the bank! Targeting should help avoid such waste and irritation to customers.
- *Targeting helps you narrow the focus of your message, making it more likely that the prospect will respond.* Although the average direct mail offer today gets less than a 2 percent response, when the list, the offer, and the message are narrowly targeted, response can go up to 10 percent or more.
- *Targeting enables organizations to build products designed for target segments and to avoid market segments for whom they have no appropriate products.* An investment company that specializes in fixed-income funds is not going to have much to offer day traders looking for fast profits

---

The Hispanic Market Buoys Bank of America

"We expect to get 80 percent of our future growth in retail banking from the Hispanic market," said Ken Lewis, CEO of Bank of America. The bank targeted this growing and underserved market segment and has become a market leader.

Growth potential is the first of numerous benefits Bank of America expects to gain by targeting the Hispanic market. The Hispanic population is not only growing faster than other groups, Hispanics have lower percentages of checking accounts or credit cards. This may change. Hispanics are becoming more economically powerful —with an estimated $540 billion in purchasing power controlled by Latinos in the United States. By segmenting, the bank focused on appropriate tactics to reach the segment, like handing out brochures and coffee to those standing in line for identification papers at Mexican consulates. The bank also advertised heavily in the Spanish-language media and increased the number of bilingual employees— in recent years, 60 percent of new hires have been bilingual.

Other advantages to targeting are the opportunities to shape products to fit the specific needs of Hispanic customers. For example, Bank of America began writing mortgages secured by the credit of an extended family. It also created a product called SafeSend, which made it easier for people to transfer money from the United States to Mexico. Once a product has been created for a particular market segment, it helps draw more customers from that segment. Given that the Hispanic segment is noted for its brand loyalty, the bank hopes to retain a large percentage of these customers over the long term.[2]

---

and shouldn't waste its money seeking them. However, if a target segment, such as retirees, is looking for a related product, like annuities, it may be sensible to investigate offering such products.

Methods of Segmentation

There are many ways to segment a market. The most common method is demographic, because demographic information is easy to acquire. Product purchase behavior is another objective type of segmentation based on information that also is readily available. Other types of segmentation require more

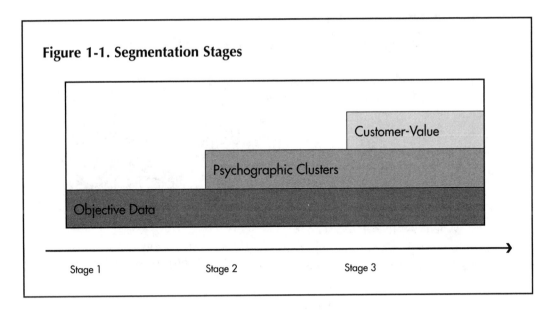

Figure 1-1. Segmentation Stages

Customer-Value

Psychographic Clusters

Objective Data

Stage 1   Stage 2   Stage 3

sophisticated data collection and analysis. Marketers usually begin with objective segmentation methods and develop these more sophisticated methods over time, as shown in **figure 1-1**.

Objective Methods of Segmentation

Demographic segmentation. Bank of America and other financial institutions pursuing the Hispanic market are practicing demographic segmentation—the most basic kind of segmentation. Other recent examples of demographic segmentation include a new effort by Wells Fargo to make its online services more accessible to the blind and visually impaired, a home mortgage–like product developed by HSBC that addresses religious law forbidding Muslims to pay or receive interest, and a sponsorship by several mutual funds (Calvert, Domini, TIAA-CREF) of a gay and lesbian conference.

The great advantage of demography as a segmentation variable is that it is based on observable, measurable characteristics. Demographic variables in the consumer market can include age, sex, race, religion, personal income, household income (HHI), marital status, number and ages of children, home ownership, education, professional status (type of job), language, ethnic group, physical disability, and sexual preference. In the business market, demography can include size of business (by number of employees, revenues, or other mea-

Geographic Segmentation for Flood Insurance

Demographic and geographic segmentation are useful because these characteristics are easy to act on. One particularly clever use of geographic data was an online promotion for State Farm insurance. It was targeted at visitors to Weather.com who live in regions of the United States that are usually warm but occasionally suffer cold spells. When weather forecasts for these regions predicted snow or freezing temperatures, a banner ad from State Farm crossed their screen, with a warning about frozen pipes. A Flash image of a boy in a scuba suit and his dog, underwater, was the punch line.

State Farm targeted local Weather.com visitors when freezing weather was forecast.

sures), type of industry, length of time in business, ownership characteristics (public corporation, privately held), management structure (hierarchical or flat), and so forth.

Geographic segmentation. Geography is also a basic, measurable segmentation variable. Clearly, a company that does business only in certain geographic regions (such as a local bank) would limit its target market to potential customers in that region. Geographic segmentation also applies to creation of sales territories and efforts to expand nationally or internationally, as well as to pinpointing potential markets by type of neighborhood, urban versus rural locales, single or multiple locations for businesses, and the like.

Life-cycle segmentation. Another common method of segmenting a market is based on the fact that customers' needs change as they enter different phases of the life cycle: for example, young marrieds are likely to buy a home, growing businesses are likely to need a line of credit. Although identifying potential clients by life cycle phase is strongly correlated with marketing success, the data points are often difficult to find. If you're looking for people who have just bought a home (say, to target for a home equity

---

Life-Cycle Event—The First Job

Welcoming consumers into the labor force (and getting a shot at their first independent income) is a goal of many marketers. Visa and MasterCard have come up with an ingenious way to do it. They offer pre-paid cards (also known as "stored value" cards), which have become popular ways for fast-food restaurants and others to pay their young employees. Since teenagers seldom have checking accounts, paychecks are inconvenient. Prepaid credit cards can be used like any other credit card. For the bank that issues the card, acquiring consumers at the beginning of their working life increases the likelihood that they will remain customers for other products later.

---

product or mortgage insurance), it's easy to find this information. If you're looking for people who are *thinking about* buying a home, the task is much more difficult.

Product segmentation. When General Motors' Alfred Sloan called in 1924 for "a car for every purse and purpose," he was segmenting his customers to match his cars—Chevrolets for the young and less affluent, Cadillacs for an older, wealthier crowd, other brands in between. Banks have also traditionally segmented their markets by product—credit card customers are in one silo, home equity loan customers in another, and certificate of deposit owners in a third. From this rudimentary information, whole customer relationship management (CRM) systems can be built, yielding valuable data on account size, profitability by product, purchasing patterns, usage (debit versus credit), number of products, churn and retention rates by product, transaction method (phone, online, in branch) and other variables.

Segmentation by Psychographic Clusters

Demographic, geographic, and purchase variables are relatively easy to find and use, but they have limitations. Take, as an example, two 30-year-old men with similar incomes and education. Both are married and childless, but one has $100,000 in investable assets, and the other has no savings. What variable explains this difference in behavior?

Attitudes and behaviors are much more difficult to observe and measure than demographics, but they can offer more insight into what customers actually buy

Table 1-1. Behavioral Segmentation by Benefit Sought

FACTOR	% CITING AS MOST IMPORTANT	SEX	AGE
Service (hours, location, speed)	72.5	Both	All
Access to branch and ATMs	68.6	Both	18–54
High interest rate paid on deposits	57.8	Both	26 and above
Financial advice	28.7	Mostly female	18–35

Source: Raj Singh Minhas and Everett M. Jacobs, "Benefit Segmentation by Factor Analysis: An Improved Method of Targeting Customers for Financial Services," *International Journal of Bank Marketing*, March 1996, 3-13.

and why. And by analyzing why customers have bought in the past, it is possible to project who would be most likely to buy in the future.

Benefits-based segmentation. One way to segment a market is by which benefits appeal to customers. For example, British researchers sent a seven-page questionnaire to some two thousand randomly selected households in order to determine why different demographic segments chose their bank. The results, shown in **table 1-1**, demonstrate their conclusion that "segmentation criteria must be relevant to the purchase criteria of customers." Based on their research, for example, a bank that offers limited access to ATMs probably shouldn't bother aiming for the youth segment, whereas a bank that has ATMs but pays lower-than-average interest on deposits would find the 18- to 26-year-old market a suitable target niche.

Knowing why customers buy is very helpful for creating targeted campaigns. For example, SouthTrust Bank's equity line of credit direct mail solicitation was segmented by the purpose of the loan: home improvement, debt consolidation, and children's education were the three leading categories. Knowing this made it easier to customize the messages for a direct mail campaign targeted to prospects in each of these segments.

Lifestyle segmentation. Lifestyle segmentation operates on the principle that "birds of a feather flock together." Similarities of interests, attitudes, and activities are common among people who live in the same neighborhood—for example, suburban soccer moms often read the same magazines, shop in the same stores, and share political and social viewpoints with their neighbors. The tools that are used to group customers and prospects into attitude and behav-

Applying Cluster Analysis

Claritas, creator of the popular PRIZM system of cluster analysis, drilled down its database to create a finance-specific lifestyle model. Called P$YCLE, it differentiates 42 clusters by financial behavior. A cluster is a zip code–based group with similar demographic and behavioral characteristics; for example, "High-Asset Exurban Boomers," have assets of between $100,000 and $1 million, income of $75,000 or more, are age 55 or older, obtained a mutual fund through the Internet, read *Inc.* magazine, and go downhill skiing. Financial marketers can plug their own customers into these databases to help determine the characteristics of their target segments. Once these customers have been clustered, their common characteristics can be used to determine media, products, and message preferences.

ioral segments include cross-tabulation analysis, data mining, predictive modeling, cluster analysis, and other statistical techniques. The resulting variables have many names, including psychographics, behavioral models, values-based analysis, and lifestyle analysis.

One common way of determining the lifestyle characteristics of one's customers is to overlay one's own database with a commercial "cluster analysis." Cluster systems, such as PRIZM, ACORN, and MOSAIC use census and other quantitative and qualitative data to divide the United States and other countries into clusters, based on demographic and lifestyle similarities.

Business customers can also be segmented by psychographic criteria and buying behavior. For example, businesses can have different types of personalities: entrepreneurial, buttoned-down, consensus-driven. Decision-making styles can vary—in some businesses, decisions are made by one individual while in others they are made by committee. Purchasing decisions may be based on different personality factors: some businesses seek name brands or added-value services, whereas others look for the cheapest solution. Some businesses are "innovators" or "early adopters," that like to be on the cutting edge. Others are followers or "laggards" in their adoption of new technology. The sales force needs information about important behavioral factors such as length of sales cycle, relationship (preferred provider versus competitive bidder), and expectations for delivery, maintenance, training, and other services.

Table 1-2. Lifestyle and Profitability Segments

	ATTITUDES	BEHAVIORS	CHARACTERISTICS
Asset managers	Astute financial manager	Frequent transactor	High income/assets
	Tax concerns	Uses electronic banking	Younger than average customer
	Interest rate sensitive	Uses many banks and non-banks	Young children Owns valuable home
Secure traditionalists	Most loyal	Average transactor	Moderate income/ high assets
	Seeks value, convenience, recognition, and personal service	Moderate electronic usage	Slightly older than average customer Owns valuable home
	Low price sensitivity	Saving for a purpose	College-age children

Customer-Value Segmentation

When lifestyle characteristics are combined with profitability data, organizations can develop deep knowledge of their customers. As customer relationship management systems have become capable of predicting and projecting, segmentation schemes have developed that can increase lifetime customer value—that is, both the length of a customer's tenure and the long-term profitability of that customer. For more on CRM and customer value, see chapter 11.

An early user of customer-value segmentation methodology was Chemical Bank (now part of J. P. Morgan Chase), which took all the various data points it had collected about its customer base and then used a lifestyle approach to append behavioral and attitudinal data. This combination of data enabled the bank to view who their most profitable customers were in terms of lifestyle characteristics. **Table 1-2** shows two of the identified groups.

The insights provided by these segmentation methods are useful in several ways: They can help a company target new prospects who resemble their current best customers. They can help cross-sell and up-sell current customers who are thought to have additional assets outside the institution. They can help

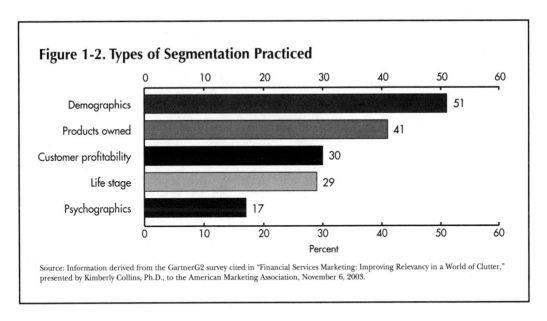

Figure 1-2. Types of Segmentation Practiced

Percent

	Percent
Demographics	51
Products owned	41
Customer profitability	30
Life stage	29
Psychographics	17

Source: Information derived from the GartnerG2 survey cited in "Financial Services Marketing: Improving Relevancy in a World of Clutter," presented by Kimberly Collins, Ph.D., to the American Marketing Association, November 6, 2003.

retain current customers by predicting life-cycle or service issues that require intervention.

Behavioral segmentation can also help determine levels of service for current customers in order to maximize profitability. This must be done carefully, however. There have been a few public relations disasters when companies have too publicly announced that they were shifting unprofitable customers to cheaper methods of service, like ATMs or online access. Further, by making this information available to branch staff, there is the risk of inadvertently revealing potentially embarrassing information to customers. At the same time, if better service is to be offered to better customers, the customer-facing staff must be aware of which profitability "bucket" the customer falls into.

Segmentation by lifetime value is still relatively rare. A 2003 survey of 97 financial firms conducted by GartnerG2 reported the percentages of firms employing segmentation, based on the criteria shown in **figure 1-2**. Respondents could list more than one type of segmentation, so totals exceed 100 percent. Some categories surveyed were omitted from this figure in order to more clearly demonstrate the usage of the types of segmentation discussed in this chapter.

Finding Your Target Segments

The science of marketing comprises fact-based research, sophisticated statistical methods, testing of hypotheses, and analyzing results. The art of marketing is based on experience, imagination, and creativity. Both art and science must go into choosing target segments.

Any financial firm that has been in business for any length of time has three potential markets: current customers, prospective customers, and former customers. This last group is often overlooked, yet can be a significant source of new business for certain products. For example, a customer who has purchased an equity loan product in the past is an excellent prospect for a future equity line.

For start-up firms or companies that are expanding their markets, the task is more difficult. Rather than analyzing current customer patterns, they need to develop profiles of potential segments based on the variables most appropriate to their situation. For each profiled segment, research must determine the following:

- *Market potential:* What is the total size of the segment in dollars or units?
- *Sales potential:* What market share percentage of this segment can you reasonably expect to develop (over one or more years)?
- *Competition:* Who are the market leaders? What strengths and vulnerabilities make this an attractive segment?
- *Ease of reach:* How will you reach this segment? Are there identifiable media that match key variables?
- *Cost:* How much will it cost to reach this market? Can you afford it?
- *Other resources:* Do you have products that appeal to this market segment? Sufficient marketing resources and expertise?
- *Fit:* Does this segment fit with your organization's objectives? Are there conflicts or synergies with other client segments? Are there changes in the environment that will make this segment more or less desirable in the future?

Identifying Current Market Segments

Your best prospects will resemble your best customers. They usually buy for the same reasons and are reached through the same media and methods.

Table 1-3. Segmentation Checklist

Demographic variables
Financial variables (such as total investable assets, size of payroll)
Geographic variables
Life-cycle variables
Product/service needs
Attitudes toward product/service
Buying behavior
Belong to (social/professional groups)
Media (specific reading/viewing habits)
Responsive to (type of marketing approach)
Market potential

Who are your most profitable customers? The old 80/20 rule still operates in most businesses: 80 percent of your revenues come from 20 percent of your customers.

What do your top 20 percent buy from you? How often? How long have they been customers? Look at last year's customer list. Are the same people still in your top 20 percent? If not, what happened? Why did some of them leave? Can you get them back if you address the issues that concern them? Are any of your other top customers likely to leave? Can you save them?

What characteristics do your top 20 percent have in common? Do they have similar demographics or other observable characteristics? Can you do a cluster analysis to find out where they live, what they read, or watch on TV? Are they in similar types of business? Do they belong to the same organizations? Do they have common relationships with lawyers, accountants, or other professionals?

How did they become customers in the first place? Was it through personal referrals, a mailing list, an ad, attendance at a trade show? This is critical information, and you should always enter this data when you first acquire a new customer.

There are several ways to collect more detailed information about your customers:

Surveys. Create a short questionnaire with key items of importance to your business (see box at right). If yours is a relationship business, you can call or e-mail your customers to ask if they are willing to participate. If you have a physical place of business, you can provide survey forms to waiting customers or have a staff member approach customers to fill out a survey.

Informal Q&A sessions. You may want to talk informally to your top customers or arrange a breakfast meeting of five or six top customers for an informal focus group. Chances are they will be flattered to be asked. If you feel a need to provide an incentive, you can offer to make a donation to their favorite charity. You should also contact former customers to find out why they left.

Industry gossip. Your sales force, suppliers, even your competitors can provide priceless information about your markets. Go to sales conferences and trade shows. Even if you don't exhibit, you will pick up the latest inside information.

Have a cluster-based overlay done on your customer database. If you have enough clients to make this worthwhile, you can get all kinds of interesting information about them, from what they watch on TV to how much their homes are worth.

CHAPTER NOTES

1. What a Capital Idea," *Banking Technology,* July–August 2002, 44.

2. Sources: Shawn Tully, "BofA Is Betting Its Future on the Hispanic Market," March 30, 2003, www.fortune.com/fortune/fortune500/articles/0.15114,438340,00.htm. Ari Weinberg, "Banks Seek Credit with Hispanics," July 30, 2003. www.forbes.com/2003/07/30/cx_aw_0730hispanic_print.html.

Get Your Customers to Tell You How to Find More Customers

Learn as much as you can about why your customers buy from you, how to get them to buy more, how to encourage them to refer others to your firm, and how to find more people like them. Here are some sample questions you might want to ask your best customers:

Needs Being Met
- Why did you begin doing business with this firm?
- How did you hear about us?
- What was your initial impression?
- What is your impression now?
- What would you say are our greatest strengths compared with our competitors?

Needs Not Being Met
- What are you dissatisfied with?
- Are there products or services that our competitors offer that we don't?
- Would you buy these services if we offered them? (How many? How often?)

Generating Referrals
- Have you told colleagues and friends about our services? Why? Why not? Would you consider doing so in the future? Would you do so if you were given a discount on a future service?

Finding Similar Customers
- Follow up on how they came to you in the first place. Were they referred? By whom? Why?
- Who else might be interested in this type of service? Try to get referrals to specific decision-influencers (like accountants or lawyers) or specific organizations (trade and professional associations, alumni groups, social organizations, neighborhood groups).
- If the customer came as a result of a marketing campaign, get specific details about the media that made them aware of your offering. Particularly in the institutional arena, find out what journals your customers read for professional development, which trade shows or conferences they attend, whether they see direct mail or unsolicited e-mail, as well as any personal information that might be appropriate (for example, if they are avid fishermen or active in a particular charitable organization).

Positioning and Branding

2

Positioning (and its close cousin, branding) defines who you are, what values you communicate, how you're different from others offering similar product sets, and why your constituencies should prefer you to your competitors.

Segmentation and positioning are basic strategies of marketing and apply to every product and service. If you don't know who your prospects are, you can't go after them. If you don't know who you are, your customers won't either. Briefly put, positioning is determining how you want others to view your company, product, or service in relation to your competition. These others can be your target markets, your sales reps, your vendors, your community, your investors, your employees. Positioning, along with its close cousin, branding, defines who you are, what values you communicate, how you're different from others offering similar product sets, and why your constituencies should prefer you to your competitors.

Positioning

The easiest way to define who you are is by comparison and contrast with your competitors. What do they stand for? What do they offer their markets? Do you offer the same or different qualities? This exercise is called "differentiation"—determining how you are unlike your competitors.

Consider consumer banking as an example. Until fairly recently, there were two kinds of consumer banks: large banks with lots of branches but impersonal service, and small banks with personal service but few branches. Then some marketing genius came along and thought, "Why not combine personal service with lots of branches?" The result was a new wave of consumer-friendly banks like Commerce Bank and Washington Mutual. These businesses positioned themselves against their competitors to come up with a new and better bank.

The Wal-Mart of Banking

When Washington Mutual has expanded into a new geographic region, its name has generally been unknown. But its positioning strategy has been so strong that it has quickly become a market leader. The bank, known familiarly as WaMu, has carved out a niche among younger and lower-income customers, particularly in urban areas, who are dissatisfied with their current banking choices. What has made WaMu different? Lower fees and friendliness.

Free checking and free ATM usage are powerful differentiators, but it has been WaMu's friendliness that has won customers' hearts. When the bank has moved into a new territory, it drew customers by having outdoor barbecues and a "WaMoola" machine for cash giveaways. Its branches were designed to resemble retail stores, not banks. Branches often included children's play areas and a "store" that sold teller dolls for kids and personal finance books for grown-ups. Tellers were not behind grilles or high counters but were approachable, and concierges greeted entering customers. With its mass-market appeal and low pricing, the bank has modeled its positioning after Wal-Mart Stores and has been achieving a comparable level of success.

Products that are undifferentiated are considered commodities, like grains or metal ores. A commodity market is one in which all products are the same (gold is gold) and cost the same. It doesn't matter to the marketplace how much it costs to extract the metal from a particular gold mine—you'll get the same price per ounce as your competitors.

Most companies want to avoid having their products turn into commodities. Even items that were once treated as commodities—basic checking, for example, are now being differentiated.

There are many ways to differentiate. Some points of difference are tangible: price, selection, terms, and delivery time. Some are intangible: quality of service, expertise, image, value, and status. Some points of differentiation are inherent in your product or service. Mutual funds, for example, compete largely on the basis of investment return. If your fund is beating its peers, you'll get business.

Companies can add value to their products in order to differentiate. Returning to the mutual fund example, the Vanguard Group has differentiated itself from its competitors by charging very low management fees, thus becoming

---

When Is a Toaster an Added-Value Differentiator?

With most deposit accounts offering similar terms, banks have gone back to a very old-fashioned means of differentiating their products—the account opening gift. In the 1950s, you would get a radio when you opened a savings account. Today, you might get an electric screwdriver, a bag of premium coffee, or a Palm Pilot.

According to one former Wells Fargo executive banks have gone back to giving gifts for account openings because, with deposit accounts being virtual commodities, "How are you going to be remembered and move potential customers to come to you?" Gifts not only "build desire and move the purchase but build the brand image as well."

The most effective gift—and the one most often offered—is cold, hard cash. Many banks offer new accounts $25 or $50. But sometimes gifts can be more memorable. Citibank (now Citigroup), for example, gave away gold and crystal pendants commemorating the Chinese New Year to customers at branches in Chinese neighborhoods who maintained balances of $15,000 or more. FleetBoston (now part of Bank of America) also segmented its gifts, giving Boston customers tickets to Red Sox games and New York customers discounts on Broadway shows. PNC Bank was successful with a promotion that made a $25 donation to a local charity chosen by the customer. Said a PNC executive, "A lot of our competitors have undifferentiated products and need premiums to stand out. When we provide premiums, we want them to be tightly linked with our stance in the community."[1]

---

a price leader. Other companies differentiate by adding broader fund selections, like Charles Schwab's supermarket approach. Still others add value by offering personal financial planning services.

Determining Positioning Strategy

If a company is offering a new product or service, it must determine, early on, how it will position itself with respect to both its target markets and competitors. Consider an investment manager who is setting up a new hedge fund. The process would consist of the following steps:

1 Examine strengths (for example, experience in international hedging strategies).

Table 2-1. Sample Positioning Strategy Grid

TARGET MARKET NEEDS	NEW HEDGE FUND	COMPETITOR A	COMPETITOR B
Expertise in foreign hedging	B	P	P
Value of principals' experience	B	P	W
Most recent 12-month performance	P	B	P
Performance consistency	B	P	W
Fees	not yet determined	B	W
Marketing strength	W	B	P

P = Parity   B = Better than competition   W = Worse than competition

2 Determine target market need. (Is there a need in the marketplace that is not adequately being met? Would a fund of hedge funds be interested in adding an international specialist to its roster?)

3 Analyze the competition. (Who else is offering international hedging strategies? What are each group's strengths and weaknesses?)

This can be set up as a grid, as shown in **table 2-1**. The rows show the characteristics that are important in the marketplace. The columns are for your company or product and its major competitors. The goal is to see where there is potential to differentiate.

In the example, New Hedge Fund is superior to its most direct competitors in its partners' experience in the international markets and in their previous jobs with well-known fund managers. Their most recent 12-month performance (at previous jobs) was about average for their peer group, but the partners have performed better than average over time. The biggest negative is that New Hedge Fund has no money to support a sales force and is competing with relatively well-known firms. An open question is whether to charge more, less, or the same as its competitors.

An exercise of this type provides insight into how to distinguish one's own company from competitors, using attributes that matter to target markets.

Once you've established your positioning strategy, you need to make sure that all elements of your product and marketing adhere to it. A private bank is going to have a very different look and feel than a mass-market bank. Its client offices will be deeply carpeted, and the walls will be covered with fine art. Its marketing materials will be elegant and sophisticated rather than bright and fun. Client-facing staff will have advanced degrees and will dress and act like the professionals they are. Such formality would be out of place in a WaMu. Positioning means knowing who you are and making sure that the face you present to the world is how you see yourself when you look in the mirror.

Branding

There are many vogue words tossed around to describe different aspects of this important concept. "Brand," "image," "corporate image," "reputation," "brand value," "identity," and "brand recognition" are some of them. Although one can quibble over precise definitions, in essence, all these words refer to the same concept.

Most marketers use the terms "positioning" and "branding" interchangeably. However, this discussion chooses to look at branding as a further refinement of positioning. Positioning defines a company or product in relation to its markets and competitors. Branding attempts to create a unique perception, an emotional or intellectual bond between product and end user. All companies and products are positioned (even if by default). Not all companies or products can be branded.

As an example, Visa and MasterCard have similar positioning in the minds of their target markets: they are both perceived as mass-market, all-purpose credit cards, particularly when compared with American Express, which has a more upscale image. Most people perceive very little difference between them in terms of product features, pricing, or other tangible qualities. If you ask people which credit card they carry, some would have to look in their wallet to see if it was a Visa or MasterCard.

Nevertheless, Visa and MasterCard have very different brand images. These are elements that are tied to the company's "vision, mission and values—the terms most often used to define the central building blocks for the brand."[2] Advertising is not the only factor in creating a brand image, but a strong advertising campaign can certainly create a values-laden brand image. For consumers, the difference between Visa and MasterCard likely comes down to their tag lines: "Visa is everywhere you want to be" versus "Some things are priceless. For everything else there's MasterCard."

Keeping the Gold in Goldman Sachs

Why do you need a brand campaign when you're already the gold standard in your industry? The media, regulators, and the stock market are uncontrollable factors that impact how a firm is perceived by its clients, staff, and other constituencies, said David W. May, vice president and director of global marketing, branding, and advertising for Goldman Sachs. To control the brand message, a company needs "to take positive steps to define its value and project it to its constituencies."

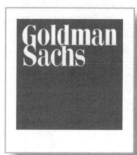

When May came to Goldman Sachs in 1996, the firm had a communications staff of one and no central advertising or brand management. But it had something any brand manager would kill for—a reputation among its peers as the "best in the business" of investment banking.

Why fix what wasn't broken? Well, in 1999, Goldman Sachs went public, which meant it had to generate awareness among a new constituency—retail investors. There was also a new class of prospective clients, such as high-tech companies and non-U.S.-based institutional investors, who did not know what the Goldman Sachs name stood for.

Goldman Sachs underwent a classic brand-building campaign, beginning with defining its core values and creating a corporate image ad campaign in the period after its initial public offering. The company made sure corporate standards for look and tone of printed and online materials projected a consistent image across all products and geographic markets. The firm used publicity to broadcast its good works. Training, seen as part of brand enhancement, emphasized adherence to company values. All the communications pieces worked together —website, printed matter, annual report, internal communications—to tell one story.

"The goal of brand building is to communicate a firm's values, not to create them," May concluded. There are many voices that influence what potential investors, clients, and recruits hear about a company. The company must make sure that its voice is heard above the others.[3]

A strong brand image, like that of American Express, has monetary value; it is a quantifiable corporate asset. This is true for several reasons:

- Brand image translates into profits because a branded product can command a higher price than an equivalent generic product. Many banks offer free travelers checks, but because American Express is a preferred brand name, it can command a premium.
- A brand image provides a shorthand way of letting constituents know what to expect from the company. A brand image has a personality, and a perceived level of quality is associated with particular brands. Sales staff, recruiters, or investor-relations managers will have a far easier time getting an audience if their target markets are already familiar with the brand image. When an American Express account manager calls up a new prospect, it will be easier to get an appointment than if that same salesperson were representing an unknown company.
- It is much cheaper to introduce a new product, or brand extension, if it is attached to a familiar brand name. An example of a "brand extension" is OPEN: The Small Business Network from American Express.
- Most important of all, a brand name is unique. It is one characteristic of your product that cannot be copied by your competitors.

Not every product or company can be successfully branded. Traditionally, branding has been used for tangible consumer goods—soaps, soft drinks, cars. Very few financial services companies have widely known brand names. In a 2002 Harris Poll, not a single financial services company made the top 10 in "reputation quotient" and only three broke into the top 50: American Express, Merrill Lynch, and Citigroup. According to a Harris spokesperson, financial services companies "do not leave an emotional impact, which is typically key to a ranking of this nature."[4] This lack of brand recognition for most financial services companies in the United States is borne out by *Fortune* magazine's "America's 2004 Most Admired Companies" list, which includes only one financial services firm—American Express—among the top ten.

Why is American Express a more recognizable name than other financial services firms? For one thing, American Express has had the same name since it was founded in 1850 and a consistent branding approach for most of that time. For another, AmEx has been a consistent advertiser and has had one of the longest-standing relationships with its advertising agency—Ogilvy & Mather—since

---

Whose Name?

In 2000, UBS (formerly Union Bank of Switzerland) purchased PaineWebber for $11 billion. Included in the company's assets was its more than 120-year-old brand name. So why, two years later, did UBS spend a reported 953 million Swiss francs to drop the PaineWebber name?[5]

Most companies, in fact, do drop the old brand name when an acquisition is made. Sometimes, as with UBS PaineWebber and Morgan Stanley Dean Witter, the old names are phased out over time. Sometimes a new compound name is retained. In the case of U.S. Bankcorp Piper Jaffray, this was a good thing. Acquired by the bank in 1998, the brokerage firm Piper Jaffray was spun off again in 2003. Sometimes multiple acquisitions create havoc, as with the Philadelphia convention center that began as the CoreStates Center, then became the First Union Center, and then the Wachovia Center.

Sometimes, if the old name is better known, it is kept, as when Chemical Bank acquired Chase Manhattan and First Union acquired Wachovia. But even though PaineWebber is far better known than UBS in the United States, UBS has a stronger brand name internationally.

An acquiring company often makes the acquisition to strengthen its own brand image, by filling in some perceived gap in product or geographic offerings. It is logical to rename the acquired company to boost the parent. UBS, which also acquired Warburg and other investment banks over the last few years, wanted all of its divisions to bolster the UBS image as an international investment banking powerhouse.

---

the 1950s. It is probably no coincidence that the agency is a strong proponent of what it calls "360-degree branding." This means that every piece of communication that passes among AmEx, its internal audience, and its clients contains the same tone and look, whether annual reports or product packaging, advertising or training manuals, websites or signage.

Very few brand strategies have had such consistency over such a long period. (Merrill Lynch, with its bull logo and "bullish on America" tag line going back to the early 1970s, is another rare example.) Part of the reason for the scarcity of recognizable financial brand names is simply that many notable brand names routinely disappear in mergers and acquisitions.

Creating a Brand Image

For a new company or product, or one without a recognizable brand image, the starting point is the name. Naming can have an enormous impact on a business's success or failure. For example, two companies that provided online trading for large volume traders were formed around the same time. One was called Harborside, for no reason except that the founder liked boats. The other was called Liquidnet. While the name was not the only factor that contributed to Liquidnet's greater success, making the nature of the company's business part of the name was certainly a plus.

In a crowded marketplace, a memorable name can stand out. In the competitive hedge fund area, most funds are named after their founder, but some managers have attempted to stand out from the crowd with names like Pirate Capital and Grizzly Bear Fund. A clever pair took the name "Dalton" from their old prep school—and got calls from alumni who were interested in investing.[6]

After the name is settled, the next step in branding is the corporate identifier or logo. A logo should be distinctive and easily recognizable. A logo can use a distinctive typeface, or it may have a visual motif, like Chubb's circle or Citicorp's "bug."

Although large companies spend millions to get the right logo design, success in this area is primarily a matter of knowing your positioning and making sure the logo reflects it. When Chemical Bank took over Manufacturers Hanover Trust in 1991, it inherited a logo of a square with diagonal lines through it. It was referred to, internally at least, as a "tire tread"—not exactly the image the bank hoped to convey.

"Borrowing" a Brand Image

Because it is so difficult to make a financial company stand out from its competitors, some companies have had success by associating with a better-known brand name. For example, many credit card companies "co-brand"—with airlines, car companies, online retailers like Amazon, and so forth. Customers may not remember whether they're carrying a MasterCard or Visa, but they do

Branding an 80-Year-Old Company

Teachers Insurance and Annuity Association—College Retirement Equities Fund (TIAA-CREF) was founded in 1918 by Andrew Carnegie as a charitable trust to provide pension fund management for college teachers. Well-regarded among its core constituency of educators, TIAA-CREF had never actively marketed itself beyond the campus until the late 1990s.

Although few people outside the university had heard of it, those who knew the brand name regarded it as "trust-worthy, prudent, principled, and value-driven," according to Richard Alpert, director of advertising and brand management. With Ogilvy & Mather, its advertising agency at the time,[7] TIAA-CREF began to build its brand image by conducting qualitative and quantitative research, finding that its target customers were highly educated, often in public service careers, and idealistic. "They are not consumed by wealth—they want to make a dollar and a difference," says Alpert. TIAA-CREF briefly considered changing its unwieldy name, but didn't want to risk losing the equity it had built among its customers or signal a radical shift in direction.

Instead, TIAA-CREF and its agency came up with a campaign focused on the tag line "Managing money for people with other things to think about," and featuring actual TIAA-CREF clients. Combining the "halo" effect of celebrity endorsement with the credibility of actual users, past and present, the effort began with TIAA-CREF's perhaps most famous customer—Albert Einstein. Other featured endorsers included the well-known author Kurt Vonnegut and DNA discoverer James Watson, as well as lesser-known names with interesting professions, such as a paleontologist and a volcano expert. Advertising, directed to opinion leaders, was supplemented with public relations and highly targeted sponsorships, such as an Einstein exhibit at the American Museum of Natural History.

Alpert states that brand awareness grew "significantly" among target segments. Just as important have been the positive effects on TIAA-CREF's own employees, branch consultants, and the financial planner intermediary segment. The success of the strategy is evidenced by the fact that TIAA-CREF was one of only three financial companies named in *Fortune*'s Fifty Most Admired Global Companies (along with Citigroup and HSBC) for 2003.[8]

remember they get points toward a new car or book every time they use it.

Co-branding helps promote both brands. First, the advertising dollars are multiplied with each additional marketer. Disney, Bank One, and Visa created a co-branded card—the Disney Visa Credit Card from Bank One—that all three support. Second, co-branding enables synergies, such as free publicity for Visa at Walt Disney World or Disney's name appearing on Visa's cards. There is also a "rub-off" effect, by which Bank One and Visa benefit from Disney's distinctive brand identity. In fact, Disney's identity was seen as so valuable that Visa paid an estimated $20 million in licensing fees.[9]

The strategy of co-branding is not limited to the consumer marketer. Wall Street Access, a NYSE member firm, has targeted strategic alliances to help build the brand image. Because one of its programs offered mutual funds through banks, the company sought out and won the exclusive endorsement of the American Bankers Association—a backing that enabled the company to grow rapidly.[10]

Not all co-branding efforts work. Sometimes the target group isn't appropriate, or the environment isn't suitable to support a co-branded activity. E*Trade entered into a partnership with Target in which the online broker opened mini-branches in Target stores. According to E*Trade's president, Jarrett Lilien, "we were not able to make it into a profitable distribution channel."[11]

Other ways to "borrow" a brand image are to use well-known names in advertising and promotion. For example, MetLife licensed the *Peanuts* comic-strip characters to lend a "warm and fuzzy" feel to its product. Companies have tried, with varying degrees of success, to use celebrity endorsers.

Another way to create a brand image is to use real clients or executives. Charles Schwab & Co. built its advertising and its brand image around the figure of Charles Schwab. "Tombstone" ads, which announce completed deals, are examples of using real client names to bolster the image of the investment bank.

Supporting a Brand Image

In maintaining a brand image, the most important quality is consistency. Both tangibles (such as brochures or premiums) and intangibles (such as commitment to quality) should conform to the brand image.

There must be consistency of message across all channels of communication, including these areas:

- Management communications through public relations (talking to the press) and investor relations (talking to analysts)

Typical Identity Guidelines

Mailing Label

The logotype is 40mm and placed at 6mm from the top and left hand side of the label.

Same rules apply to different formats.

Company name

- Typeface: Helvetica Neue bold, upper- and lower-case

- Colour: Pantone 287 (or 4-colour equivalent)

- Size: 8 pt, track amount 10, leading auto

- Position: 20mm from the top of the label, aligned with the axis of the

Corporate guidelines are usually very specific as to type style, size, colors, and position on the page. This is a guideline for a mailing label. It is part of a corporate identity system that runs to hundreds of pages, specifying nearly every piece of printed and online design that is distributed by the company.

- Internal communications with employees, vendors, and investors
- Company history and leadership
- Brick-and-mortar look and feel (offices, signage)
- Image projected by employees
- Online image
- Corporate identity system: use of name, logotype or symbol, color, and typography

In addition to consistency, brand management requires differentiating in a number of ways, such as unique product attributes/distinctiveness in market perception and appropriate sponsorships.

When It's Time to Reposition

Through acquisition and internal growth, the Bank of New York (BNY) had become one of the largest institutional brokerage and clearing firms in the world. However, its brokerage and clearing units operated independently of one another, frequently under preacquisition brand names. Opportunities to cross-sell products and services were sometimes missed. Clients were often unaware that BNY even offered clearing and brokerage services.

In 2002, BNY formed a new group-level organization over

its brokerage and clearing business units, which was later named BNY Securities. Management worked with Silver Communications, a financial marketing specialist, to improve its branding and communications practices. Silver recommended a unified branding strategy that clearly positioned individual business units as part of a single, integrated group. In addition, Silver developed a groupwide communications program, including advertising, collateral literature, and sales-support communications.

The new identity and communications strategy helped BNY Securities to achieve higher levels of awareness of the full range of its capabilities, among both existing and prospective clients and within the bank itself. The new strategy also helped BNY Securities achieve greater cumulative impact and efficiency from its communications expenditures. With unified branding and a coordinated system, all communications were mutually reinforcing, providing a greater number of exposures for the brand name and for core positioning messages.

Perhaps most important, maintaining the value of a brand image requires actively avoiding negative messages. It is not always possible to control negative messages, but there are ways to stack the odds in one's favor:

- Practice honest and proactive communications with all constituencies, including the press
- Create proactive customer-satisfaction programs
- Maintain company standards through employee recruitment and training
- Create a positive workplace environment
- Contribute through philanthropy and public service to build "reservoirs of goodwill" that will carry a good company through bad times.

Repositioning and Rebranding

Once a company has developed a positioning strategy, it can be difficult to change it. Schwab, for example, first established its identity as a discount alternative to full-service brokerages. When it wanted to move upscale in order to acquire more high-net-worth customers, it bought private bank U.S. Trust rather than try to reposition the Schwab brand name. When First Union bought Wachovia, it was happy to switch to the Wachovia name because the First Union name was attached to bad publicity about poor customer service in previous mergers.[12]

CHAPTER NOTES

1. Jeremey Quittner, "Giveaways, an Old Bank Concept, Back in Vogue," *American Banker's Financial Services Marketing*, May 29, 2002, 10A.

2. Anne Bahr Thompson, "Brand Positioning and Brand Creation," in *Brands and Branding*, ed. Rita Clifton, John Simmons, et al. (Princeton, NJ: Bloomberg Press, 2004), 86.

3. Author's interview with David May.

4. Lee Conrad "Playing the Name Game," *American Banker's Financial Services Marketing* (March–April 2002), 6-7.

5. "UBS Profit Hit by Rebranding," *Swissinfo*, February 18, 2003, www.swissinfo.org/sen/swissinfo.html?siteSect=161&sid=1639162.

6. Svea Herbst-Bayliss, "Hedge Funds Have Fun with Names," Reuters.com [biz.yahoo.com/rf/030407/financial_fund_hedges_1.html], April 7, 2003.

7. In 2003, TIAA-CREF replaced its advertising agency of the past seventeen years and appointed a small

Boston shop called Modernista.

8. Author's interview with Richard Alpert.

9. Stuart Elliot, "Advertising", *New York Times,* March 4, 2003, C6.

10.. Loretta Mock, "Brand Building and Service Delivery," Financial Communications Society Intelligence and Insight, April 7, 2003, www.fcsinteractive.com/editorials/displayarticle.aspx?articleID=160&sectionID =2.

11. Gaston F. Ceron, "E*Trade Ending Partnership with Target," *Dow Jones Business News,* June 5, 2003, biz.yahoo.com/djus/030605/1941001534_1.html.

12. Matthew De Paula, "In Wachovia Deal, First Union Tries to Avoid Past Mistakes," *American Banker's Financial Services Marketing,* May 29, 2002, 5A.

The Market Plan

3

Why create a market plan?
1) To save time. 2) To be
able to measure results.
3) To improve the
likelihood of success.

3

The market plan is the center of the marketing process. Using the information on segmenting and positioning that you have already compiled, the market planning process then asks you to set specific market objectives, as well as to develop a budget and ways to reach those goals. There are several reasons to create a market plan. First, it saves time. Although marketers complain about the hours that go into the planning process, planning lets you align limited resources with your most important objectives. Rather than running around in circles, the plan gives you a road map from where you are now to where you want to be.

The second reason for a market plan is that it permits you to measure your results. Without a clear statement of your current situation and your objectives for the future, you can't determine whether or not you've succeeded. Even if elements of your plan fail, the information will be useful. The plan enables you to fix your mistakes and try something else.

Finally, having a plan is more likely to lead to success. In large corporations, market planning is routine, but it is often considered too troublesome for smaller financial firms or for individuals, such as financial advisers, accountants, or consultants. A recent survey, however, shows that planning is associated with higher sales. Of the 716 financial advisers who responded, the higher their income, the more likely they were to have a plan.[1]

A market plan is a dynamic document that can change based on environmental factors as well as competitive product introductions, changes in competitor positioning, and shifts in your own company's strategic positioning. With each change, the market plan should be reviewed and adjusted. Even when things

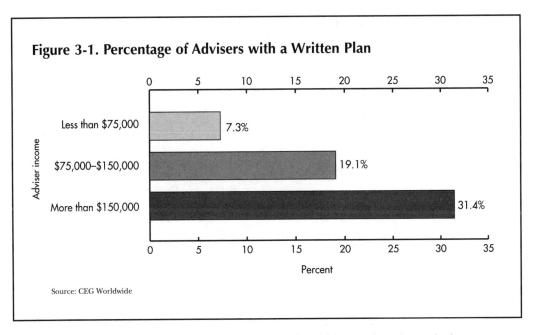

Figure 3-1. Percentage of Advisers with a Written Plan

Source: CEG Worldwide

are proceeding as expected, your market plan should be reviewed regularly to determine whether schedules need to be updated, tactics revised, and responsibilities reassigned.

Types of Marketing Plans

The type of marketing plan you develop will depend on the nature of your organization. A small business or individual practice will not have the resources to do as much market research as a large corporation. Its environmental and competitive analysis may be less developed. In a midsize company or a start-up, the marketing plan often will be developed along with the overall business plan. It will generally flow from the business plan and work in conjunction with other operating plans, such as finance, operations, and production.

In a large corporation, marketing plans may be developed by a marketing department, a line of business, a product group, a geographical region, or other business unit. Some institutions use a top-down approach to market planning, with a few key executives setting policy, which is then implemented in the field. In a bottom-up approach, each division, profit center, or line of business may develop its own plan that is then "bought into" by senior management.

Researching Your Plan

Before you can write your plan, you need data. Market research data can be quantitative or qualitative. Quantitative research usually refers to surveys and other techniques that involve large sample sizes and resulting data that can be analyzed with some degree of statistical confidence. Qualitative research relies on small groups or individuals.

Quantitative Market Research

There are two types of quantitative data: that which you derive from your own customers and that gathered from public sources.

Customer information is invaluable in helping you answer questions like these:

- Who are your most profitable customers?
- What is your average customer-retention rate?
- How do buying patterns (amount, frequency) impact retention rates and profitability?
- Are there other factors that impact retention and profitability (such as demographics, psychographics, or life cycle)?

Public information commonly used in market research includes statistical data compiled by local and federal sources, business associations (like the Chamber of Commerce), and industry trade groups. For example, comparative banking statistics are available from sources such as the Federal Reserve Board and the American Bankers Association. Census data, industry information, and much more can be found by regular reading of business and trade publications and on the Internet. Competitors' websites are also good resources for constructing comparative information on target markets, positioning, and marketing tactics.

Purchased research is available from market research firms. Syndicated research is often made available by subscription. For example, Dalbar and Cerulli Associates compile information of interest to pension plan providers from regular surveys of third-party sales professionals, plan sponsors, and plan participants. Subscribers can receive information that is industrywide or specific to their own company and its immediate competitors.

Customized research provides information based on the client's specific questions and is not shared with anyone but the client. A bank launching a new ad campaign, for example, might commission a survey to determine baseline aware-

---

Using Research to Derive More Profit from Each Customer

If you could retain each customer an average of one month longer than you currently do, what would it add to your bottom line? A North Carolina mortgage lender discovered that keeping its customers on the books for one extra month increased its net annual interest income by 6 percent. Finding this metric through analysis of its own customer data was one use of market research. Putting it to work was the next step. The lender's data analysts began by determining which independent variables affected the duration of the loan. It discovered that profitability in lending (loan size multiplied by duration) had the highest correlation with the income of the borrower, the market value of the home, and the loan amount.

In addition to analyzing its own customer data, the North Carolina lender also looked at public information. From periodicals and trade association studies, it determined average retention rates for leading practitioners in order to determine whether its own retention rate was high or low. It was found to be about average. The bank engaged a consulting firm whose staff interviewed market leaders in noncompetitive industries (such as life insurance) to learn best practices for increasing retention.

One result was a "Scoring Guide for Payoff Prediction." This model enabled managers to estimate customer tenure and intervene before customers were lost. By communicating with profitable segments in appropriate ways and developing strategies to retain them, the lender used the data to improve bottom-line results.[2]

---

ness. After the campaign launches, the bank would conduct another survey to determine whether brand awareness and positive recognition have increased. The bank might also survey whether the ads were recalled (aided or unaided), and changes in purchase intent.

Qualitative Research

Sometimes marketers want answers to questions that can't be reduced to multiple choice. Finding out client price sensitivity or how to effectively motivate third-party distributors usually involves qualitative techniques. Qualitative methods, such as focus groups and personal interviews, are often used for evaluating branding strategies and marketing campaigns. Focus groups are usually done in a series, either over time or over geographical locations. One focus group may be atypical; it takes more than one to establish a pattern. For example, a brokerage company planned to launch a massive campaign targeted to high-net-worth women. Prospective materials, including promotional and educational tools, were shown to focus groups in New York, Chicago, Dallas, and Los Angeles. Each group consisted of eight women with net incomes over $100,000 and net assets over $500,000. While there were minor regional differences, there was substantial agreement among all the groups on key issues, which were then incorporated into the materials.

Observational research is another type of qualitative data gathering. For example, "mystery shopping," in which a researcher poses as a customer, is a technique that can be used to evaluate the service proficiency of one's own employees or to learn more about competitors.

The Elements of the Plan

Although each organization will have its unique market plan format, there are elements that are common to most market plans. These include identifying your target segments, determining your positioning, setting objectives, developing tactics, establishing budgets and timetables, and setting up metrics for evaluating results.

Table 3-1. Elements of the Market Plan

- Executive summary: a synopsis of the plan and its key elements
- Environmental analysis: a SWOT (strengths, weaknesses, opportunities, and threats) analysis of your company and your competitors
- Identification of your target segment(s) (see chapter 1)
- Analyzing your positioning in relation to your competition and establishing your branding strategy (see chapter 2)
- Establishing marketing objectives
- Determining schedules, budget, human resources, responsibilities, and accountabilities
- Setting implementation tactics
- Identifying the metrics that will be used to track and measure success

The SWOT Analysis

SWOT is an acronym for strengths, weaknesses, opportunities, and threats. (SWOT analysis, which evolved during the 1950s and 1960s, came out of work at Harvard Business School in analyzing case studies. It has been widely used ever since as a tool for developing business strategy.)

SWOT Analysis for a Global Bank

A division of a multinational bank was charged with determining strategy for selling currency transaction processing services in Great Britain. This is a portion of its SWOT analysis:

STRENGTHS	WEAKNESSES
Demonstrated international expertise	Low market penetration
Offerings on par with the competition	Low market recognition
Internal client base to cover fixed expense	No decisive competitive advantage over other providers
Can provide multicurrency services	Sales force not familiar with product

OPPORTUNITIES	THREATS
Consolidation among British providers means fewer competitors	Declining global interest rates will reduce income but not operating expense
Potential outsourcing by smaller banks opens potential markets	New competition from other foreign banks
If U.K. adopts the euro, our bank will be well positioned	Technology "fixed costs" continue to grow

From this analysis, the bank determined that its most likely potential target markets were smaller U.K. banks looking to outsource their transaction processing to a recognized multinational currency leader. The SWOT analysis also helped the bank identify areas of deficiency that needed to be addressed by the marketing team, such as sales training and brand-building efforts, in order to meet revenue objectives.

Strengths are capabilities or resources of the organization (or product) that could be used to improve its competitive position. Weaknesses are the opposite. Strengths and weaknesses usually focus on the following items within the organization:

- Size of organization
- Reputation of organization
- Current market share of product
- Current market segments
- Ability to meet target market wants and needs
- Product or technological advantages/disadvantages
- Pricing advantage or disadvantage
- Market perception of product: positioning or brand image
- Operational strengths and weaknesses
- Budgetary constraints and types of resources available
- Management commitment
- Marketing/communications differentiation

Opportunities and threats come from outside the organization. Opportunities are favorable conditions in the environment that can potentially produce rewards. Threats are external barriers that may prevent a company from reaching its objectives. Opportunities and threats may come from:

- Industry trends (industry growth, maturity, or decline)
- Economic factors (interest rates, business cycle, inflation)
- Political forces (wars, changes in leadership, new legislation, or court decisions)
- Regulatory forces (new or changing regulations)
- Technology
- Demographic changes
- Societal changes (large-scale changes in attitudes or behaviors)

Competitive Analysis

The SWOT analysis can be used not only to pinpoint your own situation but also that of your competition. You can begin by identifying your top three to five competitors by name. List each competitor's strengths and weaknesses in a chart format so comparisons can be made. **Table 3-2** lists some of the items that might be included.

Table 3-2. Competitive Assessment

ASSESSMENT CRITERIA	OUR COMPANY	COMPETITOR A	COMPETITOR B	COMPETITOR C
Market share				
Estimated marketing budget ($)				
Estimated net sales ($)				
Size of sales force				
Geographic coverage				
Unique selling advantage(s)				
Pricing (high/moderate/low)				
Target segments				
Brand image				

Marketing Objectives

Marketing objectives need to take into account the company's overall business plan. When looking at priorities, it is important to determine not only what actions are needed but also how these actions will be viewed by the plan's various partners, supporters, and beneficiaries, both inside and outside the company.

Clear and achievable objectives need to be established and communicated to all parties, including the rest of the marketing department, product development, management, the sales force, service areas, and any other group within the organization on which your plan can have an impact. Your objectives should be projected over a time period—x percent over y years. (See the example in **table 3-3** on the following page.) Here are some common objectives:

- To grow profits, revenues, or market share in a certain market
- To increase the number of customers
- To increase the proportion of customers who are highly profitable or otherwise valuable (for example, as referral sources)
- To increase the size of customer accounts or the amount of activity in those accounts
- To reposition a product

Table 3-3. Goals Should Be Specific and Measurable

The marketing objectives for a small, regional bank might look like this.

	CURRENT	1-YEAR GOAL	2-YEAR GOAL	3-YEAR GOAL
Assets ($)				
Increase (%)				
Rank vs. competition				
Earnings ($)				
Increase (%)				
Rank vs. competition				
Average loan size ($)				
Increase (%)				
Rank vs. competition				
Average deposits ($)				
Increase (%)				
Rank vs. competition				
No. of deposit accounts				
Increase (%)				
Rank vs. competition				

- To build brand awareness for long-term profitability
- To increase the number of products or services you cross-sell to current customers
- To increase retention rates
- To increase share of wallet

Implementation

Before you develop tactics for meeting your objectives, you first need to determine your resources. What is your budget? How big is your staff? Will the plan be implemented by your own department or by others? How much authority do you have over those who will be charged with implementing your plan (such as an outside sales force)?

Budgets are usually outside the control of marketers; the funds available may be a percentage of sales or may be based on a formula derived from competitive analysis and marketing objectives—or, in the case of a small business, on how much cash is in the till. No marketer ever has enough money to do everything that is desired. You'll hear the complaint from those with multimillion-dollar budgets and from those with no budgets at all. Budget will indeed determine what your marketing options are, but creative marketers can accomplish far more on a small budget than they think.

Other steps in implementing the plan include the following:

Get buy-in from all concerned parties. Understand your management's and sales team's objectives and goals. Make a point of meeting with the management team to review the market plan and gain buy-in. Programs are more likely to be successful if management and sales input is solicited and incorporated.

Leverage partnerships. Take advantage of programs that may be available on a co-op basis or that are centrally managed and funded. Be alert to ways in which national advertising campaigns, corporate sponsorships, sales contests, and product launches can help you. Make sure these activities are integrated so local offices and branches are aware of the activities and can plan local events accordingly.

Establish a tracking and measurement process. A process must be put in place to capture the information and to provide the tools needed to track each program and measure success.

Continually evaluate all existing marketing programs and change or modify aspects that aren't working. The plan must be fluid and adapted to changing internal and external environments. Review progress at intervals short enough to catch developing problems early.

Assign responsibilities for implementation and tracking. The plan will not succeed unless all the people on the team know what they must do to execute the plan and measure the results.

Insure that your proposed tactics can be communicated to and executed by others. When implementing tactics over different geographic locations with different staffs, the plan must insure that the tactics are replicable and cost-effective. This may mean beta testing a tactic in one location and rolling it out across markets as results merit. If the size of the market and the cost of reaching the market vary from location to location, the plan should address how tactics will vary with those factors.

Table 3-4. Selected Implementation Tools—A Checklist

Media Advertising

- Radio
- Television spots, product placement
- Signage (billboards, subway)
- Co-op advertising
- Print (newspapers; magazine, trade, and professional journals; advertorials; Yellow Pages; specialized directories and trade books)

Public Relations

- Media relations
- Media events
- Public speaking
- Signed articles and op-ed pieces

Event and Cause Sponsorship

- Sponsorship of existing events (sporting, cultural, educational)
- Cause marketing (such as working with a charitable group by donating a portion of sales, providing goods or services, or underwriting and publicizing events)
- "Activation" events associated with a sponsorship, including contests, giveaways, special events

Direct Marketing

- Direct response advertising
- Direct mail packages
- Dimensional mailings (anything that is not a flat letter or postcard; see chapter 7)
- Telemarketing

Communicate successes early and often. Establish a means to gather program feedback—best practices or lessons learned as well as hard numbers—and identify a vehicle to communicate this feedback to the sales force, management, and other partners. Communicate any early "wins" as soon as possible. It will set the right tone and provide some immediate support for the program.

The Internet
- Banner advertising
- Key word advertising
- Customer website
- Wholesaler website
- Intranet
- Permission e-mail campaigns

Personal Selling
- Lead-generation campaigns
- Personalized letters and calls
- Customized proposals
- Presentation/sales materials
- Sales training
- Sales contests

Trade Shows and Seminars
- Exhibiting at trade shows and industry events
- Holding seminars for prospects and clients
- Convened events, such as panels, symposia, and round tables

Relationship Marketing
- Retention-marketing programs (special programs for new customers, loyalty programs)
- Cross-sell and up-sell programs
- Customer publications

Implementation Tactics

The universe of marketing communications tools is vast and ever-growing. As you brainstorm possible tactics for your campaign, the tactical tools above will give you some ideas. Chapters 4 through 11 discuss these tools in more detail.

Table 3-5. Choosing Tactics

ADVANTAGES	DISADVANTAGES	RESOURCE USAGE	OBJECTIVE
MEDIA			
Depending on vehicle selected, can reach mass audiences or highly targeted ones. Cost per thousand (CPM) is low.	Cost per prospect is often relatively high. No definitive way to measure effectiveness.	Costs range from moderate to high. For most organizations, ad specialists are outsourced.	Awareness building. Branding. Retention marketing.
PUBLIC RELATIONS			
If successful, powerful "third-party endorsement" has higher credibility than advertising.	No control over whether message appears or in what context.	Relatively low cost. Can be done with limited staff or outsourced expertise.	Awareness and brand building. Establishing name in the marketplace. Relationship building.
SPONSORSHIPS			
Opportunity to associate brand name with event or cause favored by target markets. Exclusive venue for sales team to meet with clients and prospects. Opportunities to motivate internal staff.	Sales effectiveness not easily measurable. Must be planned carefully to achieve goals.	Sponsorship costs can be low or high, but activation will cost an additional 50 to 150%. Need for large staff resources.	Awareness building. Lead generation. Relationship building.

Choosing Tactics

Given the large number of potential tactics, how does a marketer choose which to implement? From a strategic standpoint, the answers should be based on a combination of factors:

ADVANTAGES	DISADVANTAGES	RESOURCE USAGE	OBJECTIVE
DIRECT MARKETING			
Highly targeted. Results easily measured. Call to action.	Can create negative image (junk mail, telemarketing, spam).	Low on a cost per contact basis. High on CPM basis. Usually outsourced.	Sales. Sales leads. Relationship building.
INTERNET (TRANSACTIONAL WEBSITE)			
Public face of company. Opportunity to tell story in depth.	Difficult to measure effectiveness.	Cost varies. Creation is usually outsourced. Maintenance can be done in-house.	Sales. Sales leads. Image building. Relationship building.
PERSONAL SELLING			
Most personal method. Measurable results.	Highest cost. Results vary by skill and experience of salesperson.	High.	Sales. Sales leads. Image building. Relationship building.
TRADE SHOWS AND SEMINARS			
One-on-one opportunity to demonstrate expertise.	Only as good as the people who work them.	Variable. Trade shows need sufficient staff resources.	Sales leads. Image building. Relationship building.
RELATIONSHIP MARKETING			
Most profitable return on marketing dollars.	Difficult to do well.	Variable.	Retention. Referrals. Cross-sell. Up-sell.

Selected client segments. What do they read, watch, do for entertainment? What is the most effective way to reach them? How do they like to be contacted (mail, phone, in-person, Internet)?

Opportunities in the marketplace. Are there special events that lend them-selves to a seminar? For example, are there tax changes your clients should know about?

Competitive behavior. Are your competitors advertising heavily? Have com-petitors entered or exited your markets?

Short- and long-term objectives. Are you trying to generate leads for your sales force or outright sales? Are you trying to build brand awareness for the long term or generate a "quick hit"?

Budget. Although marketing dollars and staff resources shouldn't be the first consideration in tactical planning, budget will certainly have a major impact on what you can do. But bear in mind that no budget ever seems big enough. Planning and creativity can be more important than dollars.

Even with identical budgets, two companies will likely come up with different tactical marketing plans. There is no formula for choosing marketing tactics. However, the matrix in **table 3-5** can provide a starting point for prioritizing tactical decisions. Chapters 4 through 11 discuss each of these tactics in detail.

Metrics to Track and Measure Success

Tracking and measuring marketing programs can be a challenge. Depending on the nature of the program, anecdotal results may be the best that can be hoped for—an ad that gets a salesperson an appointment, which in turn leads to a big sale; positive client feedback on a new loyalty membership benefit; or good press from a new corporate sponsorship event. Although these results can and should be shared with top management, there will be disappointment that they are not quantifiable.

Senior management is increasingly demanding accountability for market-ing dollars. "Track and measure" has become a corporate mantra. There is an urgency to demonstrate the value of a program, through a payback analysis or calculation of return on investment (ROI).

The limits of measurement. Some tactical programs are easy to measure. Direct response through mail, phone, or e-mail usually yields hard sales numbers and an immediate calculation of ROI. Some tactics are measurable over time, like relationship-building and loyalty programs that are designed to increase retention and cross-sell. These can be measured against a control group or against earlier retention and cross-sell rates.

Then there are programs that involve direct, one-to-one selling. The problem here is not a lack of data but the difficulty of gathering the data. It is notoriously

---

Table 3-6. Marketing Plan Checklist

Like a last-minute check of your tires before you go on a trip, this questionnaire can help make sure you've thought of everything. When you are comfortable with the answers to these questions, you are ready to implement your market plan.

- What is the business reason for this strategy or program? Simply put, why is this program important?
- What are the specific objectives?
- By what variables will success be measured?
- Is the budget sufficient?
- Is the program sustainable and can it be replicated?
- Is there buy-in from management, the sales force, and the necessary support groups?
- Do all the right people understand the objective?
- How does this market plan fit into the company's overall priorities?
- What needs to be done to implement the market plan to achieve the company's expected results?
- Is product training needed?
- Is collateral material available?
- Have goals been established and communicated?
- Have the necessary tracking and measurement tools been put into place?

---

difficult to get salespeople to fill out tracking reports, although this problem is beginning to abate as producer optimization systems automatically track contact and sales data. Programs that involve the sales force—whether at trade shows, seminars, or in face-to-face selling—can be measured, provided the data are tracked.

The most difficult types of tactics to track and measure are advertising, public relations, event sponsorship, and other programs where sales are not directly attributable to the promotion. If the campaigns are designed to build awareness, proxy measures—such as number of ad views, recall scores, and media placements—can measure success. But the reliable correlation of increased sales (if any) to an advertising or public relations campaign is a problem still looking for a resolution.

Better tracking and measurement tools are being developed. Consulting firms, along with many of the country's top advertising agencies, have started providing their clients with measurement services. Still, most marketers are not yet using these sophisticated tools. Only 28 percent of business marketers measure "most of their communications tactics" when evaluating marketing program effectiveness, according to a survey by Mobium Creative Group.[3] In another survey conducted among members of the Business Marketing Association, the Association of National Advertisers (ANA), and other organizations, "only 37 percent of respondents track sales as a measure of success when determining the return on investment of a marketing program."[4]

Yet a third survey revealed that 72 percent of respondents lack the necessary data to assess the ROI on their marketing investments.[5] The problem may not be a lack of data so much as a lack of access to the data. The ability to track and measure activity is not solely the responsibility of the marketing department. Rather, it requires a corporatewide commitment and the cooperation of management, marketing, operations, IT, service, sales, and product management.

What to measure. Before rushing off to create a tracking process, an extremely important question needs to be asked: What needs to be tracked? For many, the answer will be sales. However, along the road to tracking sales there is a wide array of information that can also be obtained. For a trade show, for example, measurement data might include attendance numbers, clients and prospects in attendance, demographic information, sales leads, brand impressions, appointments made, cost per lead or sale, and lifetime value of customers. What can be measured is limited only by cost and the thought and planning required to set up the infrastructure.

CHAPTER NOTES

1. Survey conducted by CEG Worldwide, 2001, cited in Cliff Oberlin and Jill Powers, *Building a High-End Financial Services Practice* (Princeton, NJ: Bloomberg Press, 2004), 217.

2. David Oshan and Kristin Triplett, "The Value of Retaining Customers," Quirk's Marketing Research Review, April 1994, www.quirks.com (article no. 062).

3. "Mobium survey finds limited measurement for ROI," BtoB Online, September 22, 2003, http://www.btobonline.com/cgi-bin/article.pl?id=11637.

4. Jim Nail, "Mastering Marketing Measurement," Forrester/ANA Study, September 2002.

5. "How's Your ROI?," Reveries Magazine, August 2002, http://www.reveries.com, reverb/revolver/roi/index.html.

MARKETING TACTICS

CHAPTER FOUR

Media Advertising

4

Advertising gives potential buyers the comfort that they are making the right decision. It is easier to buy from a well-known company than to take a chance on an unknown quantity.

4

To most people, advertising *is* marketing. It is often the first tactic to come to mind when a sales or product manager is seeking to build sales. But media advertising (as opposed to direct marketing, Internet marketing, and other tactics discussed in other chapters) is just one element in the marketing mix. It is not necessarily even the best choice if the objective is building sales.[1] There are nevertheless many reasons to use media advertising—whether print, broadcast, Internet, or outdoor. These are among media advertising's most important functions:

Brand building. This is the main reason most companies use brand or "image" advertising (that is, advertising not designed to sell a particular product). Keep in mind that most financial services are bought irregularly. Buyers pay little attention to advertising for products or services that they are not looking to buy. Therefore, the task of financial advertising is to generate a sufficient level of awareness over time to be "top of mind" when the buyer is ready, say, to take out a mortgage or engage a new investment banker. A British study that compared consumer awareness of a brand and consumer "willingness to buy" showed that "the better known a company is, the more likely it is to be accepted by a customer."[2]

Familiarity. Advertising gives potential buyers the comfort that they are making the right decision. It is easier for someone to buy from a company that is well known than to take a chance on an unknown quantity. This familiarity also "softens the beaches" for the sales force. The more a company advertises, the more successful its salespeople are in making the sale.[3]

Customer retention. Advertising reinforces satisfaction among those who have already purchased from a company. In a proprietary study conducted by a leading brokerage firm, advertising was found to have no measurable impact on acquisition of new customers but had a significant effect on client retention.

Reaching third-party influencers. Institutional advertising is often aimed at senior management rather than at those who actually buy a particular product, with the aim of getting a "trickle-down" referral from the top. A British insurance company found that as its advertising campaign created greater brand awareness among consumers, it also increased the willingness of financial advisers to refer business. Financial advisers were most willing to refer business to companies that they felt were "well-known to the public."[4]

Maintaining market share. Companies may be forced into "defensive advertising" in order to keep up with their competitors' ad expenditures and avoid losing market share.

Improving employee morale. Advertising can have a positive effect on staff motivation and make recruitment easier.

As for the direct effect of advertising on sales, the results are mixed. Many advertisers believe that if advertising isn't contributing measurably and promptly to the bottom line, it isn't doing its job. They know that a targeted product campaign can lift sales of some financial products that are bought regularly, such as car insurance or certificates of deposit. But many financial products—such as mortgages or pension fund management—are purchased rarely. Advertising that generates brand awareness may take years to pay off in actual sales, and the connection between the two may never be measurable.

Media Selection

When most consumers think "advertising," they most often think "television." But television is the most costly of advertising media, both in airtime and in production costs. Although local and cable television advertising can be cost-effective for some companies, only large and nationally distributed brands can cost-justify prime-time network television advertising that can run nearly a million dollars for a thirty-second spot, not counting several million for production. Add a star (like Jerry Seinfeld for American Express), and you're talking tens of millions.

Even though prime-time television costs less on a cost-per-thousand (CPM) basis than print advertising, at least one study has shown it to be less effective

A National Campaign to Generate Brand Awareness

AXA, a well-known name in Europe, was virtually unknown in the United States when it acquired The Equitable in 1999. Working within a budget that was far smaller than those of its well-established American competitors, AXA began by doing market research to determine its target market segment. The company discovered an underserved but rapidly growing consumer segment that wanted financial advice and was willing to pay for it. Behaviorally, this segment was self-directed but sought a sounding board. These investors were looking for someone knowledgeable to evaluate their ideas. The segment wanted to have some involvement in their own affairs but didn't want to do it all by themselves.

The resulting strategy was to position AXA as the advocate for the financially independent-minded, self-directed investor. To accomplish this, AXA decided to use primarily national television advertising, complemented by out-of-home media (such

The AXA "your way" campaign raised brand awareness by more than 40 percent.

as outdoor and transit). Given the limitations of budget, the creative needed to stand out and break category conventions.

The campaign line that came out of the strategy was "AXA. Your Future. Your Way." The Martin Agency, in Richmond, Virginia, created the ads, using the song "My Way" to drive home the message. The visuals featured a series of vignettes illustrating distinctive ways in which people conduct their lives. For example, one vignette featured a woman in a wheelchair winning a race. In another, a newlywed couple jumps into a swimming pool while still dressed in wedding gown and tuxedo. By the end of the first three months, brand awareness was already up 40 percent, and the ads themselves had the third-highest recall in the entire financial services category.

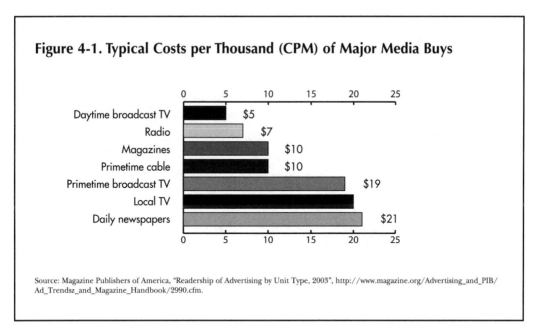

Figure 4-1. Typical Costs per Thousand (CPM) of Major Media Buys

Medium	CPM
Daytime broadcast TV	$5
Radio	$7
Magazines	$10
Primetime cable	$10
Primetime broadcast TV	$19
Local TV	
Daily newspapers	$21

Source: Magazine Publishers of America, "Readership of Advertising by Unit Type, 2003", http://www.magazine.org/Advertising_and_PIB/Ad_Trendsz_and_Magazine_Handbook/2990.cfm.

than print.[5] For companies selling investment products, in particular, when the target segment has investable assets of $100,000 or more, television is not as productive as more targeted media. Even the shows with the highest household income demographics draw huge numbers of viewers who do not meet investment minimums. As the AXA example shows (see facing page), there may be good reason for a company with little name recognition to advertise during prime time. However, many of those watching are not part of the target market.

Another concern facing television advertisers is the "zapping" of commercials by TiVo and other devices. American Express used a product placement to get its message seen in the NBC reality show, *The Restaurant*. Every time a table got its check, it came in an American Express folder; there was also a prominent American Express sign on the door. American Express was a major sponsor of the show as well. And in fact, its ad campaign featuring Rocco DiSpirito, the "star" of the restaurant, scored the highest in television ad recall among all financial services companies.[6]

Which medium should carry one's advertising message? All of them. Assuming you've got the money, each medium reinforces the other and reaches consumers in different ways. A successful campaign will use print and broadcast coupled

---

Reinforcing the Ad Message

A good example of a successful interactive campaign is the Harrisdirect campaign, which focused on "individual, fictitious direct investors and how they incorporate investing into their everyday lives," noted Eric Frenchman, director of online advertising for Harrisdirect.

Harrisdirect is the latest incarnation of what was formerly CSFBdirect (and before that DLJdirect), so the first order of business was generating brand awareness. Television and print ads developed personalities for the "direct investors," which were then carried forward by Internet ads that permitted viewers to learn more about the characters, including seeing what was on each investor's screen. These characters became so popular that they were also turned into in-store signage for Harrisdirect's investment centers.

According to Frenchman, this multimedia campaign "has been very successful in delivering new accounts at allowable costs and boosted brand awareness by 620 percent."[7]

---

with online channels, "to create an impact strong enough to elicit action, at the time when the viewer is in the most convenient position to respond to the ad," says Bryan McCarter, interactive strategist for Doremus Advertising.[8]

Print Advertising

Although a growing number of financial services companies are turning to television to help position a product or brand the company, print advertising, in the vast majority of cases, is the primary medium for conveying product information. There are three good reasons for this.

Print ads are less expensive to create and place. Of the one hundred top advertising spenders, almost all of whom rely primarily on television, only four financial companies—American Express, Visa, MasterCard, and Morgan Stanley's Discover—could afford to budget the $300 million or so required to make the list.[9]

The complexity of financial products lends itself to print. Whereas television is particularly adept at conveying emotions, print is better able to communicate facts and figures.

Print media offer the ability to target more precisely. There are hundreds of thousands of print publications, from free weekly shoppers to slick, monthly publications for pension fund managers.

Choosing the Right Publication

Print advertising includes newspapers, consumer magazines, specialized trade magazines, and directories (everything from the Yellow Pages to specialized industry directories). When deciding on print placement, here are some key questions to consider:

What publications do your target markets read? For most institutional advertisers trying to reach financial professionals, this is a simple question. There are standard trade journals that everyone in a given industry reads (for example, in money management, such publications as *Institutional Investor* and *Pensions & Investments*). There is some debate over whether institutional advertisers should ever bother advertising in general business publications, like *Business Week* or the *Wall Street Journal,* but this is largely a question of budget and ego—CEOs like to see their companies in the *Journal.*

On the consumer side, media placement is a complex and highly specialized subject. Ad agencies and specialist media firms perform sophisticated analyses to determine which of thousands of publications best match target market segments. Two key considerations for financial advertisers are budget and competition.

How much can you afford to spend? Print ads, depending on their size and the circulation of the publication, can range from several hundred dollars—for a local daily or weekly publication with a circulation of several thousand—to upwards of $75,000 for a full-page ad in the 2.2 million circulation *USA Today*—the largest-circulation U.S. daily newspaper. It is important to keep in mind that advertising page rates will vary greatly depending on whether the ad is black-and-white or color, the overall bargaining power of the advertiser, the number of pages and repeats being contracted for, and whether the ad will appear in regional or national editions, or in weekday or Sunday editions. Bargains can sometimes be found by waiting until the last minute for left-over space in a publication.

Where are your competitors advertising? This is a trick question, since a key goal is to avoid the clutter of competing ads. During the market boom of the 1990s, ads from mutual fund companies fattened consumer financial titles like

Don't Overlook Radio

Too many advertisers forget about radio, but in many markets, radio reaches more people than newspapers or other print media. Depending on the time slot, radio has these additional advantages:

It's inexpensive. Radio spots often cost less than print for equivalent CPM prospects. What's more, radio ads are not expensive to produce—if you want, you can just provide a script, and the radio deejay will read it.

It's clutter-free. People don't zap radio ads the way they do television. Listening to the radio may be the only thing the people in a car are doing other than driving, so you have a very large share of their attention.

It's targetable. In many markets, some radio stations may be reaching small ethnic and other communities that may otherwise be difficult to access. A financial adviser of West Indian background had considerable success using a radio station directed at Caribbean audiences for advertising and related publicity.

Money, Smart Money, and *Kiplinger's.* But with so many companies advertising the same type of product, the message got lost in the clutter. Smart advertisers began looking for alternatives, like shelter magazines and other publications aimed at wealthy consumers.

More Print Buying Decisions

Once you've decided where to place your advertising, there are still four more questions to consider: size, color, placement, and frequency. Size is the number of column inches the ad takes on a page. It can range from a two-line classified ad to a multipage spread. Placement refers to where the ad will appear in the publication. Frequency is the number of times the ad appears.

Size. Budget is the main determinant of size, tempered by competitive considerations. If competitors are placing full-page ads, a quarter-page may not get noticed. In newspapers, some advertisers have found that a three-quarters page can be as effective as a full page, because there is editorial matter around it.

Table 4-1. The Impact of Ad Size and Placement

SIZE AND PLACEMENT	RECALL INDEX (FULL-PAGE COLOR AD = 100)
Inside two-page spread (color)	139
Back cover (color)	120
Inside front cover (color)	112
Full page (color)	100
Inside back cover (color)	90
Inside spread (black-and-white)	95
Vertical 2/3 page (color)	81
Horizontal 1/2 page (black-and-white)	56
Vertical 1/3 page (black-and-white)	42

Source: Magazine Publishers of America, "Readership of Advertising by Unit Type, 2003," http://www.magazine.org/Advertising_and_PIB/Ad_Trendsz_and_Magazine_Handbook/2990.cfm.

Color. As **table 4-1** shows, four-color ads generally have more impact than black and white.

Placement. This is often the publication's decision, although some placements can be bought (the inside front and back covers and the outside back cover). One of the best placements is opposite the table of contents.[10] Advertisers prefer "front of the book" to "back of the book," largely because many people never get to the back of a magazine. The more an advertiser is willing to spend advertising in a publication, the greater its influence over where the ads will be placed.

Frequency. This decision is probably more important than the size or placement of the ad. Repetition in advertising is important. Multiple exposures are needed to generate awareness of the ad and the advertiser. The classic "Ebbinghaus Curve of Forgetting" showed that three-quarters of an audience forgot the message one week after exposure. Frequency reversed the pattern of forgetfulness and built recall. Many factors determine the precise number of exposures that are needed, but recall, brand familiarity, brand-quality ranking, and interest in buying all increase with repeated exposures.[11]

Creativity That Sells

The number of creative awards a campaign wins is usually not a good measure of strategic effectiveness. But solid creative input that generates attention, is memorable, is well liked, and serves strategic ends, can lead to synergies that multiply the effectiveness of a campaign. A good example of this is MasterCard's long-running "priceless" campaign.

Until 1997, MasterCard was regarded in the marketplace as the "other" card—one with no strong product differentiation. Five different brand campaigns in less than a dozen years and fifteen different agency partners globally were, in part, responsible for this muddy brand image. Following rigorous consumer research and an agency review, MasterCard picked McCann-Erickson, which devised the "price-

MasterCard's "priceless" campaign debuted in 1997 and increased purchase volume by 64 percent over the next five years. Its adaptability has been key to its success. Integrated marketing programs and promotions—including sponsorship of world soccer and major league baseball—multiply the campaign's effectiveness.

less" campaign with its tag line: "There are some things money can't buy. For everything else, there's MasterCard." Not only did the concept test well with consumers in the United States, but it was also a winner in every global market tested. The campaign has been used in over ninety countries in more than forty-five languages.

The success of the creative component has given MasterCard another advantage: cultural currency. Very few ad campaigns become part of popular culture; the publicity garnered from having Jay Leno do ten separate take-offs on the campaign, along with spoofs by David Letterman, *Saturday Night Live,* VH-1, *Will & Grace,* and many others, is—well—priceless. The campaign has received awards in the United States and worldwide. A *USA Today* AdTrack poll noted that the campaign is a "big hit with consumers," earning high scores for both likability and perceived effectiveness. Consumer awareness of the brand recorded double-digit increases.

And, most important, the campaign increased sales dramatically, and the number of MasterCard–branded cards increased by more than 52 percent over the same time period. MasterCard attributes 24 percent of its gross dollar volume to the campaign—driving six times more volume than anything they'd done before.[12]

Advertising Effectiveness

The impact of advertising on sales is notoriously difficult to measure, as it is difficult to isolate the effect of the advertising from all the other variables that impact sales. A 2002 survey of marketers published by researcher Marketing Management Analytics found that 72 percent of respondents did not have enough data to analyze the effectiveness of their marketing programs.[13] Nevertheless, there are qualitative and quantitative measures advertisers can apply to determine whether advertising is meeting its short- and long-term goals.

Advertisers may use qualitative measures of effectiveness, such as whether an ad is noticed and whether it is recalled, aided or unaided. Attitudinal changes toward the product or advertiser can also be measured through focus groups and interviews.

Quantitative measures of effectiveness can include the following:

- Number of inquiries or sales directly attributable to the campaign (generally used for direct response ads; see chapter 7)
- Variations from previous years in market share; size of customer base; purchase frequency; average size of purchase; and percentage of total assets held ("wallet share"); and profitability and length of customer tenure (lifetime value)

Advertisers can also test campaigns in spot markets and compare results against control markets. The effect of a campaign can also be measured using multivariate regression analysis. This statistical technique examines the relationships between one dependent variable (sales, for example) and multiple independent variables (for example, the individual elements of the marketing mix). This enables marketers to estimate the relative importance of each of the independent variables and to compare the financial return from each of the various inputs with its dollar cost.

Creating Effective Creative

The classic theory of advertising is that it is based on awareness, interest, desire, and action (AIDA). First you have to get the target's attention; then you have to provide a reason to listen to your message; the message needs to stimulate the desire for the product; and finally, the target needs to buy whatever it is you are selling. While overly simplistic, the AIDA model has some element of truth.

Selecting an Agency

The steps below have been adapted from the publication "Selecting an Advertising Agency," published in 2002 by the Association of National Advertisers. Many advertisers use consultants to help them through the agency selection process.

Develop an agency "job description." This document should clearly define the roles and responsibilities of the agency and list the capabilities and skills being sought:

- Identify the functions the agency will perform, such as account service, research, and media buying.
- Determine whether the assignment will be local, regional, national, or global.
- Will the agency be joining a roster of other agencies, or will there be an exclusive arrangement?
- Will the agency's work need to be coordinated with your company's in-house or outside public relations team?
- What tasks will the agency have, such as new product introductions, positioning or repositioning, brand building, and increasing market share?
- Based on all the foregoing, communicate the industry expertise that is expected (for example, whether the agency's financial services background needs to be strong in retail or institutional, high-end or down-market, in banking or with investment companies).

Effective creative (copy and illustration) should perform the first three of the AIDA functions—get noticed in a cluttered environment, be interesting, and establish a reason to buy—or at least to think of the brand the next time a potential customer is in the market for the product. The elusive "action" is usually dependent on point-of-purchase information. In the case of financial services, this is often supplied by the salesperson.

Effective advertising communicates quickly. The average person takes less than thirty seconds to look at an ad, and very few ads are noticed in the first place. In a print ad, the headline alone should tell the whole story, mentioning both the product and the key benefit. For example, consider a Fidelity Investments ad headlined: "Want to make sure your plan is on track? Fidelity can help." It's not brilliantly creative, but it is perfectly pitched for a target worried about losing money in a down market.

Determine what size agency is desirable. A smaller agency will dedicate its top people to an account that a large agency might assign to junior or less experienced staff. Clients with smaller budgets run the risk of not getting enough attention from agencies with a long roster of bigger-spending clients. On the other hand, the larger the agency, the deeper and broader its resources.

Consider potential conflicts. Are there conflicts with current clients? This is a matter of judgment. A competitor can be either broadly defined as any financial services provider (whether involved in banking, insurance, credit, or investments) or more narrowly defined to include only directly competing product lines. Or conflict can be limited, based on the marketplace the company serves. For example, a Chicago regional bank might not object to its agency handling a similar regional bank in San Francisco, as long as their markets didn't overlap.

Narrow the list of potential agencies. After you have reduced the candidates to a small group, issue a "request for proposal," seeking more information about the agency's experience, size, client list, personnel, and other matters of interest. From the questionnaire, and any personal interviews, clients will generally narrow the choice down to two or three firms. If you have the budget, you can commission each of the finalists to prepare a sample ad. Do not expect an agency to do it "on spec" (that is, without compensation).

The two most critical elements in a print ad are the headline and the visual (photo or other illustration). If neither the headline nor the visual attracts the reader's attention, it is likely the ad will be overlooked. The headline and graphic need to do all of the following: appeal specifically to the target market, describe a need or benefit, and arouse curiosity or in some way disturb the reader so the message is read.

Below are a few tips for making sure your print advertising is noticed, read, and serves your objectives, based on classic advice from David Ogilvy.[14]

- Always use headlines and an illustration.
- Relate the illustration to the headline or subheadline. Otherwise it may be misunderstood.
- Photos do a better job of attracting a reader's attention than drawings.
- Before-and-after photos are effective. So are babies and animals and sex,

What Makes Great Creative?

The Financial Communications Society has sponsored the annual Portfolio awards for best financial advertising since 1994. When asked, "What makes great creative?" Bill Wreaks, president of the society and publisher of the *Journal of Financial Advertising & Marketing,* looks for "creative messaging that is relevant, resonant, and simple." Veteran graphic designer Piet Halberstadt asks, "Does it enhance the product and inform the consumer?" Bob Kupperman, president of DDB Needham, also thinks simplicity is the key to notable financial advertising, although, as Mark Dimassimo, president and creative director of Dimassimo Advertising points out, "a lot of simple campaigns out there are simply awful."

The Citigroup "live richly" campaign, created by Fallon Worldwide, demonstrates the qualities of a multiple FCS Portfolio winner. Both simple and informative, it also contains an element often missing from financial advertising—emotion. Says Kupperman, "financial advertising does not have to be dry and devoid of emotion. . . . [Good advertising] connects with emotions of what really matters in life."[15]

though the last is probably not appropriate for most financial ads. Many financial ads show "aspirational" images, such as luxurious settings, romantic retirement travel, and well-heeled clients whose finances seem to be well looked-after.

● Celebrities or well-known people will increase recognition and recall. Spokespeople do not have to be movie stars. Steve Martin was a less effective spokesman for Merrill Lynch than Peter Lynch was for Fidelity, even though Martin

What's Wrong with This Ad?

Although this advertiser has only seconds to grab attention, it will take the target that long just to figure out how to read the headline, much less comprehend it. This is an art director's ad—pretty, but difficult to read. The headline is all caps, the body copy is in reverse, sans serif type, justified.

The good news is that the illustration is dramatic and eye-catching. Readers might stop long enough to look at the picture—but what will they take away from the headline? The brand name is not mentioned. There is no benefit beyond a vague claim that client companies (nature unspecified) are helped to seize opportunities of some kind. For the advertiser, an opportunity has been wasted.

is better known. The ads with Lynch were effective because he was known to the target market and was closely related to the company and its message.

- Avoid negative words in a headline (no, not, nothing, none). Readers skip over them and may associate the product with a negative quality.
- Don't be afraid of long copy. If the target is interested, more information is better than less. When using long copy, break up the copy with bullet points, numbers, or graphic elements.
- Use a call to action—a phone number or website—so the reader can act on any interest the ad has created.
- Don't make ads difficult to read. Keep layouts simple. Do not use reverse type (white on black). Avoid sans serif type except in headlines. Avoid justified type with a rigid right-hand margin—or worse, centered type—for body copy. Always make headlines in upper and lower case. If the targets can't read the ad easily, they won't.

The Creative Brief

It is important to have an unambiguous understanding of goals before creative work begins. One way to help ensure that is to provide the agency with a "creative brief." This document clearly and succinctly (usually in two to three pages) spells out the purpose of the ad and the key benefits that need to be communicated.

Problem. What problem is the ad trying to solve?

Objectives. How will this campaign solve the problem? Be as specific as possible—for example, increase awareness of product/brand by 20 percent, or increase market share by 3 percent in one year.

Target markets. Whom are you trying to reach with this campaign? Describe each market segment in as much detail as possible.

Competitive positioning. What is your competitors' positioning? How do you want to differentiate?

Target market positioning. How do you want this brand/product to be perceived by its target markets?

Product features. What features of the product will appeal to this target?

Product benefits. How can you translate the features into specific benefits that the target markets can relate to? For example, "24-hour service" is a feature; "world-wide trades are executed as efficiently and accurately as all other trades" is a benefit.

Key benefit/unique selling proposition (USP). If possible, identify one key benefit that stands out. This will become the theme—and tagline, if any—of the campaign.

Supporting sales concepts. Which product benefits support the USP?

Creative theme/concept. Derives from the USP.

Legal and Regulatory Considerations

After pharmaceuticals, financial services are probably the most highly regulated of all industries when it comes to advertising. Like all advertisers, financial services companies must comply with general advertising guidelines prohibiting advertising that is untruthful, deceptive, or unfair. But financial advertisers have many additional regulatory requirements—mandated by the federal government (such as the Federal Trade Commission and the Securities and Exchange

Commission), industry associations (the National Association of Securities Dealers, the New York Stock Exchange), and various departments within each individual state (state banking department, attorney general's office, insurance office). In fact, financial services may be the only industry in which some advertising is prohibited altogether: for example, the SEC has fined hedge funds that advertise in consumer publications.

What can happen if a financial services firm runs afoul of these laws? Fines, substantial penalties, and potential lawsuits. For example, a bank was sued under the federal Truth in Lending Act for advertising "no annual fee," and then charging such a fee six months later. The court ruled against the bank, despite other language in the ads giving it the right to change terms.

For marketers, the severity of regulation means a lot of small print in advertising. (But not too small—Rule 420(a) of the Securities Act mandates that all copy, including footnotes, be in "roman type at least as large and as legible as 8-point modern type.") It also means reviews by legal and compliance officers, sending marketing copy to Washington, D.C., for preapproval, and generally a lot of interference with what the creatives want to do. Further discussion of the impact of regulation on marketing can be found in chapter 7.

Field Advertising and Co-op Programs

Financial companies with field offices usually offer funding to their sales forces to offset the cost of local advertising. A 2002 MarketScan Report from LIMRA International (formerly the Life Insurance and Market Research Association) on "Field Advertising Programs" revealed that twelve of the fifteen insurance companies that responded to the survey offered corporately subsidized local advertising programs for the sales force. The objectives of the advertising programs varied, but most focused on building prospects' awareness of the local office. The study also produced other information:

- Ten of the fifteen companies offered co-op advertising. This allowed the salesperson to share the cost of the advertising 50/50 with headquarters.
- All twelve companies made preapproved ads available either via the Internet or hard copy from headquarters. All ads could be personalized with copy and/or photos.
- Ten companies offered programs that allowed salespeople to create their own ads as long as company guidelines were followed.

- Ads were available for a variety of media, including newspapers, magazines, radio, cable TV, bulletins, and Yellow Pages.
- Five companies monitored their programs for incorrect or nonapproved usage. Violators faced a reduction in funding or termination.
- Overall, the companies reported that approximately half of their salespeople or field offices participated in the programs.

There is an apocryphal quote, sometimes attributed to department store magnate and innovator John Wanamaker (1838–1922), to the effect that "I know half my advertising is wasted, but I don't know which half." With senior management demanding greater accountability for marketing return on investment, marketers are increasingly turning to measurable promotional channels, including direct mail, online, and relationship marketing efforts. Still, it is unlikely that traditional media advertising will disappear anytime soon. Although financial services companies are, individually, not among the top media advertisers, the industry as a whole ranks sixth among the top ten categories of advertising, spending $4.7 billion in 2002.[16]

Resources

The two major advertising trade papers are *Adweek* (http://www.adweek.com) and *Advertising Age* (http://www.adage.com). The American Association of Advertising Agencies (http://www.aaaa.org), often colloquially referred to as "Four-A's," is the major association of advertising agencies, while the Association of National Advertisers (http://www.ana.net) represents the interests of large, national advertisers. A good starting place for background on advertising is the Advertising Education Foundation (http://www.aef.com). For more information and resources, please see our related Financial Services Marketing Handbook website at http://www.fsmhandbook.com.

CHAPTER NOTES

1. According to market research firm Marketing Management Analytics, return on advertising investment does not pay back in profits over the short term. Using a model of one-year contribution of advertising to total brand sales, minus the fixed and variable cost of goods, divided by the cost of the advertising, they arrived at "payback," or "advertising-delivered profit before taxes." For consumer packaged-goods marketers, one dollar in advertising resulted in an average payback of 54 cents. For nonpackaged-goods consumer products and services, the payback was higher—87 cents—but still negative. Erwin Ephron and Gerry Pollack, "The Curse of the Leverhulmes," http://mma.com/resources/knowledge_center, February 2003.

2. Mark Stockdale, "Best Practice in Financial Services Advertising," *Admap*, May 1995.

3. A five-year study by McGraw-Hill showed that results from sales calls increased proportionally with ad spending. Cited in *An Advertising Handbook for Financial Marketers*, published by Pensions & Investments, 1999, 12.

4. Stockdale, "Best Practice."

5. The MMA data cited in Note 1 also showed that the marketing mix affects payback, with television offering the lowest return on advertising dollars.

6. Intermedia Advertising Group (IAG), "Ten Most Recalled Television Ads by Financial Services Firms, 2003," *Fund Marketing Alert*, January 11, 2004, www.fundmarketing.com.

7. Source: Joseph Jaffe, "Harrisdirect Adds a Human Touch," July 8, 2003, http://www.imediaconnection .com.

8. Bill Wreaks interview with Bryan McCarter, February 2004.

9. "One Hundred Leading National Advertisers," *Advertising Age*, June 23, 2003, www.adage.com.

10. According to studies published in the Magazine Publishers of America's *MPA Research Newsletter*, no. 60, "Advertising Positioning," ads opposite the table of contents were among the highest-scoring group.

11. *An Advertising Handbook for Financial Marketers*, see Note 3.

12. Debra M. Coughlin, "The Power of the Brand," *The Advertiser* (Association of National Advertisers), October 2002.

13. *Reveries Magazine*, 2002, http://www.reveries.com/reverb/research/ROMI.

14. David Ogilvy, *Ogilvy on Advertising* (New York: Vintage Books, 1985).

15. Bill Wreaks interview with all individuals quoted, February 2004.

16. "Top Megabrand Spending by Category and Medium, 2003 ed.," Adage.com, February 8, 2004, http://www.adage.com/page.cms?pageID=1016. The top five industry spenders were as follows: automotive; retail; movies, media, and advertising; food, beverages, and confectionary; and medicines and proprietary remedies. Rounding out the top ten were financial services; telecommunications; toiletries, cosmetics, and personal care; airline travel, hotel, and resorts; and restaurants.

Public Relations

5

Too many marketers fail to exploit the image-building potential of public relations. PR is the most effective means of shaping attitudes and building credibility for a person, company, or product.

How much of the financial services advertising that you see or read each day do you act on? When was the last time you discussed a financial ad with a friend or colleague? Now, consider your reaction to a recent news story—whether print or television—concerning the financial industry. How much of your attention did it receive? Did you discuss it with a friend or colleague? It is likely that you spent more time thinking about the news story than the advertisement. That is also the bottom line when comparing advertising with public relations. Too many marketers, particularly in financial services, give short shrift to public relations as a tactic for image building for their company or product. Public relations is one of the most effective means of shaping attitudes and building credibility for you, your organization, and its products.

If you asked a group of consumers or even professionals to define public relations, you invariably would hear it described as "free advertising." This is not a good definition because PR isn't advertising, and it isn't free. Rather, public relations is a means of positioning your products or company through a perceived third-party endorsement.

Third-Party Endorsement

When an outside source lends you or your company credibility, you have received a third-party endorsement. It could be inclusion in a magazine list of the best local banks for service. It could be an article you wrote, under your own byline, that appears in a trade magazine or local newspaper, thereby establishing your expertise on the subject matter. It could be a quotation attributed to you by a

Table 5-1. Advertising versus Public Relations

	ADVERTISING	PUBLIC RELATIONS
Cost	High to moderate	Moderate to low
Objective	Build/maintain awareness	Establish credibility and build awareness
Placement	Advertiser chooses time and place	Editor or producer decides where and whether to include
Who controls the message?	Advertiser	Editor or producer
Market perception	Puffery	Objective third-party endorsement

reporter who interviewed you as a source for a story. It might be a presentation you make at a professional conference. By selecting you as a speaker, the organization is, in effect, acknowledging your skills and abilities. It is the third-party, presumably objective, nature of this endorsement that brings you and your organization believability.

Consider the difference in impact between announcing something yourself and having a third party say the same thing about you. When you tell people "I just received a major industry award," or "the company just landed a major client," whether in person or through advertising, it is perceived as puffery. When someone else says or writes something about the same event, it has far more credibility.

PR is not better than advertising—it's different (see **table 5-1**). One key difference is that you cannot control what is written or broadcast about you or your company. An editor may reject your press release as too self-serving or lacking in interest to readers, members, or viewers. Conversely, the story idea you pitch may turn out to be of tremendous interest to a reporter, but you may see little, if anything, about your company in the finished piece.

Getting positive press is the most effective way to create favorable public opinion. By directing your message to the audiences you want to reach, your goals are to generate positive feelings toward your firm, differentiate the company from its competitors, and help position the company in the marketplace.

The Tarnished Image of Financial Services

Financial services have received much media attention since 2000, and very little of it has been positive. Commercial and investment bankers were tarnished in the accounting scandals surrounding Enron, WorldCom, and other companies. Stock brokerage firms have spent billions to remedy charges of giving companies favorable investment ratings in exchange for investment banking business. The mutual fund industry has been investigated by both federal and state prosecutors for a variety of charges, ranging from market-timing irregularities to excessive fees. Many financial companies have merged, acquired other companies, or gone out of business, upsetting communities, laying off workers, and raising fees as competition has lessened. And each severe stock market decline makes financial companies easy targets for stories about those who lose their life savings. The New York Stock Exchange itself has come under fire for ineffective self-governance and for permitting conflicts of interest.

Bankers and stockbrokers were once viewed as pillars of the community, but now those pillars have crumbled. In a November 2002 poll by Harris Interactive, respondents were asked, "Would you generally trust each of the following types of people to tell the truth or not?" Only 51 percent said they would trust commercial bankers, and only 23 percent trusted stockbrokers (the lowest percentage of all groups surveyed). The most-trusted group were teachers, with 80 percent.[1] In another study conducted by Golin/Harris, insurance was ranked No. 2 and brokerages No. 3 among the "least-trusted" industries in the country. (The most mistrusted industry in the country was oil and gas.)[2] As a sector whose livelihood depends on its customers' trust, financial services clearly needs to repair its image on a major scale.

The Tools of Public Relations

PR encompasses a wide variety of disciplines, including investor relations, crisis management, internal communications, influencing government policy, and community relations. This chapter will look primarily at PR as a marketing tactic —that is, how to use public relations to achieve your marketing objectives.

Press kits. The classic PR tool is the press release or press kit. A press release is a structured document. It is written like a news story, beginning with the headline. The headline should convey something newsworthy or something contrary to expectations, and must serve your objective. "Barracuda Bank to Take Over Local Small Bank" is a newsworthy headline for a local paper, but probably puts the wrong spin on the acquisition if you're writing for Barracuda. A better head-line might be "[Name of Town] to Get Big-City Banking Benefits."

The press release continues in newspaper style, with the most important points of the story coming in the first paragraph. The second paragraph often contains a quote from one of those involved in the story. The idea is to make it simple for an editor to use your release as it is written. If the editor has space for only two paragraphs, make sure your first two paragraphs are the ones that get printed.

The traditional press kit provides additional information. It can be mailed, distributed during a press conference or event, or given personally to a reporter. A press kit may contain any or all of the following:

- Press releases (see boxed examples on the following page)
- Backgrounders or fact sheets about the company or product
- White papers about industry or a particular issue of importance
- Biographies and photographs of the principals
- Suggested interview questions, with sample answers
- Brochures, newsletters, and other marketing material
- The URL of your website, which should post all of your press releases and supply background pages that reporters can refer to for information

If possible, it is a good idea to include illustrations in your press kit. Editors and reporters look for visuals to illustrate a story, and they may be more likely to pay attention to the information if it comes with a photo, slide, chart, graph, or other relevant piece of artwork. Make sure the materials you include are relevant.

Video news releases (VNRs). These tapes can be sent to local television stations, which may run a VNR as part of a news show, often as a feature, and sometimes without even mentioning that it came from a corporation. Local news budgets are low, and a slickly produced feature story about, say, a bicycle race sponsored by a local bank could well make the cut. The more a VNR looks like a real news segment and is tied to news of interest to a general audience, the more likely it is to run.

The VNR needs to be of equal or better quality than the footage shown on the news program. According to *Business World News* (www.businessworld news.com), the typical costs for a professionally produced VNR can range

Examples of a Bad Press Release and Its Rewrite

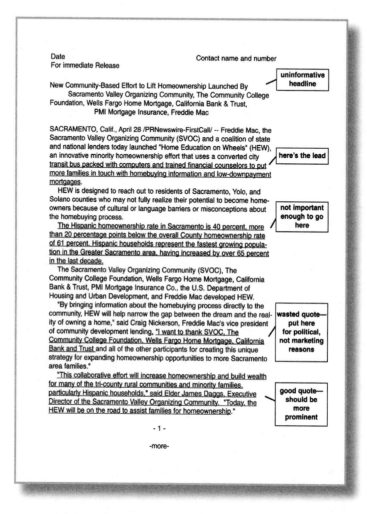

Date   Contact name and number
For immediate Release

New Community-Based Effort to Lift Homeownership Launched By
       Sacramento Valley Organizing Community, The Community College
Foundation, Wells Fargo Home Mortgage, California Bank & Trust,
              PMI Mortgage Insurance, Freddie Mac

[uninformative headline]

SACRAMENTO, Calif., April 28 /PRNewswire-FirstCall/ -- Freddie Mac, the
Sacramento Valley Organizing Community (SVOC) and a coalition of state
and national lenders today launched "Home Education on Wheels" (HEW),
an innovative minority homeownership effort that uses a converted city
transit bus packed with computers and trained financial counselors to put
more families in touch with homebuying information and low-downpayment
mortgages.

[here's the lead]

HEW is designed to reach out to residents of Sacramento, Yolo, and
Solano counties who may not fully realize their potential to become homeowners because of cultural or language barriers or misconceptions about
the homebuying process.
     The Hispanic homeownership rate in Sacramento is 40 percent, more
than 20 percentage points below the overall County homeownership rate
of 61 percent. Hispanic households represent the fastest growing population in the Greater Sacramento area, having increased by over 65 percent
in the last decade.

[not important enough to go here]

     The Sacramento Valley Organizing Community (SVOC), The
Community College Foundation, Wells Fargo Home Mortgage, California
Bank & Trust, PMI Mortgage Insurance Co., the U.S. Department of
Housing and Urban Development, and Freddie Mac developed HEW.
     "By bringing information about the homebuying process directly to the
community, HEW will help narrow the gap between the dream and the reality of owning a home," said Craig Nickerson, Freddie Mac's vice president
of community development lending. "I want to thank SVOC, The
Community College Foundation, Wells Fargo Home Mortgage, California
Bank and Trust and all of the other participants for creating this unique
strategy for expanding homeownership opportunities to more Sacramento
area families."

[wasted quote— put here for political, not marketing reasons]

     "This collaborative effort will increase homeownership and build wealth
for many of the tri-county rural communities and minority families,
particularly Hispanic households," said Elder James Daggs, Executive
Director of the Sacramento Valley Organizing Community. "Today, the
HEW will be on the road to assist families for homeownership."

[good quote— should be more prominent]

- 1 -

-more-

from $10,000 to $20,000. If a satellite uplink is added, the amount can rise to
$30,000. And there is no guarantee that the VNR will ever receive airtime. The
magazine reports that "a carefully crafted three-minute VNR often ends up
as a mere twelve-second sound bite airing only once during a non-prime-time
hour. Even worse, the newsroom may choose to take an unflattering angle on
the story."

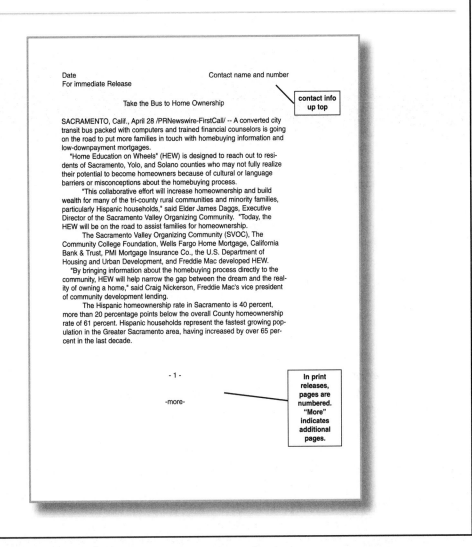

Date   Contact name and number
For immediate Release

contact info up top

Take the Bus to Home Ownership

SACRAMENTO, Calif., April 28 /PRNewswire-FirstCall/ -- A converted city transit bus packed with computers and trained financial counselors is going on the road to put more families in touch with homebuying information and low-downpayment mortgages.

"Home Education on Wheels" (HEW) is designed to reach out to residents of Sacramento, Yolo, and Solano counties who may not fully realize their potential to become homeowners because of cultural or language barriers or misconceptions about the homebuying process.

"This collaborative effort will increase homeownership and build wealth for many of the tri-county rural communities and minority families, particularly Hispanic households," said Elder James Daggs, Executive Director of the Sacramento Valley Organizing Community. "Today, the HEW will be on the road to assist families for homeownership.

The Sacramento Valley Organizing Community (SVOC), The Community College Foundation, Wells Fargo Home Mortgage, California Bank & Trust, PMI Mortgage Insurance Co., the U.S. Department of Housing and Urban Development, and Freddie Mac developed HEW.

"By bringing information about the homebuying process directly to the community, HEW will help narrow the gap between the dream and the reality of owning a home," said Craig Nickerson, Freddie Mac's vice president of community development lending.

The Hispanic homeownership rate in Sacramento is 40 percent, more than 20 percentage points below the overall County homeownership rate of 61 percent. Hispanic households represent the fastest growing population in the Greater Sacramento area, having increased by over 65 percent in the last decade.

- 1 -

-more-

In print releases, pages are numbered. "More" indicates additional pages.

Radio. Although radio may not reach as broad an audience as television, it should be considered for every press campaign. It is a highly segmented medium, which means that there is probably a radio program in your local market that is targeted to your particular demographic segment. There are stations directed at every age group and ethnicity. There are thousands of talk radio shows, all looking for editorial content—that is, someone to speak intelligently about a topic of interest to listeners. Radio interviews can be conducted at the studio or by phone and can be done on a low budget.

Public Relations for Every Budget

Public relations is generally considered a relatively inexpensive marketing tool, but the costs can add up depending on what you are trying to achieve. Still, effective PR can be achieved on any budget.

No Budget

- *Add a short (one-sentence) message to your e-mail signature,* such as "Hank Smith, CFP, can help with your insurance and investment planning."
- *When reprinting your business cards, add a sales message.* If you have a website, make sure you include your URL on all communications—e-mail, business cards, letters.
- *Research local organizations that might be interested in having you as a speaker.* If you're a financial planner or certified public accountant, for example, you will likely be welcome to talk to a wide variety of groups—from garden clubs to church groups to local parent/teacher organizations and local civic associations. If your service is more specific, find an organization that fits your target market.
- *Find out if a local or trade publication is interested in a signed article or white paper.* Send a letter to the editor with some possible topics. For example, a CPA might offer to write about changes in tax laws or business deductions that are often overlooked. A professional concentrating on retirement planning within the health-care industry could write an article for a hospital newsletter or a journal such as *Advance for Nurses* or the *American Journal of Nursing.* If the article is successful, speak with the editor about a regular column. Unlike a press release, or even a press interview, an article with a byline allows the writer to maintain control of the content, under the premise that an expert is providing valuable information and sharing knowledge with the publication's readership.
- *Contact local radio station news and community-service programs to suggest interview topics.* Let them know of your availability to discuss financial topics of interest to listeners.
- *Make yourself available to the press as an expert.*

Small Budget (up to $2,000)

● *Create a special event in conjunction with a nonprofit partner.* For example, a bank branch might sponsor a local church picnic or a Girl Scout camping trip. Make sure the local press knows about it. (See related sponsorship and event information in chapter 6.)

● *Send out press releases whenever you or your firm does something newsworthy (no more than once a month).* Keep your list of press contacts up to date by calling to confirm every six months.

● *Attend targeted trade shows and conferences, even if you can't afford to have a booth.* Talk to vendors about their business needs. Meet with organizers and officials to discuss the criteria for conducting a seminar or participating as a panelist at upcoming events.

Bigger Bucks (more than $2,000)

● *Hire a PR agency to spread the good word about you and your firm.* A retainer arrangement can run from a few thousand dollars for a small agency doing routine press releases to $25,000 a month or more for a large PR firm that performs numerous tasks beyond basic publicity, including development of communications strategies and media training for top executives. Shorter-term services—two to six months—often can be engaged à la carte for a specific campaign or announcement. A good PR firm buys you much more than its ability to write and distribute press releases. In most instances, a well-regarded firm can open doors to reporters and editors, as well as local "centers of influence" that may be closed to the average businessperson. Professional PR executives network and invest a large amount of time and energy developing relationships with local community and business leaders and media influencers.

● *Sponsor or cosponsor an event.* This option, which can cost from $2,000–$100,000 or more, is not for those with weak hearts or thin wallets. A title sponsorship of major professional golf or tennis tournaments, for example, typically costs in the millions of dollars per event. (See chapter 6).

● *Create a sponsored publication.* Costs range from $200 an issue for a "canned" newsletter to more than $10,000 an issue for a custom publication. (See chapter 11 for more information.)

● *Plan a media tour.* Hire a spokesperson who can appear as a guest on TV news segments and talk shows, representing your company. Have your agency prepare video press releases featuring you or your spokesperson ($15,000–$75,000).

Getting Press Coverage

Selecting the media to target is somewhat similar to deciding where to run advertising. Some publications will run your press releases or articles with a byline as a quid pro quo for your advertising, but these tend to be special-purpose journals, such as those organized around a trade conference. Most responsible journalists erect a "Chinese wall" between editorial and advertising. Being an advertiser does not automatically entitle you to news coverage (although it certainly doesn't hurt).

When picking the media to whom you will send your press release or press kit, keep their target market in mind, as well as your own. Everyone likes to see one's name in large-circulation media like the *Wall Street Journal* or *Business Week.* But a trade journal, such as *Bond Buyer* or *Institutional Investor,* can not only be a better placement, given your target market, but can also be easier to get into. Trade journals don't get the volume of press releases that general interest publications do. They have limited staff with limited time, so a usable press release may get run as it is written—something unheard of among the large-circulation general media. If you send a release to *Fortune* or the *Washington Post,* at best you may pique the interest of a reporter who will do his or her own research on the topic.

To cultivate the journalists who cover your market, make sure to introduce yourself at trade shows. Let them know if there are important breaking stories. Invite them to attend if you or your spokespeople are giving a speech or holding an event. Put them on your list for any white papers or other materials of interest. Getting on a reporter's Rolodex as a subject-matter expert or someone to bounce ideas off can lead to a gold mine of publicity. Each time you or your spokespeople are quoted as industry experts, your company's reputation is reinforced.

Think of reporters and editors as if they were very special clients. Remember, their days are deadline-driven, so always ask if it's a good time to talk if you call them. And remember that even if they cultivate you as a source, they don't work for you. Their job is to write fairly, not necessarily favorably. The following practices will help you to work effectively with the press:

● *Be positive at all times.* Adversarial relationships will not go far. Reporters are not the enemy. They have stories to write and deadlines to meet—what is important to you may not be important to them. Make sure you and your spokespeople deal with every reporter objectively and honestly.

Building Business by Becoming an Industry Expert

A small mortgage broker grew into a much bigger company through the steady use of PR. The firm's principal began by giving talks about "qualifying for a mortgage" and "current directions in mortgage rates" at local community organizations, like the YMCA. She would then send press kits, including her speech, her bio, and background information about the firm to local newspapers, inviting them to call her if they needed information about the subject. Pretty soon, the local papers were quoting her name and the name of her firm every time they did a story about mortgages. Success breeds success, and she was soon the local authority on mortgage stories—to the extent that she had to hire eight more brokers to join her staff.

- *Know the publication and its target audience.* It is important to read back issues of the publication to understand the audience and make sure your message will be relevant to the reader. Learn what the editor is interested in. Look at who the advertisers are and what ads say to readers.
- *Take the time to know the kind of information the reporter will be looking for.* Review the reporter's past stories. What type of detail does she like to include?
- *Take time to build a relationship.* Don't just go to a publication when you have something to say in the interest of your own product or business. Share industry information. Be willing to serve as an industry expert, to provide someone from your firm, or even to refer a reporter to your competitor if appropriate.
- *Know the difference between news and information.* Make sure you call reporters only when you have something that is newsworthy. Not everything your company does is worth shouting from the rooftops.
- *Don't use industry jargon or acronyms.* A reporter doesn't have the time to interpret what you are saying.
- *Know what you are going to say before you call a reporter, editor, or producer.* Before you get on the phone, jot down your talking points. Introduce yourself and be clear and concise when pitching your story.

- *Never promise what you can't deliver.* If you commit to getting information for a reporter, make sure you provide it before his deadline. If you can't deliver, let the reporter know as soon as possible.
- *Determine if charts, graphs, or illustrations are appropriate.*
- *When possible, make executives available for questions.* Don't offer identical interviews to different publications, particularly if it is not breaking news. You can damage any relationship you have built if the same interview appears in competing newspapers or on competing radio or television programs.
- *Make sure you or your spokespeople are trained in handling the media, especially for broadcast interviews, where you need to respond quickly and clearly.* Having a session or two with a professional media trainer will give you far more confidence, as well as some knowledge of how to better control the interview.
- *Follow up intelligently.* It is a good idea, after sending a press release, to follow up with a phone call. Editors can get hundreds, even thousands, of press releases every day and don't necessarily read every one. Reminding an editor of the subject of your press release may pique her interest. She may ask you to send the release again. Do so, marking it clearly "Information requested by [name and date]." Then follow-up once more. The more relevant the information is to the audience, the more likely the press release will be used and phone calls returned.
- *Don't keep calling to find out if or when your press release or interview will appear.* This is one case in which the squeaky wheel not only doesn't get the grease, it may end up in the junk pile.

Above all be ethical. Never misinform, and be careful what you omit in the service of spinning your story. If you don't know the answer, say so, and get the answer. If you can't reveal certain information, say so.

Many corporations discourage employees from speaking directly with the press about company activities. From a corporate perspective, controlling the message assures consistency, as well as the ability to address press inquiries in an organized fashion. It also reduces the need for "damage control" when an unauthorized spokesperson makes a mistake. On the other hand, this policy does limit the ability of a local sales executive to build local visibility and credibility and may frustrate a reporter or editor who is looking for a local expert to quote.

Finding the Right Publications and Editors

Media directories abound, both print and online, that identify everything from general interest magazines to tiny special-interest publications. These directories may be organized by geography or by subject and include such information as geographical address, e-mail address, phone and fax numbers, circulation, frequency (daily, weekly, monthly), and the names and phone numbers or e-mail addresses for the publisher and the various editors. Be aware, however, that editors' names are often out of date. You should call the publication directly to make sure of the name of the editor you want to reach. When you call, ask the editor or assistant whether he or she is the right contact for your information, and if not, who at the publication might be interested.

For business-to-business publications, good places to start are the websites of industry trade associations. For example, the website of the Futures Industry Association (http://www.futuresindustry.org) has a list of fifteen publications relating to futures trading. For more information, see the Resources section at the end of this chapter.

If direct access to the press is important to you, build a relationship with your public relations or corporate communications group, just as you would with the press. Know the press guidelines established by your company and adhere to them. If a press opportunity arises, contact the appropriate people before making a comment, but do try to find out the nature of the press inquiry, the type of story being written, your role (whether the reporter is looking for a single comment that can be taken over the phone or a sit-down interview) and the deadline the reporter is under. Have this information available before you call corporate communications.

Given the financial industry's strict regulations, licensed financial advisers should not offer any financial advice to the media before talking to your compliance department or your attorney. If not already required, ask a member of the corporate communications group to monitor any press interview that you schedule. This will not only protect your licenses, but will also help convince them that you are a knowledgeable and responsible spokesperson. Many calls from the press go directly to corporate communications. Let those colleagues know your area of expertise and your willingness to address press inquiries. If you are asked to become a local spokesperson, ask for media training. If not available internally, find a successful local PR firm that can provide one-on-one training. Expect to pay a fee to any outside firm.

In this post-Enron era, the press is taking a more critical look at the words and actions of the business community. Reporters will be more cautious and less likely to take what is said at face value. Many feel duped and manipulated by events over the past several years. In response, you can expect that statistics and recommendations will be scrutinized and held to a higher standard of proof than in the past.

Dealing with Bad Press

When you or your company receives bad press, your first inclination may be to fight back. Usually, that's a mistake. If the charges are true, the best course is to publicly acknowledge the problem and fix it. Although confirming bad news—even if it's not your fault—can hurt your reputation in the short run, the pain will pass quickly, and you can move on. In the long run, your reputation will probably be strengthened by your quick action. Of course, if there is any risk of legal liability, you should consult your attorneys before making any statements.

Financial services firms have not always been willing to admit their mistakes or to publicly offer corrective action. The bad press surrounding

---

Solving a Problem a Bank Didn't Create

Sometimes companies do the right thing, even if they don't think they're wrong. In 2002, Wells Fargo was the only bank to refuse to sign a $57 million Holocaust-reparations settlement with Belgium's Jewish community. Wells Fargo maintained, plausibly, that it was under no obligation to pay a $267,000 obligation it had inherited at three removes when it acquired First Interstate Bancorp in 1996. But when the *Los Angeles Times* picked up the story, Wells Fargo found itself with more than $267,000 worth of bad press. The bank quickly reversed the decision and issued a press release apologizing to the Jewish community for "any misunderstanding that our original decision may have caused."[3]

Table 5-2. Responses to a Crisis

SITUATION	STRATEGY	ADVANTAGES	DISADVANTAGES
Misinformation being spread about your company	Go on the offensive with the accusers or the media for spreading rumors	Gives stakeholders rebuttal points; gets your story out	May fan the flames and cause the media to look for other potential wrongdoing
Information is true but not presented fairly	Defend your position by making spokespeople available, being open to the press	Gives your company the opportunity to set the facts straight and improve employee morale	Spokespeople may appear defensive
Your company cannot respond for legal or other reasons	Avoid press as much as possible; apologize and explain reasons for avoidance	Reduces potential legal liability	Makes company look like it's hiding something
Your company is at fault	Engage the media; hold a press conference announcing changes to address the problem; use the Internet to reach stakeholders	Gets the story out and over	Only works if you really fix the problem

Source: Adapted from Irv Schenkler and Tony Herrling, *Guide to Media Relations, Prentice Hall Series in Advanced Business Communications* (Upper Saddle River, NJ: Prentice Hall, 2003).

research analysts who touted companies that did investment banking business with their firms was not helped by denials, destroyed e-mail correspondence, and failure to punish the guilty. A firm that took a strong stand and said, "we've made a mistake, and we are correcting the problem, and here's how we're doing it," would be in a far better position.

Although crisis management is outside the scope of this discussion, **table 5-2** gives a brief overview of possible responses. In the event of an actual crisis, be sure to consult a professional.

Resources

Some of the major media directories include Standard Rate and Data Service (www .srds.com), Bacon's (http://www.bacons.com), Gebbie (http://www.gebbieinc.com), Burrelle's (http://www.burrellesLuce.com), and MediaMap (http://www.mediamap.com). These services are available by subscription or in some public libraries.

The Securities Industry Association has an excellent resources section with links to dozens of financial trade associations and government entities at http://www .sia.com/resource_links/#exchange.

Another good resource is PR Newswire (http://www.prnewswire.com), a service that distributes press releases to publications worldwide. The major trade association for the public relations industry is the Public Relations Society of America (http:// www.prsa.org). Other good reference sources include O'Dwyer's Public Relations Daily (http://www.odwyerpr.com) and Public Relations Online (http://www.public-relations-online.net). For more resources on public relations, see our Financial Services Marketing Handbook website at www.fsmhandbook.com.

CHAPTER NOTES

1. "Trust in Priests and Clergy Falls 26 Points in Twelve Months," *The Harris Poll* #63, http://www.harris interactive.com, Harris Poll Library, November 27, 2002.

2. "Faith in Business Rapidly Eroding," http://www.worldpreferred.com/pub/infoCentre/newsDetail.asp? NewsId=18, February 28, 2002.

3. "Kovacevich Commits a Rare Gaffe," *Institutional Investor,* April 2003, 16.

Sponsorship and Event Marketing

6

Sponsorships build credibility for the company, demonstrate corporate caring and good citizenship, communicate the brand's philosophy to the public, and build employee morale by involving employees with their communities.

6

The last time you attended a sporting or other event, how receptive were you to the products and services being promoted? Did you walk away more knowledgeable about the sponsor? With more interest in its products and services? That was the hope of the companies around the world that invested more than $25 billion in event and cause sponsorships, an increase of 220 percent over the last ten years. Sponsorship of events and causes is a subset of public relations. It is used primarily as a brand-building strategy, although it has other potential benefits, such as building customer loyalty and motivating employees. Unlike, say, trade show or seminar marketing (discussed in chapter 10), its primary goals are not immediate leads or sales.

There are tens of thousands of sponsorship properties chasing businesses that are looking to have their names associated with an event, cause, or organization. Sponsorship properties are available to address every corporate strategy and every marketing budget, and if an appropriate opportunity doesn't already exist, it can be created for you. If golf is your game, and you have $5 million or more available, your company can be the title sponsor of a prestigious PGA event. For $10 million or more, your company's logo can be splashed across a car going more than 170 miles an hour as part of a NASCAR sponsorship. If football reaches your target audience, title sponsorship of college bowl games can be had for anywhere from $500,000 to several million dollars. If your company is a supporter of the arts, there are museum exhibits, concerts, and hundreds of worthwhile organizations that support artists of all types. If you prefer educational initiatives, there is not a high school or college in the country that wouldn't name a scholarship after your company, as long as you fund it. Not all sponsorships cost a lot of money. A community bank or branch of a larger bank might sponsor two local Little League teams for less than $1,000. In exchange, the bank's name is emblazoned on each team member's uniform.

Like anything else, sponsorship fees and the benefits your company receives from its investment are negotiable. Obviously, the larger the investment, the greater your ability to negotiate fees or services. There is no lack of opportunity. The challenge is finding the event or sponsorship that best meets your objectives.

What Is the Value of Sponsorships?

One reason for the steady increase in sponsorship spending is the perceived long-term value associated with an event. A worldwide study of 13,000 people, conducted by Mediaedge:cia's MediaLab in 2003, found that 45 percent noticed the companies and products that sponsor events, 42 percent believed that the companies and products that sponsor events are of high quality, and 28 percent claimed they would buy from the companies that sponsor these events.[1] For example, NASCAR is particularly known for its devoted fans. Depending on the product and driver, as many as 94 percent of fans purchase the product of the NASCAR sponsor over any other product in the category. They are also more likely to have positive feelings about NASCAR sponsors than about nonsponsors of competing products.

For financial services companies (unlike, say, beverage producers), sponsorships are not primarily meant to generate immediate sales. But they do have numerous other benefits:

- Build brand awareness by associating a company's product with an event of importance to its target market. Brand awareness is further extended through advertising, public relations, and other efforts that surround the sponsorship.
- Shorten the sales cycle. Getting the company's name known through events and sponsorships helps purchasers relate the company's products to a cause or event that customers also support. When given a choice, consumers would rather purchase a product with which they have an affinity.
- Maintain and strengthen existing relationships. Events provide opportunities to entertain clients in ways not typically available to the general public. Client-only receptions, celebrity "meet and greets," and event packages including tickets and parties can be created for clients and key prospects.

What's German for "Tiger Woods"?

The world's No. 1 bank wants to be better known in the United States. Deutsche Bank purchased Bankers Trust in 1999 but only began an active brand-building campaign in the United States in August 2003, when it sponsored the Deutsche Bank Championship golf tournament at Boston's Tournament Players Club. The bank chose the locale because it was convenient to both American and European clients. The key benefit Deutsche hoped to gain was the opportunity to do some "heavy-duty shmoozing" with clients. Each part of the bank was allowed to bring clients and reserve places in the professional-amateur golf day before the tournament started.

Looking for more bang for its buck, Deutsche assigned the proceeds of the event to support the Tiger Woods Foundation. Not only did the bank hope doing so would improve its image, but it also hoped it would improve the chances that Tiger would show up for the event. He did.[2]

- Demonstrate to attendees a company's expertise through seminars and exhibits.
- Improve employee morale by providing employees with tickets to an event, creating an employee-only hospitality area, or holding internal contests for event-related prizes.

Locally, sponsorships help to identify and link a company to the community it is serving. Sponsorships build credibility, demonstrate a sense of corporate caring and giving, communicate the brand's philosophy to the general public, and most important, get employees and management out into the community among clients and prospects. As competition among financial services companies grows for share of the consumer's wallet and mind, advertising has become cluttered, and consumers are less able to differentiate products. Financial companies, in particular, are looking for new and versatile ways to sell relationships, not just products.

A prioritized list of the benefits you are seeking will guide your evaluation of the kinds of events to consider. Bank of America, which spends some $50 million in sponsorships annually, has different goals for different local markets. In regions where the bank is dominant, it sponsors community-based activities, as a means of building relationships and loyalty. Where competitors dominate,

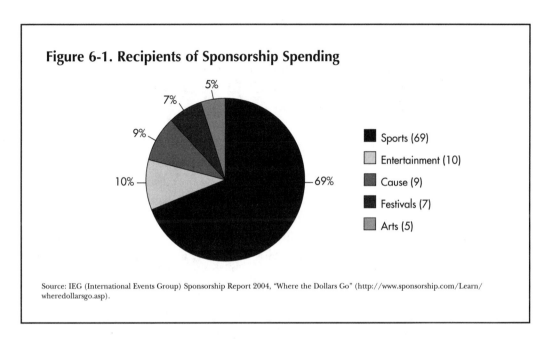

Figure 6-1. Recipients of Sponsorship Spending

- Sports (69)
- Entertainment (10)
- Cause (9)
- Festivals (7)
- Arts (5)

Source: IEG (International Events Group) Sponsorship Report 2004, "Where the Dollars Go" (http://www.sponsorship.com/Learn/wheredollarsgo.asp).

BofA looks for higher-profile sponsorship opportunities in order to build brand awareness.[3]

Sponsorships allow versatility, creativity, and interaction so that companies can communicate with their audiences in personal and direct ways. For example, MetLife looks for exclusive sponsorships that permit the insurer to target human resources professionals, to whom it sells employee-benefits programs. As a result, MetLife has become the exclusive sponsor of *Workforce* magazine's Optimas HR awards.[4]

The billions of dollars spent annually on events, nearly 70 percent of which goes to sports, is intended to help fans know that Visa, for example, understands sports fans and what is important to them. As the tagline says, "Visa, it's everywhere you want to be." Visa's more than $15 million sponsorship of the National Football League works to drive the point home. Spending by financial services firms on sponsorships has steadily risen over the past ten years. In 2002, nine financial services companies—Visa, MasterCard, Bank of America, John Hancock, J. P. Morgan Chase, American Express, MBNA, Charles Schwab, and Wachovia—together paid in excess of $320 million in sponsorship fees.

Financial and other companies will continue to spend more on sponsorships, but the distribution of those dollars is changing. According to the

International Events Group (IEG) Sponsorship Report (2003) "expansion will come as the result of partnerships with a wider array of nontraditional partners." Sponsors are focusing more on interaction and experiential marketing—not just inviting clients to watch the game, say, but also giving them the chance to participate in some way.

Cause Marketing

Tying into sponsorship of a charitable event or creating a program in support of a charitable cause can greatly increase the value of the investment. The 2003 global study by Mediaedge:cia's MediaLab, found that 56 percent noticed the companies and products that sponsored good causes, 43 percent believed these companies were of high quality, and 53 percent would buy from them.

American Express virtually invented cause marketing with its 1983 sponsorship of the refurbishing of the Statue of Liberty. By pledging to contribute a portion of each dollar spent on the card, American Express greatly increased card usage. AmEx saw that linking its name to a good cause offered multiple benefits. For example, since 1993, AmEx has supported Share Our Strength, an antihunger program. Originally, AmEx was looking for a way to mollify restaurateurs who were complaining about the costs of accepting the AmEx card. Contributing part of every dollar spent on a meal in a restaurant not only raised millions for the charity, but served numerous marketing ends, including increased usage of the AmEx card and increased business for participating restaurants; improved image in the community of both the restaurants and AmEx; measurably improved cardmember satisfaction; and enhanced pride of employees working for American Express, increasing their participation in community activities related to the promotion.[5]

FNB Corporation, a banking company, moved its headquarters from Hermitage, Pennsylvania, to Naples, Florida, in search of high-net-worth clients. To let the community know about its services, FNB has put 90 percent of its advertising budget "into community and civic support for things like Habitat for Humanity, United Way, and the YMCA," according to Clay Cone, a vice president. "If people see that you're out there supporting the community, they will bank with you. [Community sponsorship] has served us very well."[6]

Local Cause Sponsorship Pays Big Dividends

On a local level, tying business and charity together can be particularly effective. Not only are there opportunities for the business to promote the charity but there may also be opportunities for the charity to promote the business. For example, when Washington Mutual entered the New York City market, it sought a way to extend its brand image as a community-centered bank. It sponsored a photojournalism program in association with the public schools that provided each school with a digital camera. Students' entries were judged by a Pulitzer Prize–winning photographer, and winners were exhibited at the New York Historical Society.

The promotion intersected with WaMu's brand image and sales objectives in several ways. Local community newspapers were delighted to publish winning pictures from their area. Press coverage also included a kickoff event and opening night at the Historical Society. WaMu also had students and teachers drop entries off at the new WaMu branches in their communities—immediately introducing the branch to the community and leading to new accounts.[7]

Activating a Sponsorship Program

Sponsorship spending statistics do not reflect the cost of ancillary activities, events, and programs developed to leverage a sponsorship. Typically, a company will budget anywhere from $0.50 to $1.50 for each sponsorship dollar spent, in order to "activate" their programs. By that rule of thumb, Visa—which spent $80 million on sponsorships in 2002—was likely to have spent an additional $40 million to $120 million to activate its sponsorship programs. Activation programs include many elements:

- *Contests.* Offering a free trip to an event is a strong draw for customers. Visa and Sovereign Bank of Boston upped the ante by offering free trips to five events in conjunction with Visa's "Be There" promotion in the fall of 2002. Local and national publicity surrounding the contest was enhanced by the nature of the prizes. The winners, limited to Sovereign Bank Visa card users, received all-expenses-paid trips to Visa-sponsored events, including Super Bowl XXXVII in San Diego, the 2003 Daytona 500, the 129th Kentucky

Derby, the 57th Annual American Theatre Wing's Tony Awards in New York City, and the 2004 Summer Olympic Games in Athens.

- *Giveaways (premiums).* These are items such as balls, caps, and other products with the sponsor's logo. To amplify the effect of American Express's sponsorship of the 2002 U.S. Open tennis tournament, the company created an on-site promotion called American Express Radio. Spectators were provided with special radios that provided audio feeds of the tournament.
- *Corporate entertainment.* Luxury boxes at sporting events and concerts fall under this category.
- *Opportunities to meet the stars.* Introductions to professional athletes, artists, and other celebrities are another successful tactic.
- *Advertising tie-ins.* As a sponsor of the 2002 Winter Olympics, Bank of America invested $49 million in related advertising. The campaign featured bank employees "competing" in skiing, skating, and bobsledding—with slapstick results. The voice-over began, "At Bank of America, we really wanted to participate in the Olympic Winter Games," and continued, "but we decided to stick with what we know best." Pre- and post-Olympics surveys showed that unaided awareness of the sponsorship increased from 3 to 13 percent, and the campaign ranked highest among all advertisers in unaided awareness. The campaign also led 94 percent of bank employees to say that the sponsorship made them proud to work there.[8]
- *Client communications.* These can take the form of statement stuffers, newsletters, or membership magazines. The communication can be targeted (for instance, sent only to customers who will be able to take part in the event), or it can be disseminated to the entire client base, particularly when it supports a charitable cause. Letting clients know about such activities builds goodwill.

One of the benefits offered by sponsorships that other marketing tactics can't hope to achieve is the ability to provide an extraordinary experience—something the client will remember for a lifetime. Sponsor a team, and you can bring clients onto the field just before the start of the game or fly them with the team to a game of their choice. Sponsor a racecar, and a client can experience first-hand the feeling of going 170 miles per hour around a racetrack. Sponsor an exhibit, and guests can see it before it opens to the public. If concerts are more to your purpose, your clientele can meet the musicians, sit in the best seats during the concert, and go backstage afterward. A New York Stock Exchange specialist firm has invited clients to equestrian events featuring horses owned and trained by one of its senior executives. Going to the winners' circle is an event not easily replicated.

Planning to Maximize Sponsorship Value

Whereas companies once determined the success of an event based on attendance or the thank-you notes sent to the CEO from grateful guests, today, return on investment is the measure for success. As marketing programs come under increasing scrutiny, it is critical to maximize the value of a sponsorship event.

Unless you plan thoroughly and manage the sponsorship, you can do more harm than good. Poorly executed events will damage your company's reputation, alienate your guests, leave potential clients with a poor perception of your company's capabilities, and negatively impact other sponsors, event organizers, and related vendors.

Before you agree to become a sponsor, understand the implications associated with being a major sponsor versus a smaller sponsor. Take a hard look at your budget. Does this sponsorship restrict the company's ability to participate in other sponsorships? Can you do what it takes to activate the sponsorship? These two questions need to be asked regardless of the sponsorship level and cost. To determine if a sponsorship is right for you, here are some additional questions to consider:

- What do you want to accomplish with the sponsorship (quantify, if possible) —increased sales, brand building, client appreciation, employee motivation, or other aims?
- What type of organizations or activities do you want to be associated with?
- Does the sponsorship reach your desired audience? What are the demographics of the audience? Request an analysis of past or projected attendees.
- Is the sponsorship compatible with the company's segmentation and branding strategies?
- Does it have buy-in from your sales force?
- Does it have management's support? Will it be viewed as frivolous or lacking the anticipated ROI?
- Is ROI measurable? How will you track results?
- Is the event local, regional, or national? If national, are there regional or local opportunities and how can these be leveraged?

Making the Most of Your Sponsorship

Sponsorship planning should take a three-phase approach:

Prior to the Event

- Determine the company's primary objective. Is it sales, local or corporate brand building, brand repositioning, product communication, or something else?
- Communicate the company's involvement to the target audience through letters, flyers, invitations, and print ads. It is important to let the target audience know about the sponsorship and the company's role in it.
- Determine if opportunities exist to create a "mini-event" for key clients and prospects that will give more value to the sponsorship.
- Determine where and how the company name will be displayed. What signage is provided by the organizers? Where will the company's logo appear?
- Determine if speaking opportunities are available. If so, meet with event organizers early in the planning to discuss potential opportunities.
- If an event attendee list is available, mail information to attendees highlighting your sponsorship and the company's place in the community.
- Schedule time to meet with key clients, prospects, or community leaders. Make tickets available to them.

During the Event

- Be visible. Make sure the company is well represented at the event. Provide company attendees with shirts, jackets, or sweaters that can be easily spotted in a crowd.

- When is the event being held? Does it conflict with other corporate initiatives? Is there enough preparation time to handle the sponsorship correctly?
- Are the cosponsors companies with which you want to be associated?
- Is category exclusivity available?
- What marketing opportunities will support the event? What is the organizer doing to market the event and promote the sponsors?

Building internal support for an event is a key element for success. Garnering the necessary support should begin only after you are satisfied that the event fits strategically with the company's objectives and a clear set of metrics has been identified to measure the event's success. Once this

- Schedule informal meetings with clients or prospects. Use meals or refreshments as a reason for getting together.
- Be prepared. Have extra tickets or event passes available for your best clients or key community leaders.
- If appropriate, set up a hospitality area for employees, clients, prospects, and other guests. A hospitality area makes a great meeting location and gives invited guests a rendezvous point.
- If the budget permits, have a photographer on hand. Pictures make a great keepsake for guests and can be used in follow-up communications, such as newsletters.

Following the Event

- Send thank-you notes and pictures to guests.
- Follow-up on business-related conversations that took place during the event.
- Meet with event sponsors to discuss what went right and wrong. Determine what can be corrected before agreeing to participate again.

Promote the event throughout the year in communications to clients and prospects. Even a small sponsorship position can be made larger by promoting the event. Let the event sponsors know your intention. Negotiate for a higher level sponsorship because of the added publicity.

is accomplished, a number of other tasks lie ahead:

- Communicate the proposed sponsorship to your various constituencies— senior management, the sales force, key marketing teams, corporate communications department, and any other area that will be directly impacted by the sponsorship.
- Build a team of cross-functional experts to assist in the planning, implementation, marketing, and internal and external communication of the sponsorship. If internal resources are not sufficient, there are outside companies that can be hired to help with event planning.
- Establish weekly, biweekly, or monthly update meetings where information and ideas can be shared with all involved parties.

- Establish an activation budget, and make it everyone's responsibility to stay within it.
- Create internal excitement for the event. Develop programs that allow employees and the sales force an opportunity to attend the event.

Measuring the Effectiveness of Sponsorship

When planning a sponsorship, you should set both short- and long-term objectives for awareness building, increased market share, increase in customers and revenues, and profitability. Also, set criteria for evaluating how the event will help achieve desired marketing objectives. Most important, make sure the event has a strategic fit with your company's image, position, products, and services.

The success of an event can be measured by the value gained minus the costs. Value is assessed in relation to the following factors:

Revenue. This is measured in terms of sales associated with the event. These numbers must often be estimated using "close ratios" and "average value of sale" applied to the number of prospects seen at an event and committed to a follow-up activity.

Cost reductions. Reduced expenses can be achieved through efficiencies in selling and operations accomplished through an event. For example, cost savings may derive from shortening the sales cycle or reuse of collateral and properties developed for an event.

Direct Connection between Sponsorship and Sales Increases

J. P. Morgan Chase has segmented its Asian (primarily Chinese and Korean) client base in the New York metro region and has developed a number of special events for high-net-worth members of this group. Research showed that this particular segment was very supportive of classical music. Chase therefore became a sponsor of the Chamber Music Society of Lincoln Center, which designed events to maximize value for J.P. Morgan Chase. One event featured new work by well-known Chinese composer Tan Dun, who attended a pre-concert reception with clients. A post-concert dinner, which included several Asian musicians who had participated in the concert, was an enormous success. From this one event, for some sixty attendees, Chase traced several million dollars in new assets from the invited customer base.

Equivalent value. This is measured by applying a budget number to the value of the pre-event publicity or direct marketing; event-based promotion such as banners, workshops, or seminars; or other marketing tactics that are run in conjunction with an event. The impact of these tactics has a value equivalent to the cost of advertising, public relations, or other marketing activity normally required to accomplish similar awareness or brand development goals.

"Successful event managers gather all examples of payback," notes Ed Jones, of event-marketing firm Nth Degree. "They should include performance-tracking ratios, such as cost per visitor, average cost per sales lead or sales call, average cost of adding a new prospect to the marketing database, and other relevant metrics when reporting progress to management."[9] Tracking and measuring outcomes not only lets you know whether your event was successful but also enables you to make necessary changes to enhance future results.

Resources

Organizations: International Events Group/IEG Sponsorship Report (http://www.sponsorship.com); TSNN Events Network (http://www.events-network.com); Cause marketingforum.com (http://causemarketingforum.com).

Publications: *Special Events* magazine (http://www.primedia.com); *Event Marketer* magazine (http://www.eventmarketer.com); *Team Marketing Report* (http://www.team marketing.com); *Event Marketing* magazine (http://www.promomagazine.com/event _marketing).

CHAPTER NOTES

1. "Cause Marketing's Power Shown in MediaLab Study," Causemarketingforum.com (http://www.cause marketingforum.com), 9/1/03.

2. Adrian Michaels, "Deutsche Bank tees off in US branding drive," *FT.com*, August 27, 2003.

3. Bonnie McGeer, "B of A's Strategy to Improve Sponsorship Payoff," *American Banker*, April 29, 2003, 35.

4. Kate Maddox, "Sponsorships now part of media mix," *BtoB*, October 13, 2003, 16.

5. http://www.strength.org/meet/partnerships/charge/becoming.htm.

6. "Reaching Old Money Consumers in Naples, Fla.," *American Demographics,* June 2003, 35.

7. *Event Marketer* magazine, 2003 EX Awards, http://www.eventmarketer.com.

8. Bonnie McGeer, "B of A's Strategy to Improve Sponsorship Payoff," *American Banker,* April 29, 2003, 11.

9. Author's interview with Ed Jones.

Direct Marketing

7

Media advertising is meant to stimulate awareness, interest, and desire. Direct methods are different. They are meant to stimulate action—by selling products or services to customers, generating leads for the sales force, or driving traffic to a branch. Direct marketing also makes it relatively easy to measure results.

7

irect marketing is not new. The classic way of finding new customers for insurance and brokerage accounts has long been cold calling. It is a method detested by most callers and recipients. But for those without a book of business, it has been regarded by sales managers as the way for newcomers to start. And it has been successful enough to persist. Banks have traditionally used direct methods of getting new customers, such as handing out flyers to bring new customers in the door at a branch. Credit card companies are major users of direct mail and e-mail. What distinguishes direct marketing methods from indirect methods is the person-to-person communication involved. Mass media methods of marketing, such as advertising and public relations, are one-way communications from the marketer to the customer.

Marketer ⟶ *Consumer*

Direct marketing is a two-way communication between the marketer and the consumer.

Marketer ⟷ *Consumer*

Direct marketing encompasses numerous tactics, including direct response, direct mail, telemarketing, Internet marketing (see chapter 8), personal selling (see chapters 9 and 10), and relationship marketing (see chapter 11). Direct response refers to media advertising (in print, radio, TV) that calls for immediate action, usually through a toll-free number or reply coupon. Cable shopping channels and infomercials are also examples of direct response, as are catalog mailings, coupon packs, and door-to-door promotions, such as sample packs left hanging on a door.

Among nonpractitioners, direct marketing has a bad rap. Some of the terms applied to it include "junk" mail, "nuisance" calls, and "spam." But when your credit card company sends you an offer you want—say, a joint program with a car rental company that will give you free rentals—it is no longer junk or a nuisance. Or, when Amazon.com e-mails you an offer for frequent book-buying points by acquiring a particular credit card, it's no longer spam. The difference: Welcomed offers tend to come from companies you already do business with.

Techniques and Goals of Direct Methods

Direct methods work differently than media advertising. Of the four AIDA goals of advertising, the primary aims of media advertising are awareness, interest, and desire. Direct methods, on the other hand, are meant to stimulate the action component, and specifically to sell products or services to new customers, generate leads for sales force or other follow-up, or drive traffic to the retail outlet or branch.

It's not just the goals that distinguish direct marketing from media advertising. It's also the ability to measure whether the goals are achieved. Since media advertising doesn't necessarily result in an immediate sale, there is rarely any swift and sure method to determine how successful it is at reaching its goals. With direct methods, you will often know how successful a campaign is within weeks (for direct mail), days (for telemarketing), or hours (for online promotions). Not only does this enable you to find out quickly whether a given promotion will achieve its goals, but it also permits you to test and make changes "on the fly" to bolster results.

Literally everything in a direct offer can be tested, from the color of the background on an HTML e-mail message to the use of a stamp or a meter on a direct mail envelope. Professional direct marketers incorporate tests into every campaign, either by breaking lists up into "cells" that test different variables, or by testing new packages against controls. By constantly testing and tweaking the package, offer, and other variables, one should, in theory, continually improve results.

Targeting for Tax Season

H&R Block spent more than $100 million during the 2002 tax season on an integrated campaign that included media advertising, direct TV, and a 20 million-piece direct mail campaign. Unlike previous years, Block did not send generic messages to broad target groups like singles, retirees, and investors, but decided instead to tailor each message to a distinctive life-cycle segment. Targets included new movers, new parents, new homeowners, and newlyweds. In 2001, Block used eighty-four versions of five creative pieces; in 2002, the company used ninety-nine versions of nineteen different pieces.

One version of the piece targeting recent movers read, "New digs. New deductions!," with copy expanding on the message. The names and addresses of nearby H&R Block locations were laser-printed onto the mailing piece. "We're really trying to focus on getting the right messages to key segments," noted Joe Sevcik, the campaign's manager. Two months after the first mailings, which were dropped in December and January, Block had already seen a 4 percent increase in the number of clients over the previous year—and this was six weeks before April 15.[1]

Although the improvements may be minor (less than 0.1 percent in some cases), a million-piece promotion that is improved by 0.1 percent will still bring in 1,000 more responses. For smaller mailings, these kinds of tests may not be as important, although it is always a good idea to test the performance of different lists.

Personalization

In addition to different goals, direct marketing employs different methods of persuasion than does media advertising. One key difference is that direct methods can be personalized. Personalization can be as basic as using the prospect's name in the salutation or as complex as greeting an online customer with a listing of recent purchases and suggestions for new purchases. The most important component of personalization is choosing the right offer for the right list. Making sure that the offer is going to the right people (or conversely, making sure that the people you are planning to reach are getting the right offer) will spell the difference between success and failure.

Finding the Best Lists

There are two basic ways of getting a mailing list of prospects: buying or compiling your own. For example, credit card companies generally buy lists from credit agencies, based on credit variables such as paying outstanding balances on time or carrying a balance. This is one reason why everyone with a certain credit score receives similar offers from different credit card companies. It is also a good reason to avoid lists that your competitors are using heavily.

Purchased lists. One of the great advantages of direct mail is that lists can be purchased for almost every variable: For example, if you're selling college funding advice, you could buy a list of parents with children under age 10 who live in the Chicago metro region and have incomes of $50,000 or more. These lists will be of two kinds—people who have purchased products by mail, and "other." Other lists may include subscribers to publications (for example, subscribers to *Highlights* magazine, broken out by age of child, location, and income of parents); membership lists (for example, the Chicago-area PTA); or cluster-type lists based on census data.

As a general rule, mail-order responder lists are better than other types of lists, for the simple reason that people who respond to one mailing are more likely to respond to another. But not all response lists will pull equally. The more similar the product purchased in the past, the better the response to the current mailing. A good list broker will help you determine the right variables to select and identify several lists that you can test before committing to a large mailing.

Compiled lists. There are several ways of compiling your own lists. One way is to run a direct-response ad in a publication, on the radio, or on cable TV. The people who respond to your offer (which could be a free consultation) are prime prospects for a product sale. For example, if you market lending services to professionals, you could run an ad in a newsletter directed to doctors or dentists offering a free booklet on financing a practice. From the group that responds, you could then follow up with a one-on-one sales call, either by phone or in person.

You can compile lists from any number of sources. It is common to compile lists of prospects who visit your booth at a trade show for follow up by the sales team. You can clip trade magazine announcements about personnel changes at various companies in your industry. A financial planner looking for parents of children under age 5 could search through the local newspaper from five years earlier and check the birth announcements, then use the phone directory to

---

Cleaning a Purchased List

A bank did a mailing directed to human resources directors of New York–area institutions with more than 500 employees. The bank purchased the list, which included the name of the HR director. The initial response to the bank's mailing was disappointing. Telemarketing follow-up revealed that many of the names on the list were inaccurate, and consequently, the HR director never received the mailing. This is a common problem. The names of people occupying a given corporate title turn over constantly—by one estimate, more than 30 percent each year. For the next mailing, telemarketing calls were made prior to the mailing. Even if the contact person was not reached, the telemarketer verified the name (including spelling), title, correct address (including floor or suite), and phone number. Response to this mailing, with the same creative and offer, exceeded 33 percent.

---

determine current addresses and phone numbers. Keep in mind, however, that mailing lists date rapidly. About 10 percent of consumer households change addresses each year, and corporate turnover is even higher. You should make sure your lists are kept up-to-date by calling the names on a periodic basis.

Factors Affecting Direct Mail Response

There is a common conception that typical direct mail response is between 1 and 2 percent. But these numbers are meaningless. There are extremely profitable mailings that may only get a 0.5 percent response. There are mailings that get a 50 percent or more response rate. In a 2003 survey, the Direct Marketing Association (DMA) found average response to direct mail campaigns was 2.5 percent. But there was wide variation by industry, ranging from below 2 percent to 5.4 percent. A follow-up survey of financial services campaigns showed that responses varied from 2.5 to 13.7 percent, depending on the offer and the type of list.[2] The most important measure is not how many responses you get but the cost of getting those responses and their quality. If the campaign is profitable, even if you only get one new customer, it was a successful campaign. One of the campaigns in the DMA financial services survey had an average order size of $150,000. You don't need too many of those to make a campaign worthwhile.

It would seem a simple matter to measure the break-even point of a campaign: the sales generated through the current promotion divided by its cost. But for many direct marketing efforts, full value is not realized until well after the promotion ends. Credit card issuers, for example, may not realize profitability on any one mailing for years. They have developed metrics to enable them to estimate what percentage of new cardholders will remain, for how long, and how much profit they'll bring. Using this estimate of lifetime value enables the issuers to include future returns in their profitability analyses.

Other ways of measuring return on a promotion include the value of referrals to the sales force. Keeping the sales channel filled with quality new leads is an important aspect of many financial service promotions on both the consumer and institutional side. Although it may take months or even years to convert a lead into a sale, the profitability analysis of the campaign needs to account for expected future sales. The most important factors affecting response are these:

- **The list.** The list will have the greatest impact on response. Clearly, a list of your own customers will usually pull better than a list of people who have never done business with you. Lists of former customers will also usually do well. Targeting and testing are critical to raising the response of whatever lists you are using.

- **The goal.** Direct mail seeking leads is usually going to generate a higher response than that seeking outright sales. Offering a free consultation or the chance to win a sweepstakes is going to draw more response than the sale of a life insurance policy.

- **The offer.** The cost, value, and uniqueness of the product or service will affect response. A $49 book will get more response than a $1,200 newsletter. The first affiliation-based credit card offer will get more response than the fifteenth.

- **Integrated marketing.** Other marketing efforts that supplement your direct mail will lift response. Advertising and public relations will help build your brand identity, making prospects more responsive to your direct mail pitch. Outbound telemarketing before and/or after a mailing can lift response by a factor of 5. Including your website URL on a mailing piece will also increase response, because it gives prospects the opportunity to get more information without committing themselves to a call.

- **The company making the offer.** A familiar company is going to get a greater response than an unknown company. If your company is not well known, you may want to implement an integrated marketing strategy before and during your direct marketing efforts. Another option is to find a better-known partner for co-marketing.

- **Re-mailing.** A second try will increase response. People don't always respond to the first offer and may put it aside for later action. Studies have shown that it can take five mailings to get a satisfactory response. One investment company raised the number of re-mailings to those who had responded to an offer for a free portfolio analysis from two mailings to five. Doing so raised the number converted from leads to clients from 30 to 66 percent.
- **Creative.** The creative aspects of a mailing—the letter, the artwork, the number of pieces, and so forth—are less important than the factors cited above. Sending a poorly conceived offer to a good list will result in far more responses than sending a brilliant concept to a bad list. But creative issues can make a difference. For example, a clever teaser line on the outer envelope will get more people to open the mailing, thus improving response. Response will increase with each piece in the mailing, such as a "lift" letter (an additional piece designed to improve response by giving the reader just one more reason to buy), business reply card (BRC), reply envelope, involvement device (such as a peel-off sticker), and other tricks of the trade.

Getting Past the Gatekeeper

Mailings to institutional prospects have long been problematic. Personnel move around from position to position and company to company, but the major barrier to using direct marketing to high-level executives is getting past the gatekeeper. Many companies' mailrooms, for example, will not deliver third-class mail or mail that is addressed to a title rather than an individual. Once your piece gets through the mailroom, it then has to get by the executive's assistant or secretary, who often opens the mail and discards anything that looks like junk.

There are several schools of thought as to the best way to get past these gate-keepers. One tactic is to make the mailing look as much like a regular business letter as possible: a number-10 envelope with return address and no other copy, metered, or stamped first class. This will get it through the mailroom, though perhaps not past the secretary. If the letter really is personal—say from a sales-person to someone she met at a conference—it will be read by the assistant and

What's a Dime Worth?

This mailing contained a real dime, which was glued onto the front cover of the mailing piece. Response was in the 10 percent range, higher than expected for a mailing to heads of human resources and finance for large companies. Was the dime the "extra" factor? The theory is that assistants were reluctant to throw away anything with real cash—even a measly dime. Note, though, that the mailing was expensive—not so much because of the 10 cents, as because of the additional handwork required to glue the dime and its extra weight.

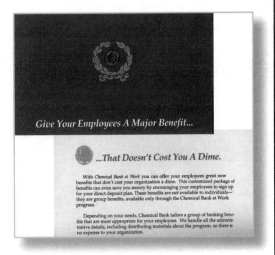

A dime is worth a lot if it gets past the gatekeeper.

passed on if it looks genuine. It's very important to make sure that it does not contain misspellings, incorrect grammar, typos, and other flaws that could get it tossed in the trash. Another approach is to enclose something valuable—even if the value is minimal. One mailer enclosed a $1 lottery ticket with a survey and increased response sevenfold.

A surefire way to get past most gatekeepers is to send the mailing via courier or overnight express. However, this is an expensive solution best saved for very targeted, high-value prospects. Prospects may handle their own mail, so marketers sometimes use a postcard or other type of self-mailer—that is, something that does not need to be opened. The idea here is that the executive may take a quick look at the offer. If there were an envelope instead, he might just toss it out without opening it.

Dimensionals, Premiums, and Other Gimmicks

A more expensive solution is a dimensional mailing, which is something sent in a box or other container. Dimensionals are expensive even if the item itself

---

The $1,200-per-Piece Direct Mailing

The marketing director who handled investment products for Bankers Trust (now part of Deutsche Bank) was looking for a way to help salespeople get in to see pension advisers. The bank sent out a series of high-end gifts, each with a presentation box that featured a sales message. One was a hand-carved wooden duck decoy carrying the message "we help you get your ducks in a row." The total costs of the mailing were $1,200 per recipient, but the program opened the door to 33 percent of the recipients—more than paying for itself in new business.

---

is not. Usually the container must be custom-made and printed, the items individually packed and mailed. But clever dimensionals can be effective in getting through the door—in one study, using a dimensional improved response rates by 75 percent.[3]

Sending a series of items can be a good foot-in-the-door technique. For example, a person looking for foreign-exchange business could send one attractive granite bookend in the shape of a dollar sign with a cover note explaining that he would bring the other bookend, in the shape of a Euro sign, to a personal meeting with the prospect. A technology company selling to commercial banks used this technique when DVDs were new. The chief technology officer received a promotional DVD disc, with the promise of a DVD player to be delivered by the sales rep at their first meeting. Be sure, however, the item is consistent in tone and content with both your image and the recipient. Obviously, expensive premiums should be limited to A-list targets only.

A word of caution: if your promotion is too valuable, it may run afoul of corporate gift policies and IRS regulations limiting the deductibility of gifts to $25. Although the IRS would generally allow companies to treat such promotional items as advertising expenses, it may be best to add your corporate logo to the item to avoid any question. As to whether this would satisfy the rules of the receiving organization, it may be wise to check with your own legal counsel for guidance.

> ### Dimensionals for Consumer Mailing
>
> According to *American Banker,* Fifth Third Bancorp has found that retaining customers in an acquisition is made easier by mailing a video that walks the new customers through the welcome booklet. The bank's marketing team found that many people will watch a video who will not read the pamphlet. Although the mailing and production costs are higher, the bank's tests have found the retention rate to be sufficiently improved to make the effort cost-effective.[4]

Costs

How much should a direct response campaign cost? Clearly, there is a wide variation, based on the type and size of the promotion. Costs per unit can range from pennies for a multimillion-piece mailing or telemarketing campaign to hundreds of dollars for limited distribution of a dimensional. While some marketers try to equate the cost of direct methods to common advertising charges, CPM (cost per thousand) is not a useful metric for most efforts. On an overall CPM basis, direct mail costs are far higher than media advertising. However, on the basis of targeted CPM—reaching those who are likely to buy the product—costs are usually lower than for comparable media buys. Similarly, return on investment (ROI) is generally higher for direct response.

Direct mail is expensive because it is complex. These are just the major elements that need to be budgeted:

- List purchase
- List hygiene (merge/purge, pre-sort)
- Creative costs (copywriting, design, photography, illustration)
- Printing and bindery costs
- Lettershop (personalization, inserting, addressing, sorting, mailing)
- Postage for mail piece and return piece

Elements of the Package

There is no standard format for a direct mail package. Formats can range from a single 4.25- by 6-inch postcard to elaborate, custom-made packages. The mass mailing sent by Fleet to small-business prospects, illustrated at right, is typical.

It includes an outer envelope (OE), a personalized letter, a four-color brochure, and a "lift" letter. In addition, the package contains a separate, personalized application and a business reply envelope (BRE) for the return of the application. These are all common pieces in a large direct mailing (to one hundred thousand or more).

The outer envelope is the most important element. The teaser—"Get up to $100,000 for your growing business. You're pre-qualified for Prime-1%"—is highly targeted to its small-business market and should get the envelope opened by any small business that needs money (and which doesn't?). Note the stamp on the envelope. This is a pre-sorted first-class-mail stamp. Affixing this stamp, rather than using a preprinted indicia, and using first-class mail will add to the costs. But clearly, in its mail tests, Fleet found that the increase in response was worth the extra expense. (Bulk mail is not forwarded or returned by the post office.)

The next thing the prospect will likely look at is the letter. There are several pieces of valuable "real estate" on a direct mail letter—the first sentence, the P.S., and a "Johnson box," if any. The Johnson box, named for copywriter Frank H. Johnson, allows for a short teaser in a box (often formed of asterisks) that sits across from the personalized name. This letter does not make the best possible use of its key real estate. There is no Johnson box—which makes for a cleaner, more business-looking letter but also removes an opportunity to grab the prospect by the lapels and sell. The first sentence reads, "I know how valuable your time is and want to remind you of your pre-qualification for a Small Business Credit Express line of credit." The acknowledgement of the reader's time is polite, but the first line of the letter needs to sell (not to mention that the end of the sentence is a non sequitur). A better opening might be: "Busy business owners like you need two things—time and money. We can't help you with time, but here's some money." The P.S. uses the standard technique of a time limit—"you only have until March 28 to respond." Using a deadline helps get the prospect to respond now, instead of sticking the offer in a drawer to deal with later.

The purpose of the brochure is to keep the sales pitch going by answering questions the reader may have. This can be done without a brochure by using longer letters. Consumer mailings are often multipage letters—some as long as ten or twelve pages. As David Ogilvy points out in his classic book, "Direct response copywriters know that short copy doesn't sell. In split-run tests, long copy invariably outsells short copy."[5] Copy must be long enough to answer the prospect's questions and make the sale. Note that the "lift" note in this case contains the current interest rate. This is smart, because the information must be up-to-date, and the lift note can be printed and inserted at the last minute. Although the letter could also be per-

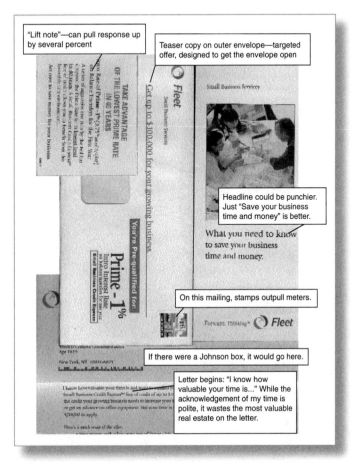

A typical mailing package: personalized letter, brochure, "lift" note and outer envelope. The outer envelope is the most important element.

sonalized with current interest rate information, the lift note is a more effective device for bringing it to the reader's attention.

Telemarketing

According to the 2004 DMA survey cited earlier, 21.5 percent of financial marketers used telemarketing in 2003. That percentage will decrease because of the passage of the "do not call" registry that went into effect in October 2003 (see discussion of regulations, below). Nevertheless, telemarketing will continue to be a valuable resource for some marketers, both to their own house lists and to business prospects (both of which are permitted under the new regulations). That's because telemarketing is relatively inexpensive on a cost-per-sale basis. Among mail, online, and telemarketing channels, telemarketing had the highest response rates, with an average of 7.4 percent.

There are two types of telemarketing: inbound and outbound. When someone calls on a toll-free number in response to a promotion, it's inbound. When your dinner is disturbed by an unsolicited call, it's outbound. Annoying as it is to many recipients, telemarketing nonetheless has its usefulness.

Telemarketing is expensive, especially in the business-to-business arena. But it is far less costly than a personal sales call. Many companies seeking to reach business decision makers employ an inside telesales staff to make the initial calls. This staff tracks down the appropriate decision makers, then attempts to qualify them and to set up an appointment for a meeting with an outside sales person.

There are several reasons why telemarketing continues to be a valuable tool to the marketer:

- **Speed of set-up.** Setting up a telemarketing program can be done much more quickly than most other types of programs. If you need to act quickly—because you have a limited-time offer, as with an initial public offering, or a need to beat a competitor who has launched an ad campaign—telemarketing, along with e-mail, is the way to go.
- **Response is immediate.** As with an e-mail campaign, you can know within hours whether your promotion is working. If you are testing a new offer, call list, or sales script, telemarketing will give you quick results so that you can make necessary changes or scrap the program if it does not appear to be profitable.
- **Contact is personal and interactive.** Like direct sales, telemarketing allows you to modify your pitch as you're making it, in response to questions and objections from the prospect. If your telemarketing staff is working from a script, you probably don't want them making impromptu changes, especially when regulatory compliance issues are involved. But as you observe their calls, you can quickly make changes in the script to reflect new objections or misunderstanding of the offer.
- **Lists can be easily updated.** Too often, telemarketers fail to use the opportunity to build and clean their prospect and customer lists. Especially

in business-to-business situations, telesales calls can serve double-duty as both a sales introduction and a determination of the name and title of the decision maker.

Regulations Affecting Direct Marketers

Telemarketing may be an endangered species. A federal do-not-call registry drew an overwhelming response as soon as it was announced in June 2003—with threatened fines of up to $11,000 per unwanted call. There are, of course, exceptions to the do-not-call rules, but direct marketing methods of all kinds are subject to numerous regulations and laws. Even before do-not-call registries, telemarketers were bound by Federal Trade Commission rules governing the hours when they could call, how quickly a live representative had to get on the line, identification of the caller, the length of time records must be kept, and more.

New telemarketing rules are just the beginning of the regulatory maze for direct marketers. Federal and state regulations on privacy are of particular concern to financial marketers. Federal regulations have allowed diversified financial companies to use "opt out" provisions for sharing personal customer data among different divisions. For example, Citigroup's Smith Barney investment division and Citibank could share data as long as the customer did not specifically request that his or her information not be shared. But California became the first state, in 2003, to require that financial marketers specifically get permission (opt in) from customers to share information within the corporation. Although the California law was subsequently superseded by federal law, the issue of "opt in" and "opt out" remains a contentious one.

State and federal regulations also apply to fax marketers and those who market to children. With revulsion against spam growing, federal regulations have already been enacted, and more rules affecting e-mail marketers are sure to come. Direct mailers have fewer legal constraints, but ethical direct mailers adhere to the Direct Marketing Association's guidelines, which include omitting names on a mail preference service for those who do not wish to receive direct mail.

Resources

The main trade association for the direct marketing industry is the Direct Marketing Association (http://www.the-dma.org). The DMA has a Financial Services Council and a Direct Marketing Education Foundation.

Standard industry publications include: Direct (http://www.directmag.com), *BtoB* (http://www.btobonline.com), and DM News (http://www.dmnews.com).

CHAPTER NOTES

1. Patricia Odell, "H&R Block Ramps Up DR in $100 Million Campaign," *Direct,* March 15, 2002, http://directmag.com.

2. Larry Riggs, "Financial DMers Prefer Mail:Survey," *Direct,* http://directmag.com/ar/marketing_financial_dmers_prefer/index.htm, February 2004.

3. G. Stephen Slagle, "Cutting through the Clutter," *Sales & Marketing Strategies and News,* May 1998.

4. Amanda Fung, "Fifth Third Uses Videotapes to Introduce Itself," *American Banker's Financial Services Marketing,* May 29, 2002, 6A.

5. *Ogilvy on Advertising* (New York, NY: Vintage Books, 1985), 88.

CHAPTER EIGHT

The Internet

8

For most financial companies, the Internet has become an important brand-building and relationship-marketing tool. Among the key uses of the Internet are to provide information, support the sales force, offer customer service, enable customer transactions, and support retention and cross-sell.

In the delirious days of the dot-com frenzy, it seemed the entire financial sector was abandoning brick and mortar for pixels. The business media fanned the flames, plugging "pure Net plays"—online banks and brokerages—and chastising old guard companies like Merrill Lynch for their slowness in adapting online models. Fearful of losing out on the next new thing, the old guard responded by throwing money at anything with a dot-com in its name. Citicorp, for example, set up an Internet-only bank called Citi F/I in 1997. When the future of online-only banks began to dim, Citibank pulled the plug, but not before losing what was reported to be in the hundreds of millions of dollars on this and other Internet ventures.[1]

From today's vantage point, it is clear that the industry overreacted to the perceived threat of the Internet as a competitor. In some industries—travel is a good example—the Internet did, in fact, transform the industry and put many brick-and-mortar service providers out of business. Many expected the same thing to happen in brokerage, as day traders flocked to the online discount broker du jour that offered the lowest fee. But the stock market crash of 2000 finished off most of the day traders and the online trading companies they supported. In 1999, there were about 200 online-only brokerages. By the end of 2002, there were less than half that number.[2]

The Internet as One Channel among Many

The war between online and brick-and-mortar financial services firms has been won, surprisingly, by brick and mortar. At the close of the dot-com boom, name brands made a comeback, bringing their brand strength online. This was true in

---

Integrating Online and Offline Business

Customers prefer their online banks to have offline branches—that's been shown in surveys and real-world experience. For example, Wells Fargo is second only to Bank of America in percentage of customers who bank online and number of online customers. One reason for its success is that Wells Fargo closely integrates its online and offline businesses. For example, home equity loan customers can apply at the branch, by telephone, or online. They can even "chat" online with a service representative and get a follow-up phone call from the bank. Wells Fargo has found that its fifty-four hundred branches are crucial to its success on the Web. Four out of five customers who research a loan product online buy it in a branch, not online, the bank has determined. But however they choose to apply, customers can check the status of their application online and receive personalized e-mail updates. Wells Fargo credits the multiplicity of channels for the fact its average customer household uses 4.3 of its products, more than twice the industry average.[3]

---

consumer products (The Gap, Barnes and Noble) and in consumer financial services. While the online "channel" has grown exponentially, most of that growth has come from traditional institutions offering online services as one among a variety of options. A Jupiter Consumer Survey found that consumers were more likely to bank online with a company that also offered easy access to customer service (54.6 percent), nearby ATM machines (52.4 percent), and convenient branches (52.3 percent).[4]

Although the add-on benefit of the Internet channel is most apparent in consumer banking, no area of financial services has remained unaffected by the Internet's potential. In retirement services, for example, the Internet has allowed plan participants easier access to their retirement accounts, as well as to interactive planners, investment advice, and other information. At the same time, the Internet channel has lowered the cost of servicing for plan providers. As a result, the Internet has spurred the growth of qualified retirement accounts, especially to small business.

In institutional financial services, the Internet has created a new channel for transactions that is, like its consumer counterpart, often an adjunct to other methods of access. Most trade-execution firms already had some sort of computerized access to trade data, account information, and electronic communications networks (ECNs). These proprietary links often still exist alongside their Web-based counterparts. As in the consumer arena, the Web seems to be offering more choices rather than becoming an alternative to conventional methods of transactions.

The Internet as a Marketing Tool

If the grandiose claims first made for the Internet have been toned down by experience, there are, nonetheless, major transformations wrought by the emergence of online technology. For example, even though Citibank shut down its early and expensive online-only bank, it remains a leader in using the Internet as a marketing tool. Its Web portal, Citibank.com, is designed to be the customer's first stop on any Web-surfing expedition. Customers can control what their account home pages look like and can include content from other sites. Citibank offered one of the first account-aggregation services, allowing customers to access everything from their credit card balances to their frequent flyer accounts. The idea is to get customers accustomed to coming to the site, so that when they are in the market for a car loan, insurance, or a mutual fund, one of Citibank's services will be the first they turn to. An ancillary benefit is that as customers add more personal information to their accounts, Citibank can use the information to develop customer profiles to cross-sell other products.

Although account aggregation has had a mixed record of success, many companies are positioning their websites as important resources for brand building, customer retention, and cross-selling. To that end, they seek any advantage that will make their home page the customer's default page.

Improving Website Usability

The earliest financial websites were crowded and difficult to use. They also tended to be download-heavy and slow to load. Today's financial websites are cleaner to view and simpler to use. Many, like those of Citibank and other major banks, use the portal

Citibank's home page is a portal, with clear paths indicating where to find information.

What Makes a Web Page Effective?

This site, for a New York Stock Exchange–member firm, was first designed in the late 1990s and redesigned in 2002. The earlier version is typical of first-round home page design, whereas the update is cleaner and easier to navigate.

Background. The earlier site is difficult to read, with blue or white lettering on a black background. The new site uses easier-to-read dark type on a light ground.

Format. There is no grid holding the elements in the earlier site together, and the buttons are inconsistent, so the page seems random. In the updated site, all the elements below the header are lined up on a six-column grid, giving the page a sense of order and making it easier to follow.

Images. The central illustration clutters the earlier site and serves no purpose. A different type of montage works in the later version because it is tied together by the image of the cornice of the New York Stock

Old

New

Exchange. The image is much smaller and is used as a decorative element rather than the central one. The revised site also makes the logo more discreet.

Text. The first site does not use text on its home page. If visitors to the site don't make it to the next page, they will get no information at all about this company. The redesign incorporates text on the home page. Without making the page look crowded or difficult to read, far more information is conveyed in the second version.

model, in which the home page primarily provides an overview of the contents to be found inside. Citibank's website is consistently cited as one of the best. Gomez.com, a leading Internet analyst, praises the site for its accessible interface, intuitive applications, and amount of information provided. The Tower Group ranked Citibank's site among the top three, along with Wells Fargo and Bank of America, in services offered (such as electronic bill delivery and self-service functionality) and in ease of use.[5]

Website Content

When the Internet first became a viable marketing medium, most companies looked at it primarily as an acquisition tool. The key question was, "How do we get people to come to our website and sell them stuff?" Today, websites are seen primarily as a tool for brand building, retention, and cross-selling. The goal is less to attract "visitors" than to provide a service to current customers.

Content on the Web serves diverse ends, depending on the company's goals, competitive pressures, and the needs of the target markets. The following discussion outlines seven functions online content can serve.

Company Information

The term "brochure-ware" was coined to denigrate sites with nothing but informational copy. Early Web enthusiasts maintained that a website had to be interactive to be engaging, but brochure-ware serves a purpose. Many companies simply reproduce their print brochures on the Web, and such a use of the Web may be appropriate. For example, brochure-ware can be an improvement over a print brochure by providing useful background information for institutional salespeople and client decision makers. It is easier and cheaper to update than a printed piece. It can also save the salesperson time—instead of mailing a brochure to prospects, the salesperson can refer them to the company website. That institutional buyers do go online for information is confirmed in a 2002 survey among treasury and finance professionals. It found that bank sites were the most popular online source of finance-related news and research, with 56 percent reporting at least a weekly visit.[6]

On the consumer side, some type of brand-specific information is almost always included on the site. This is important, because numerous studies have shown that most consumers use the Web for gathering information about financial products and services. A survey by Harris Research in 2002 showed the Internet ranked as the top media source used by retail banking customers to obtain information about financial products.[7] The website should bear a close family resemblance to the company's other graphics to ensure brand recognition. In the Citibank example, the "Welcome to Citibank" headline uses the same design style as the company's advertising campaign. Even though many banks have similar-looking websites, this one is clearly Citibank's.

Educational Information

Brochure-ware is primarily about the company and its products. Educational information includes general service articles, like those found in magazines; interactive tools, such as retirement planners; real-time stock quotes; and other useful data. Unfortunately, many sites have exactly the same types of information, which diminishes the differential advantages of providing extensive (and expensive) resources. But clever marketers have found ways to differentiate their sites and attract qualified prospects.

For example, Chubb has created a separate site at Chubbcollectors.com that contains articles by specialists on topics of interest to collectors, such as oriental rugs, stamps, and cars. What is clever about this site as a marketing tool is that when people who are interested in oriental rugs type that term into a search engine, it refers them to the Chubb site. Thus, Chubb gets the benefit of key-word targeting without paying for key-word ads (those that appear on the search site when particular words are keyed in). These site visitors are qualified insurance prospects. The site, which encourages visitors to subscribe to a monthly newsletter, stores the visitor's e-mail address for other potential marketing purposes.

As noted, the Web is the primary source of financial information for both consumers and institutions. In fact, Nielsen/NetRatings reported in 2002 that financial websites were among the "stickiest" on the Web, with an average stay of twenty-one minutes—far longer than the second-ranked news sites, where the average visitor lingered for only fifteen minutes.[8] A 2002 survey by Nationwide Financial of high-income professionals found that 81 percent researched specific investments on the Web and that 51 percent used the Web for general research on financial planning, retirement, and estate planning.[9] Because the Web has become the first source for customers and prospects seeking information, smart marketers will make sure that their websites contain useful items that will fulfill those search needs.

Customer Service

Customer service is one website application that is rapidly growing in importance. Allowing customers to perform service functions on a website (such as recording a change of address or transferring money between accounts) provides numerous benefits, including loyalty building—customers with online access to service functions have a higher level of satisfaction—and improved service. Customer service is the crucial differentiator among many financial institutions. If online customer service is well designed and well supported, it can improve the overall reputation of the institution. Customers like being able to handle their business online. One study indicated that 56 percent of respondents felt that online service was their most positive customer experience.[10]

Just as good service can improve customer satisfaction and retention, bad service can do the opposite. Particularly disliked are slow response times in answering customers' online questions and unreliable site performance. In one study, 31 percent of those who banked online considered switching banks because of dissatisfaction with their Web experience.[11]

Sales Support

At the beginning of the Web era, sales professionals feared that the Internet would become a competitor. And, in fact, some commissions that might have gone to a stockbroker or insurance agent went instead to online-only firms. But after the stock market crashed in 2000, many customers turned to individual financial advisers who might help them avoid the worst of the market's ups and downs.

On balance, the Internet has emerged as a valuable source of support for both captive and independent sales forces. In the case of the captive channel, most firms have created a separate website for their agents and brokers. These sites may contain everything from personal information (such as commissions earned) to sales training materials to downloadable customer promotional materials (such as brochures, letters, and signed articles). Companies also make information available for independent producers, either through an extranet or through a password-protected area on their main website.

A particularly sales-friendly use of the Internet has been the agent locator tool, which has become common on many insurance provider sites. If the viewer wants a quote or more information, these websites direct them to a nearby agent. Another positive trend for the sales force is using two-way communications (personal digital assistants, or PDAs, e-mail, and Web-enabled cell phones) to update

---

Increasing Agent Business by Moving It Online

Mortgage lender Principal Financial Group of Des Moines, Iowa, created a Correspondent Lending Center to enable independent agents to access mortgage rates, upload loan origination documents, generate reports, and troubleshoot. With real-time information on what's holding up a loan, agents can get information without all the faxes and phone calls previously required. This makes the loan process faster and less aggravating to the agents, who have responded by directing more business to Principal.[12]

---

customers on investment performance issues and to communicate new buy or sell recommendations. The more regular contact the salespeople have with their customers, the higher the customers' satisfaction. Because salespeople have limited time for phone calls, automated but personalized interactions can help them maintain the one-on-one contact that customers desire. Some firms are also using the Internet to provide cross-sell leads to their sales people. UBS, for example, offers a link to the client's financial adviser on each page of the client account area. If clients are surfing the site and find something of interest, they can follow up directly with their financial adviser.

Transactions

While large companies have had some capacity to transact directly with a financial institution since the late 1980s, prior to the spread of the Internet, those transactions were made over proprietary networks using proprietary software. For example, Bankers Trust had an accounting system for its custody clients in the early 1990s that enabled clients to directly access their accounts and render financial statements, general ledger, and other reports. Until the late 1990s, this system was available only through private networks, using customized software. After Bankers Trust was acquired by Deutsche Bank in 1999, a new system was introduced that permitted access via the Internet, along with faxes, SWIFT (Society for Worldwide Interbank Financial Telecommunication) mainframe transmissions, and private networks.

On the consumer side, the pioneers in financial transactions were credit card companies. Once they had worked out the security issues, online shopping took

Figure 8-1. Growth in Online Banking versus Online Brokerage

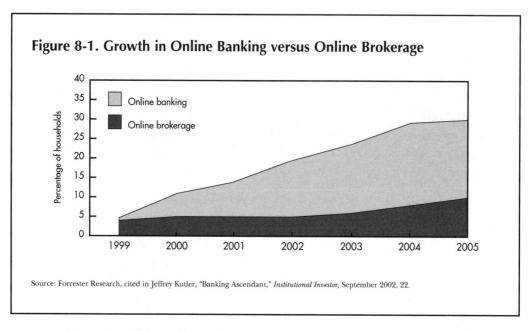

Source: Forrester Research, cited in Jeffrey Kutler, "Banking Ascendant," *Institutional Investor*, September 2002, 22.

off—and so did credit card profits. The next major financial application was online stock trading, which was buoyed by wide-scale advertising, publicity, the effervescent stock market of the late 1990s, and the rise of day traders.

At the height of the market boom, about 4 percent of U.S. households used online brokers. Many expected online brokerage to be the online "killer" application that would transform financial services. But it was online banking, not brokerage, that altered the way many people transact online. According to a 2002 Pew study, 12 percent of Internet users traded stocks online in 2000 versus 17 percent who banked online. By 2002, the percentage trading online had remained at 12 percent, while the online banking percentage had risen to 32 percent.[13] With far more consumers having bank accounts than brokerage accounts, online banking is predicted to continue growing at a compound annual growth rate of 14 percent, according to Jupiter Research.[14] Even with the market uptick in 2003, which increased traffic to brokerage sites significantly, by 39 percent from April to June alone,[15] growth for online brokerage is expected to be much slower than for banking. In fact, by 2003 online banking had become the Web's third-most-popular service, right behind auctions and dating services.[16]

The growth in online banking transactions has significance for marketers in several ways. Online customers tend to have higher retention rates, be higher-value customers, and offer more opportunities for cross-selling and referrals.

On the institutional side, hooking clients into a provider's systems has been a key marketing tactic for many years. After all, it is difficult for clients to change providers if they have to adopt an entirely new system to do so. Consumer marketers with transaction-based products have found the same to be true. Banks, brokers, mutual fund companies, and providers of loan products like credit cards and mortgages are all finding that online customers are the most loyal customers. For example, Bank of America has become increasingly profitable as its customer-retention rate has increased. One way it has improved the retention rate has been by dropping fees for online bill paying. Bank of America has found that online bill payers close accounts at one-fifth the average rate.[17]

Not only are online customers more likely to stay with the institution, but they are also likely to be more profitable. Bank of America's online customers maintained loan balances that were 45 percent higher and were 21 percent more profitable over a thirty-one-month period following enrollment than comparable customers who did not bank online.[18] The Boston Consulting Group estimates that the average online customer is 33 percent more profitable than the average offline customer, and those who pay their bills online are 98 percent more profitable.[19] Of the four major banking channels (online, ATMs, branch, and phone), the more channels the customers used, the more profitable those customers were. These multichannel users tend to have higher net worth and purchase more high-margin products like certificates of deposit and IRAs.

Speed and convenience drive online transactions. What are customers doing online? On the investment side, clients can check account statements and transfer money between accounts. Some brokerages and mutual fund sites offer search engines that can pinpoint investments by category, help clients develop appropriate asset-allocation models, and rebalance. Online-only brokers are also likely to have streaming real-time quotes and access to ECNs. On the banking side, most banks give clients the ability to check balances; transfer funds between checking and savings; download account information to financial software, like Quicken; and pay bills. Some offer online bill delivery. Few banks successfully integrate all the client's debit, credit, and investment accounts with that bank. Account aggregation (the ability to see accounts from many different providers in one place) was a big buzzword in the early 2000s, but technical constraints and customer resistance to sharing information have slowed down acceptance.

Schwab Increases Customer Profitability through E-mail Marketing

Charles Schwab & Co. has been publishing online research for its customers since early in the Internet era. Like many companies, its e-mail publications began in response to the needs of various product and service areas to communicate with customers. Eventually, Schwab centralized the function. A companywide e-mail calendar was set up to control the number of editorial, marketing, and customer service e-mails, in order to cut down on e-mailbox clutter.

An innovation was to introduce links on most client account pages, which led to a page with a complete listing of e-mail opt-in options. Another automatic function notifies customers of related e-mail services. For example, a customer initiating an online trade is reminded of Schwab's online trade confirmation service. Schwab also introduced a self-service wizard to help clients determine which e-mail services would be most useful to them. Internal research showed there was a high correlation between subscribing to online notification services and customer profitability. Those who subscribed to one particular e-mail service had five times the average trading activity as those who did not.[20]

An estimated 75 percent of online adults use the Internet to help manage their finances.[21] Financial services companies need to find ways to enable these users to do business more efficiently. As an example, one can imagine a consumer going from online tax preparation, to writing a check or taking out a loan, to filing with the IRS—all on one site. This is similar to the goal of straight-through processing, long-sought by institutions, where a single interaction controls everything from order entry through transaction to settlement. In both cases, the goal is an all-encompassing Internet-based capability that will attach the user to a single vendor.

Relationship-Based Marketing

There are effective ways to improve customer relationships using the online channel. Merely communicating with customers on a regular basis can strengthen the relationship. One study found that 88 percent of online consumers made a purchase as a result of receiving permission-based e-mail from their own finan-

---

Cross-Selling Success Online

Online or off, cross-selling current customers is more cost-effective than acquiring new ones. Mortgage.com, which is now part of ABN AMRO, spent so much in overall advertising in the late 1990s that each new mortgage customer cost it an average of $1,500. By focusing all of its marketing efforts on cross-selling ABN AMRO customers, the company increased its conversion rate by more than 500 percent and lowered its acquisitions costs to about $50 per account.[22] E*Trade also used cross-selling as a means of getting more revenue per customer. Over half of its new bank accounts and 30 percent of its mortgages came from its brokerage customers in 2002.[23]

---

cial institution.[24] But few financial services companies are taking advantage of the opportunities for one-on-one relationship building via e-mail. Of 18 percent of U.S. consumers who said they had given their e-mail address to their bank, only half actually received anything from the bank.[25]

There are two major kinds of permission-based e-mail. One is highly customized, literally one-on-one, and is generally used to provide information of importance to customers about their accounts. Some examples of this type of service include banks' sending an e-mail warning when a customer's account drops below a preset amount or has insufficient funds to cover a check. Another example is a brokerage firm that sends e-mail alerts when a customer's account shows variance from its desired asset allocation. Active traders with some companies can get e-mail (or wireless) alerts related to prices of their holdings. Brokerage firms that handle trades through a salesperson generally do not provide this type of automated e-mail service, lest they interfere with the relationship between client and account adviser. The advisers, in turn, are reluctant to use e-mail for the simple reason that all written communications (including e-mail) are subject to compliance review. Those firms that sell investments directly to the customer are thus in a better position to make use of this technology to build relationships.

The second type of permission based e-mail is personalized but not customized. It may consist of, say, stock research on a particular industry segment that is sent to everyone who has signed up for it. Or it may be an online newsletter,

---

Increasing Online Mortgage Volume

Rather than responding to an online ad or e-mail, a consumer seeking a mortgage is more likely to go to a site that compares rates and terms. Some sites are strictly informational, such as those maintained by state banking departments. Others are commercial and direct consumers to sponsors who pay the intermediary a fee. These intermediaries, or online mortgage brokers, can be effective in helping lenders acquire new customers, because the cost of acquisition for the lender is relatively low. For example, Ohio-based Provident Bank relies on Lending Tree to generate "a significant source of volume," at one-tenth the cost of other marketing methods.[26]

Another effective use of the online channel is through joint marketing with other companies, such as realtors, home insurers, and moving companies. The advantage of such cross-marketing is twofold: not only are the number of sites where a prospective buyer may find a particular mortgage lender increased but the lender can also offer a package price that makes it more difficult for the consumer to make apples-to-apples comparisons. By bundling value-added services, cost becomes less important as the driver of the mortgage selection decision.

---

distributed to anyone who has expressed interest, whether a customer or not. The idea behind these communications is to build a database of names associated with particular product interests. E-mail marketing to both customers and prospects has proven very effective, although the CAN-SPAM Act of 2003 put restrictions on sending e-mail unless the e-mailer has received explicit permission. Before the new regulations were enacted in 2003, e-mail to both customers and prospects generated the highest ROI of any direct marketing medium for financial services marketers. This was attributed in part to the low cost of the medium (average cost-per-contact was 17 cents) and the relatively high hit rate of 1.3 percent.[27]

Customer Acquisition

The effectiveness of the Internet as a means of attracting new customers varies considerably by the type of product or service being sold. Credit products (loans, mortgages) and simple insurance products (term life, auto) are more likely to be investigated on the Internet than other types of products. But even

Advertising without Trying

Netherlands-based bank ING developed a particularly clever format for an online campaign. When viewers pulled up a page (such as the sports site to the right), every "ing" on the page turned orange. It was, says the creative team, a way to show the brand as "fun, frank, and self-aware" and to concretely demonstrate ING's claim to fresh thinking.

MLB Home · Scoreboard · Standings · Schedules · Stats · Teams · Players · Transactions · Injuries

a Streak For The Ages: A's On Historic Winning Run

Sept. 4, 2002

OAKLAND, Calif. (AP) Although no manager in 55 years has led a team on such an epic winning streak, Art Howe's perspective on the Oakland Athletics' 19 straight victories doesn't stretch beyond last week.

Advertisement

Start seeing ING in a new way.
(It's pronounced I-N-G)

"I'm just happy people are talking baseball again," Howe said. "We spent a long time talking about the strike. We're doing something really unexpected and special, and it's great to focus on what's happening on the field."

What's happening on the field has been somewhat magical. The Amazing A's just

ING's online ad cleverly inserts its name into the editorial content of the Web page.

when consumers do their research online, many prefer to do business with a live representative. One study found that 61 percent of those who shopped for credit cards online applied online, but only 23 percent of those shopping for mortgages applied online.[28] Because of the greater complexity of the mortgage application and the amount of information required, most applicants preferred to meet a mortgage specialist face-to-face or over the phone.

Advertising on the Web

The debate over whether Web advertising works has been going on since the first banner ad appeared on Hotwired.com in 1994. The evidence is contradictory, but some general trends have emerged.

The Internet is part of an integrated ad campaign. As with other types of media advertising, the goal of most Internet advertising is primarily awareness building rather than making an outright sale. Web advertising can also serve as an adjunct to other media advertising by giving customers a chance to explore products and services in more depth.

New formats appear all the time. The standard banner ad is no longer the standard. It is being challenged by skyscraper and other oversize banners, rich media like Flash, video, sound, interstitials, pop-ups, pop-unders, Shoshkeles,

---

Pay-per-Click Pays

AAA Life Insurance, a part of the American Automobile Association, has been running a successful search-based campaign on more than six thousand sites, including
insurance sites, search engines, directories, and community sites. The goal was to
leverage the click-through into a subscription for a free e-mail newsletter, and the
campaign generated ten thousand subscribers in its first three months.[29]

People's Bank has taken search advertising even further—by running ads that
look like pay-per-click on its own website. Having determined that 20 percent of site
visitors were using the search box to find what they were looking for, the bank added
a yellow-boxed ad, featuring a product, in response to viewer searches for keywords.
Visitors clicking on the "ad" go to a landing page with more information, along with
the choice of receiving an immediate phone call, starting a live online chat with a
sales rep, or filling out a form. Conversions to sales from those who click on the ads
is "astonishing," according to People's Bank's senior information architect—"sometimes as high as 100 percent."[30]

---

wallpaper, Unicaster, and other formats. Whereas standard banners are now
showing click-through rates of around 0.3 percent, other formats have seen
rates as high as 15 percent.[31] Some advertisers have claimed good results for
"surround" advertising, which shows different sizes of banner ads surrounding the text. Ameritrade, for example, has used this format on the *New York
Times* website.

Paid searches are popular. Among the most effective forms of Web advertising for financial marketers are search-based ads. These are ads which appear
on search and other sites only when the viewer has entered relevant key words
("online banking," for example). In most cases, the advertiser does not pay
unless the ad is clicked on—hence, their other name of "pay-per-click." Google,
for one, claims that its keyword-based ads have an average click-through rate of
2 percent. So effective have these ads become that they now make up 35 percent
of overall online ad revenues.[32]

Advertising on the Web is relatively inexpensive. In 2000, Morgan Stanley
Dean Witter ranked the Internet lowest in cost-per-thousand (CPM) impressions,
and by 2002, per impression rates for banner ads had dropped another 70 per-

cent. With the rise in pay-per-click, advertising costs have declined even more, since these ads require little or no payment unless they are clicked.

Financial services advertising on the Web is declining. Although Bank of America and other advertisers continue to find value in banner advertising on popular websites such as Yahoo, financial companies are no longer the Web's major advertisers. In June 2001, Nielsen/NetRatings reported that three of the top five online advertisers were financial companies. In September 2002, only one financial company, Bank One, was even in the top ten, and by July 2003, there were none.[33]

In the end, the Internet is neither a fearsome competitor nor a panacea. No financial marketer can afford to ignore the power of the Internet as a distribution channel, as a source of information, as a relationship-building tool, and as a brand builder. But ways of using the Internet effectively continue to evolve, and financial marketers need to keep on top of trends and best practices.

Resources

There is no single trade organization for Web-based marketers. The Direct Marketing Association's online affiliate is the Association of Interactive Marketing (http://www.imarketing.org). Another industry group is the Emarketing Association (http://emarketing association.com).

There are many websites devoted to marketing on the Internet. Among them are clickz.com (http://www.clickz.com), which superseded the cyberatlas site, Web Marketing Magazine (http://www.dmlr.org), Web marketing today (http://www.wilsonweb.com), and email sherpa (http://www.emailsherpa.com).

CHAPTER NOTES

1. Meg Mitchell Moore, "Turn on a Dime," http://www.darwinmag.com, October 2001.

2. Eileen Colkin Cuneo, "E-Trading Hangs On," http://www.informationweek.com, December 9, 2002.

3. "Richard Kovacevich Profile," *Institutional Investor,* January 2004, 46.

4. "Users Bank on the Internet," http://cyberatlas.com, December 16, 2001.

5. "Why Online Banking Is Like a Box of Chocolates," *Bank Systems & Technology* (http://www.banktech.com), October 28, 2003.

6. "Usage Flat Among Financial Pros," http://cyberatlas.com, November 25, 2002.

7. ""Websites: Where You Find Affluent Customers," *ABA Bank Marketing,* May 2002, 52.

8. "Finance Sites the Stickiest Online," http://cyberatlas.com, February 28, 2002.

9. "Broker First, Web Second," http://cyberatlas.com, July 18, 2002.

10. "Personalization Makes for Satisfied Customers," http://cyberatlas.com, March 11, 2002.

11. Gomez survey, cited in "Connecting Channels Key to Online Banking," http://cyberatlas.com, October 25, 2001.

12. "Web Site Key to Principal's Success," http://www.informationweek.com, December 10, 2001.

13. Pew Internet and American Life Project, "Online Activities, 2000-2002," http://www.pewinternet.org/reports/chart asp?img=77_bankact.jpg, September 2002.

14. "Interest in Online Banking Grows," http://www.clickz.com, December 30, 2003.

15. "Traffic Up as Stocks Gain," http://www.clickz.com, June 19, 2003.

16. Jeffrey Kutler, "Bank Shot," *Institutional Investor,* September 2003, 150.

17. Ibid., 151.

18. "The Anatomy of an Anomaly," *Bank Technology News,* http://www.futurebanker.com, May 2003.

19. See note 16, 151.

20. "Schwab Research Reveals E-mail Alert Subscribers Place Five Times More Trades," *Marketing Sherpa* (http://www.marketingsherpa.com), January 16, 2002.

21. Survey Conducted by the Dieringer Research Group, cited in press release, "Online Banking and Bill Paying Rising Steadily," on http://biz.yahoo.com/prnews/021119/mntu005_1.html, November 19, 2002.

22. "Mortgage.com Reincarnated," http://www.efinanceinsider.com, January 25, 2002.

23. See Note 2.

24. Research by Doubleclick, reported in *Accutips* (http://www.accutips.com), December 2002. Note that permission-based e-mail refers to e-mail for which viewers have specifically opted-in (that is, a check box asking whether they would like to receive a publication has not been pre-checked). Sending e-mail without any kind of permission is spam and is not addressed in this discussion.

25. Dieringer survey, cited in note 21.

26. Dean Foust, "Lending Tree: Steadily Spreading its Roots," http://businessweek.com, February 7, 2002.

27. Financial DMers Prefer Mail:Survey," *Direct* (http://directmag.com/ar/marketing_financial_dmers_prefer/index.htm), February 2004.

28. "Consumers Shop, but Don't Buy Credit Online," http://cyberatlas.com, April 24, 2000.

29. "Birth of a Mailing List," http://www.clickz.com, January 23, 2003.

30. "How People's Bank Uses Internal Search Analytics to Turn More Browsers into Customers," http://marketingsherpa.com, February 10, 2004.

31. "What Advertisers Want," http://newarchitectmag.com, February 2003.

32. Kate Maddox, "Search Advertising Leads Online Growth," *BtoB,* May 3, 2004, 17.

33. http://www.nielsen-netratings.com, June 2001, September 2002, July 2003.

Personal Selling

9

Traditionally, financial services have been sales-driven. In most companies, marketers do not have direct access to the firm's clients. But as the industry has changed, the role of marketing has become more central. In the past, salespeople often felt marketers were obstacles rather than supporters. There is a dawning recognition that each party needs the other.

9

It is possible that financial companies have the most complex sales structures of any industry. Consider, for example, a company like Fidelity Investments. These are some of the selling relationships for its investment management/mutual fund product set:

- In-house (captive) phone sales
- In-house (captive) branch sales
- Third-party independent advisers (e.g., fee-only planners and independent brokers)
- Third-party wire house brokers (e.g., Merrill Lynch)
- Third-party diversified financial brokers (e.g., AXA)
- Third-party bank brokers (e.g., Chase Investments)
- Third-party direct marketers (e.g., Charles Schwab)
- In-house institutional sales reps who sell retirement plans to plan sponsors
- In-house institutional sales reps who sell retirement plans to plan providers
- Third-party pension brokers who sell retirement plans to plan sponsors
- In-house institutional sales reps who sell managed accounts to wire houses
- Brokers at these firms who offer managed accounts to their clients
- In-house sales reps who offer managed accounts directly to end customers

That's at least thirteen different sales channels for just one type of product.

The old saying is that financial products aren't bought but sold. This has certainly long been true in life insurance. For most people, buying financial services is a chore. It is not fun to shop for a mortgage, an annuity, or a retirement plan.

If it weren't for a salesperson's persistence, many people would choose to avoid the whole decision-making process.

The sales channel is critical in most financial subsegments. With few exceptions, financial marketers do not have direct access to their end customers. One of the reasons a disciplined marketing approach has been slow to develop in this industry is that, traditionally, financial services have been sales-driven. Where marketers functioned at all, it was to support the sales team. But there have been major changes in the industry over the past ten years—changes that have made the role of the marketer more important than before: competition across subsegments (overlapping insurance, bank, and brokerage firms); industry consolidation leading to bigger competitors; and the increasing role of technology, particularly CRM, to name a few.

There have also been significant changes in how the sales force works. Selling commissioned products, like insurance or stocks, used to be relatively straightforward. You sold a stock, you got a commission. Today, sales force compensation emphasizes asset-gathering, not individual transactions. The goal is to keep the customer for the long term, to build a relationship. Consequently, the role of marketing has become more central. Marketing can provide the tools that enable the sales rep to anticipate client needs. Analytical software can let a financial adviser know when clients are at critical points—when there is a danger of their leaving, when there is an opportunity to sell them something, when they need a call to keep them satisfied. In the past, salespeople often felt marketers were irrelevant, obstacles rather than supporters. There is a dawning recognition that each party needs the other.

Traditional Relationships between Sales and Marketing

The relationship between sales and marketing differs significantly among the various financial subsegments. Some segments have no sales function. Marketers that deal directly with the end user—such as credit card issuers, no-load mutual funds, and direct insurance sales—acquire and service their customers without the aid of a relationship-based sales force.

Some subsegments, such as banks and credit unions, sell primarily through a noncommissioned sales force. This is an example of "top-down marketing" in which a central group—either a product group or marketing group—sets

A BRAG Book for Branch Marketing

Although the central marketing and product functions control the overall marketing effort, individual bank branches often have some flexibility and some (limited) budget to create their own local marketing efforts. Sometimes these efforts are supported by a central marketing group. For example, Chase Manhattan Bank created a local marketing group that served as a kind of

A customized local postcard campaign for Chase branches in the Bronx.

internal promotions agency, creating both customized and generic materials for the branches. The local marketing group even supplied a print (and later, online) catalog, called the BRAG book (Branch Resource Action Guide) listing the various materials available to branch sales staff. These materials included everything from ads, press releases, and by-lined articles to signage, seminar kits, direct response postcards, and many other items.

goals and then instructs its staff to fulfill the directives. For example, a bank may decide that spring is a good time to sell home equity products. The marketing department oversees an ad campaign, branch signage, perhaps creation of a customer incentive, and telemarketing, direct mail, and Internet campaigns. Each branch is given a sales goal, and contests or other means are used to "mobilize the troops." The branches with the most home equity loans originated are given a special prize, or the branch manager takes them all out for a pizza.

Consumer banks have a mix of commissioned and noncommissioned sales personnel. The commissioned people include institutional sales executives, middle-market and small-business calling officers, insurance and investment brokers, and mortgage bankers. The platform workers (tellers, supervisors, branch managers) are not on commission, even though they are usually expected to push products. Top-down marketing is efficient—all decisions are centralized and marketing budgets can be allocated on a rational basis. Campaign effectiveness can be easily measured, promotions stay "on brand," and niche markets can easily be targeted.

"Bottom-Up" Marketing

Unlike branch staff, commissioned salespeople tend to think like entrepreneurs. They are only interested in a marketing program if it will translate to their bottom line. Sometimes called "bottom-up" marketing, in this arrangement marketing must "sell" the sales force first and then the end client. As an example, a major brokerage company wanted to consolidate and centralize client information in order to be able to handle any client inquiry seamlessly, whether the inquiry was to the broker, the customer service center, or online. In a bank this would be routine practice. But in the brokerage industry, the sales force has traditionally maintained its own records for each rep's personal use. A broker considers his "book of business" his personal property, notwithstanding lawsuits that routinely take place when a broker leaves one firm for another and takes his clients with him. In this example, marketing and sales were at loggerheads. Marketing won, but not without a great deal of reluctance and ill will on the part of the sales force.

In most bottom-up industries, which include brokerages, insurance, and institutional sales, in-house commissioned salespeople have nearly exclusive access to clients. If the marketing department wants to reach a client, they must work through the salesperson. Finding a way to convince the salesperson that a particular product will lead to more sales may involve creating costly materials. Items such as sales guides (how to sell the product), PowerPoint presentations, sales letters, articles for the sales force to place in local publications under their bylines, local customizable print ads, and radio spots are routinely provided by marketing or product management.

In order to sell the sales force, marketers have to budget more for any promotion. Yet, at the same time, they have less control over results. Prospect leads generated by advertising, direct mail, telemarketing, or online campaigns are turned over to individual salespeople (or their branch managers) for conversion. Thus, a successful lead generation campaign could well prove unprofitable if the conversion rate is low. And sales staff are notorious for ignoring sales leads generated by

Sales and Marketing Working Together

"The brand is central to everything the organization does," noted Lisa Gregg, director of sales development at American Express. "The challenge is to move away from the silos created over the years...between sales and marketing." To make sure the sales force always stayed "on message" and to help salespeople with increasingly complex sales, sales and marketing joined together to create a centralized sales intelligence center called "Sales Force Online." It gave the sales force centralized access to some 500 different marketing programs, including downloadable product literature, customizable presentations, and background information—such as product information, customer testimonials, and survey findings—that would help make a sale.

The sales organization chose a steering committee to identify and prioritize the most useful functions. This group of sales leaders then became the program's champions. Marketing benefited from better marketing intelligence, as it analyzed how the sales force used various programs as a proxy for what the end-users wanted. For the sales force, productivity went up significantly: presentation preparation time was cut in half, acquisition costs declined substantially, and customers were getting more focussed messages that led to higher close rates.[1]

such campaigns. By one estimate, 80 percent of marketing expenditures on lead generation and sales collateral are wasted because these efforts are ignored by the sales force.[2] Another difficulty encountered by bottom-up marketers is overlapping responsibilities between the marketing and sales management organizations. In most firms, sales management controls commission rates, bonuses, sales contests, and all other forms of compensation. With its limited input over the most crucial sales motivator, marketing has limited impact on sales results.

Third-Party Sales

If the job of a marketer selling to a captive sales force sounds difficult, consider the plight of the marketer whose target is a third-party salesperson. Commissioned sales representatives may be independents, or work for banks, brokerage, or diversified financial firms. In insurance, for example, companies without a captive sales force may sell their policies through independent insurance brokers, who can recommend anyone's policy to their clients. Similarly, mutual funds, retire-

---

Why Sales Forces Don't Sell Your Product

Getting the attention of sales agents is not an easy task. Guardian Life Insurance exited the retirement plan business because it could not get enough brokers—captive or independent—to sell the product. Why? Most of the salespeople at Guardian's own agencies did not have the necessary licensing to sell investment products—and were not sufficiently motivated to commit the time, money, and effort needed to get licensed. On the other hand, independent retirement plan specialists, who were licensed to sell annuities, already had relationships with a small group of retirement plan providers and saw no reason to expand the list. Even though Guardian offered higher commission rates, agents were not interested in learning a new product line, dealing with underwriters who might balk at their clients, or putting their reputation on the line for a company they weren't sure was going to stay in the business.

---

ment funds, and other investment vehicles often sell through third parties.

In the early 1990s, about 40 percent of mutual funds were sold directly by fund management to end consumers, as no-load funds (that is, without an added sales commission). By 2003, only 18 percent of funds were sold directly to consumers. Of the rest, 37 percent were sold through financial supermarkets, such as those offered by Schwab and Fidelity. (These funds may be sold with or without loads at the discretion of fund management.) And 45 percent were sold through brokers as load funds, up from 32 percent in 1998.[3]

When selling through brokers, companies that previously offered only no-load mutual funds developed new share classes that carried loads—including front end, back end, and contingent loads. Then these companies had to develop mechanisms for selling these load funds to brokers. Since there are more than eight thousand mutual funds in the United States, getting a mutual fund (or closed-end fund or annuity or money manager/wrap account) in front of a third party has become as difficult as getting a new grocery product on a shelf. And like groceries, brokerages started charging for "shelf space." In this arrangement, fund families paid "revenue-sharing" fees to the brokerage firm in order to gain access to the brokerage's sales force. In addition, some funds used "directed brokerage" in which a fund company agreed to direct a specified amount of trades to a brokerage in exchange for greater access to its sales force.

Along with other questionable sales practices, such as compensating sales forces with 12b-1 fees and using sales contests to raise commissions for brokers who sold certain funds, these actions have drawn the scrutiny of regulators. And even if these particular practices have been reformed, fund marketers still face the problem of breaking through the clutter to sell to third-party brokers.

High-Net-Worth Sales

The high-net-worth (HNW) market is served by many types of financial firms, from trust departments, private banks, and upscale investment banking firms to individual financial advisers or "wealth managers." Although $500,000 in investable assets will get someone HNW status with some financial advisers and firms, it may take $5 million or more to qualify for a private banker. For Goldman Sachs to handle a portfolio, the cost of entry will be $25 million or more.

One of the most competitive areas is the managed-account business, in which money managers compete to handle the accounts of individuals through their brokers or bankers. The money-management company must first be selected by the institution to participate in its managed-account program and then must be picked from the list of approved managers by the individual adviser for his or her client. Not only is there intense competition among money managers but the number of banking and brokerage firms that offer managed accounts has skyrocketed in recent years as they have become popular with HNW clients.

Institutional Sales

People who become commissioned sales reps tend to be independent, which makes them difficult for marketers to influence. As one goes up the selling ladder to those who deal with the really big-ticket sales, particularly to institutions, the role of marketing becomes less and less important. These are sales that require a painstaking, one-on-one process, often involving long intervals between initial contact and closing the sale.

Consumer sales cycles can take hours (for e-mail campaigns), days, or perhaps weeks. Institutional sales cycles—getting a new client for securities trading, investment banking, institutional asset management, plan consulting, credit analysis, risk management, prime brokerage, back-office services, or technology—routinely take years. There are several reasons why this is true. First, the number of people involved in making a decision is usually high, which means going back over the same ground again and again. Second, some of these prod-

Selling to the Corner Office

Brokers who sell separately managed accounts (SMAs) tend to be those with the biggest books of business—the ones whose success has put them in the corner office. In fact, just 5 percent of the adviser force at most wire houses and regional broker-dealers generates 80 to 90 percent of managed-account business.[4] To reach these superstars, Neuberger Berman, a midsize money manager, created a targeted campaign. Its "Influential Advisors" were invited to an intense, three-day training program featuring a roster of well-known portfolio managers, wealth management specialists, and featured speakers—and of course, high-end entertainment.

A newsletter sent to third party financial advisers by a money management company helps keep its product top of mind.

Director of Marketing Andrea Trachtenberg, who started her career with brokerage Merrill Lynch, understood that what brokers need most is support—and Neuberger Berman supplied it. Neuberger Berman's sales reps sat down with heads of brokerage sales areas and found out what kinds of programs brokers find most useful. Neuberger Berman provided modeling and profiling tools, seminars, programs to which brokers could invite their own clients, customizable newsletters, presentations, white papers, and other tools to help brokers keep abreast of new ideas and build their practices. "The real key is in the execution," noted Trachtenberg. "It's not enough to give the salespeople interesting information. It has to be actionable." As an example, she cited a survey Neuberger Berman conducted on entrepreneurial wealth. Rather than simply presenting the survey results, the company put together a sales kit that walked brokers through the information and showed them how to use it to interact with their own clients and prospects. These were expensive programs, but they paid off for Neuberger Berman. According to Trachtenberg, the return in new business was as much as one thousand times the amount spent.[5]

Consumer Tactics for Institutional Sales

Traditionally, the institutional sales force has been supported with marketing tactics such as booths at trade shows, sponsorship of specialized road shows or product exhibitions, and other events for clients (golf and tennis tournaments or training seminars held at lush resorts). The purpose of these events is to give the salesperson the opportunity to get to know the client and build a relationship—or put another way, to "schmooze" the client in order to build long-term good will and to cross-sell.

The treasury services department of a major bank has found success by modifying tactics traditionally associated with consumer marketing. For example, when the treasury services area entered a new geographic marketplace, the sales representative for the region compiled a list of his top prospects and asked the marketing department for help in getting through to the chief financial officers of these large corporations. Marketing came up with an appropriate premium—a silver key chain whose hang-tag was a Mercator map with the company's logo—and created a custom box, letter, and brochure. The salesperson sent a few of these items out each week, by messenger, to serve as an icebreaker. As a result, he was successful in securing appointments with most of his prospects. Two months later, the marketing staff followed up with a reception for these new contacts at a prestigious private club that featured other areas of the bank, thus leveraging the earlier promotion into a companywide sales success.

ucts are only purchased by a given customer once in a blue moon: for example, a company only seeks an underwriter for an initial public offering or a specialist firm for its stock listing when it is going public. Third, it is very difficult for outsiders to reach the decision makers. They are hidden behind support staff and subordinates. Last, many of these business decisions have traditionally been made for personal reasons. Selection of an investment banker, trading broker, or trustee is still likely to be based on which club the buyer and seller belong to or having been fraternity brothers in college.

At the highest levels, the people who make the sales do not think of themselves as salespeople, but as partners, underwriters, or bankers. They don't market—they network. A marketing expense might be flying a potential buyer in one's private plane to Ireland for a round of golf.[6] But even below this rarefied level, systematic market planning and plan execution is not much practiced. Instead, most institutional sales take place opportunistically. A salesperson whose commission-based income can exceed that of the firm's CEO will call clients regularly, looking for cross-selling opportunities or referrals to potential new clients. Or she may expand her network by serving on boards of nonprofit or trade organizations, joining special-interest groups involved in industry issues (lobbying Washington, for example), and attending high-level industry conferences. This relationship building may be supplemented with seminar and trade show selling, event sponsorship, and other "marketing" tactics, but for the most part, institutional sales are passive rather than active. Most institutional salespeople disdain retail-type tactics such as direct marketing. Although this attitude is changing and institutional sellers are beginning to think more strategically, most wholesale institutions have a long way to go before they are true marketers.

Changes in the Sales Distribution Model

The holy grail in marketing today is relationship building. Almost all companies—not just financial firms—have shifted their emphasis from one-time transactions to ongoing relationships. Financial firms whose sales reps possess personal, one-on-one relationships with the client have a built-in advantage when it comes to relationship building. And yet, many organizations that have the good fortune to have strong ties between their customers and their sales reps are trying to nudge the salesperson out of the picture. Many brokerage firms, for example, are "migrating" clients with lower assets to online and phone channels. At Merrill Lynch, for example, clients have to invest at least $100,000 before they qualify for their own full-service broker. Below that amount, they are serviced by a call center, whose three hundred brokers serve one million retail customers.[7]

It is understandable that firms such as Merrill are seeking to change the relationship between client and broker-adviser. For one thing, there's the matter of cost—each full-service client costs the firm an estimated $500 a year, more than some smaller clients provide in profits. Second, the cost of brokers at the call center is much lower, both in commissions and in overhead. More crucial for the firm, the goal is to redirect the relationship from client-broker to client-firm. The broker model has always presented a problem for firms with commissioned sales forces. If the broker decides to leave, in most cases the client will go along.

To counter this, companies have put complex systems in place to initiate communication with clients as soon as a salesperson resigns. Firms know they have very little time in which to retain the client. To many clients, the salesperson *is* the company. If clients are happy with the advice being received, they will follow the adviser. The reality is that there is no way to prevent clients from moving their accounts to other firms if they so choose.

This perception that the broker "owns" the client makes brokers hard to manage. Firms that attempt to cut commission rates may see a massive outflow of their top salespeople, who can always find another brokerage that will give them a bonus for making the move with their book of business. These individuals can also become independent and collect 70–90 percent commission payouts on sales compared with the 25 to 45 percent they typically get at a major Wall Street firm.[8]

In a situation such as a change of ownership, this exodus can have major repercussions. For example, sales of products by Prudential Securities brokers declined an estimated $50 million in the first five months of 2003, following the sale of its brokerage division to Wachovia. Wachovia lost nearly 15 percent of Prudential brokers, who jumped to rival firms following the acquisition.[9]

As a result of all these factors, brokerages and other commission-driven firms are looking for ways to move clients to a new relationship with the institution, not the broker. Even high-value clients are encouraged to use all available transaction channels, including online and phone, as well as transacting through their broker. Brokers are getting new tools that enable them to work with clients over the Internet on an instant messaging model. While these tools are designed to improve broker productivity, they also loosen the bonds between brokers and their clients. The more tied-in the client is to a given company's systems, the less likely the client is to follow a broker to another firm.

Ironically, while commission-based companies are trying to wean customers off personal relationships with brokers, commercial banks are heading the other way. Chase, for example, has instituted a personal "relationship manager" to service its small-business customers who combine personal and business balances. Why? Because small-business owners often have significant personal assets that can be captured by building a relationship based on business banking.

That bank salespeople may not be quite up to the task is borne out by the results of a "mystery shop" conducted by *American Banker* in 2002. Visiting several Chicago-area bank branches, the reporter and a consultant asked to open a minimum-deposit checking account, but also dropped broad hints at additional

Table 9-1. Why Clients Change Advisers

REASON	PERCENTAGE
Another adviser was more appealing	63%
Dissatisfaction with investment performance	54%
Adviser did not communicate frequently enough	54%
Adviser did not provide enough information or choices	54%
Adviser did not have their best interest in mind	34%

Source: Nationwide Financial Services survey, 2002

assets (buying a home on the Gold Coast, owning a small business). While some bankers did pick up the hints, the response seemed haphazard at best. Half the bankers did not ask their names; none asked for a follow-up visit or phone number to contact the prospects.[10]

So which way is best? Encourage or discourage personal relations between clients and salespeople? The data are mixed. On the one hand, a 2002 survey commissioned by Dow Jones & Co. found that "while affluent investors did not regard any financial firm overwhelmingly as a trusted partner, almost two-thirds reported a significantly high level of trust and reliability in their primary broker."[11] Buttressing the finding that clients still seek advice from their own brokers is a Hartford Financial Survey in 2003, that found that even though their portfolios were down significantly, 56 percent of those surveyed were satisfied with their current financial adviser. And this was despite the fact that 33 percent had not talked to their adviser in the last six months.[12]

Advisers who keep their client relationships strong are likely to benefit their firms as well. When UBS initiated a major ad campaign announcing its brokerage's name change from UBS PaineWebber, its financial advisers were required to contact each client to explain the change. The result was few client defections and more asset inflow. On the other hand, surveys show that clients want better service from their advisers and are willing to use the Internet as a substitute. A survey by Nationwide Financial in 2002 found that 35 percent of affluent investors had used the Internet for financial planning assistance. Of those, 11 percent used the Internet as their only source. The survey showed a significant drop in the use of advisers. The use of stockbrokers, for example, dropped from 54 per-

Bull versus Opossum

Many years ago, before Merrill Lynch had a marketing department to support its institutional products, a floor trader decided he wanted his own marketing brochure. Since the trader handled mortgage options, he thought it would be clever to brand them as "options to purchase or sell specified mortgage-backed securities," or

An appropriate corporate symbol?

OPOSSMS, and had a design firm come up with a cute little opossum logo. When the brochure was printed and distributed to clients and the press, there was a fair amount of buzz about the "new" product. Everyone was happy until the head of retail marketing called the perpetrators on the carpet. "Merrill Lynch is associated with noble beasts," she thundered, "bulls and tigers [a product of the time]—not road kill." She was right. OPOSSMS violated many years and dollars of brand-building effort, and even though the buzz served the product, it threatened to diminish the brand as a whole.

cent in 2001 to 32 percent in 2002, although this figure was not supported by other studies.[13] (For more on relationship marketing, see chapter 11.)

How Sales Can Help Marketing Help Sales

The relationship between sales and marketing is a little bit like the relationship between teenagers and their parents. Parents (marketers) try to guide the teens (sales force) in the right direction, and prevent them from making mistakes. Teens resent parents telling them what to do and insist on making their own decisions. But also like teens, the sales force may be too focused on the present and not always have the best interests of the organization in mind for the long term. For example, marketers complain when their in-house salespeople create their own client materials rather than use the materials so expensively crafted by the marketing department. Salespeople claim they know better what will appeal to their clients. What they fail to understand is that the marketer is looking at the best interests of the firm.

Sales-created promotions can trigger a number of potential problems:

● Legal and compliance errors

- Poor impression on the part of the client if there are typos, misspellings, grammar mistakes, or an amateurish writing style
- Failure to conform to brand image—the presentation of a consistent look and feel across the enterprise

Like parents, marketers can be good or bad. Good marketers support the sales force with essential information and client materials, including prospecting tools, lead-generation campaigns, help with developing successful sales techniques, product training, generic promotional material (brochures, ads, newsletters), customized material (proposals, sales letters, client reports), and trade show and seminar marketing. In return, good salespeople give feedback to marketing, letting them know what works and what doesn't, what they need, and how marketing can best support them.

Many traditional sales organizations have begun asking the sales force to think more like marketers. For practical demonstrations of how sales people can use marketing techniques and tactics, see the appendix, "Applying Marketing Principles to Sales Practice."

Resources

There are numerous associations and publications aimed at brokers, insurance agents, fee-only financial planners, and other financial advisers. Associations include the Investment Management Consultants Association (http://www.imca.org), National Association of Personal Financial Advisors (http://www.napfa.org), Independent Insurance Agents & Brokers of America (http://www.iiaba.org), Million Dollar Roundtable (http://www.mdrt.org), and National Association of Professional Insurance Agents (http://pianet.com).

Publications include *Bank Investment Marketing* (http://www.bankinvestment mktg.com), *Life Insurance Selling* (http://www.lifeinsurancselling.com), *Registered Rep* (http://registeredrep.com), and *Bloomberg Wealth Manager* (http://wealth .bloomberg.com).

Associations serving sales and sales management in general include the National Association of Sales Professionals (http://www.nasp.com) and Sales and Marketing Executives International (http://www.smei.org). The best-known general sales publication is *Sales & Marketing Management* (http://salesandmarketing.com).

CHAPTER NOTES

1. "CMM Case Study: American Express' Sales Force Online," *Marketing News,* June 24, 2002, 12-13.

2. Research by the Aberdeen Group, cited in Carol Krol, "Why can't marketing and sales get along?" *BtoB,* http://www.btob.com, April 14, 2003.

3. Financial Research Corp. estimates cited in Rich Blake, "Misdirected Brokerage," *Institutional Investor,* June 2003, 49-50.

4. Jessica Toonkel, "Cross-Marketing Seen as Key for SMA," *Fund Marketing Alert,* August 14, 2003.

5. Author's interview with Andrea Trachtenberg.

6. See, for example, "Golf and Power: Inside the Secret Refuge of the Business Elite," http://www.fortune.com, March 30, 2003.

7. Anitha Reddy, "Bye-Bye Small Fry: Brokers Increasingly Concentrate on the Rich," *Washington Post,* May 18, 2003, F01.

8. Lynn Cowan and Cheryl Winokur Munk, "Pool of Independent Brokers Grows as Wall Street's Falls," *Dow Jones Business News,* http://biz.yahoo.com/djus/030416/1237001115_1.html, April 16, 2003.

9. Imogen Rose-Smith, "Pru Tallies Cost of Talent Exodus," *Wall Street Letter,* June 11, 2003.

10. Lavonne Kuykendall, "'Mystery Shop' Shows Some Missed Opportunities," *American Banker,* December 10, 2002, 8.

11. Harris Interactive, "Affluent Investors Feel Self-Confident and Empowered, Yet Are Looking for a Trusted Financial Partner," News release, http://www.harrisinteractive.com/news/newscats.asp?NewsID=518, October 1, 2002.

12. The Hartford Financial Services Group, "Clients to Brokers: 'Call Me,'" *PR Newswire,* http://biz.yahoo.com.prnews/030609/nem003_1.html, June 9, 2003.

13. Nationwide Financial Services survey, "Sources of Financial Planning Help for High-Income Professionals," cited in "Broker First, Web Second," http://cyberatlas.com, July 18, 2002.

Trade Shows and Seminars

10

Trade shows and seminars provide face-to-face contact with prospects who otherwise might be difficult to reach. They are usually qualified and are receptive to learning about products and services. The challenge is getting them to focus on *your* products and services.

10

Whether captive or independent, the sales force is facing an increasingly difficult prospecting environment. With the coming of do-not-call regulations, cold calling is no longer the method of first, or last, resort. From a marketing perspective, this is probably not a bad thing. "Dialing for dollars," as cold calling has been popularly known, ignores most of the fundamental principles of marketing, such as segmentation, positioning, and taking advantage of marketplace opportunities.

Sales tools like seminars and trade shows require more planning than cold calling. But they also reward those who plan well. These sales methods require choosing appropriate target market segments, approaching these segments in a consistent and professional manner, and searching out opportunities competitors may have missed. Trade shows and seminars provide face-to-face contact with prospects who otherwise might be difficult to reach. As a function of their attendance at the event, these individuals have mentally and psychologically "opted-in" to an environment in which they are open to learning about products and services. The challenge is getting these receptive eyes and ears to focus on your products and services.

Whether you are exhibiting at a trade show or hosting a seminar, a number of steps are necessary to help insure success. Commonalities in planning and execution exist between the two kinds of events, but each has unique elements that must be considered and planned for.

Trade Shows

The largest challenge most trade show exhibitors face is getting attendees to visit their exhibit space. When there are often hundreds of exhibitors competing for the attendees' attention, a combination of planning, creativity, and thoughtful targeting is needed to bring the crowds to your space. Here are some crucial considerations for preparation, activation, and follow-up to a trade show:

- Assess the value of exhibiting. If you can't identify the benefit, there probably isn't any. Don't exhibit just because a competitor chooses to; it's far more important that you exhibit where your potential customers are.

- Accordingly, select the trade show based on where your target markets will be. Thousands of local, regional, and national trade shows take place each year. Consider only those that reach your target audience(s). For example, banks and mortgage lenders can often be found at home improvement and garden shows, because most attendees own homes and may be looking to use the equity to make improvements. Institutional sales executives choose shows that draw their particular industry focus. For example, prime brokerage services providers often exhibit at MarHedge, a conference for hedge fund managers.

- Investigate whether a show's size, anticipated attendees, other exhibitors, and past success meet your objectives. Contact the show's organizers to obtain a show kit, which will provide important information about exhibitors, statistics about past attendees and show hours, set-up and take-down dates and times, shipping information, and other important details.

- Budget comprehensively. Know what the total costs will be. The price of the trade show space is just the first in a long list of expenses. In addition to the fee for the space, plan on paying additional charges for chairs, carpeting, display lighting, wastepaper baskets, display racks, set-up and take-down, shipping, materials, and give-away items. Other expenses include travel, hotel, and meals for staff who will be handling the booth, the cost of any receptions you host, and other client entertainment. These additional expenses add up quickly and may be considerably more than the exhibition's costs.

- Organize all of the elements of the show in advance. Develop a schedule and assign people to work the booth. Share all of the show information with them. To determine staffing needs, determine the number of expected attendees and number of hours the exhibit is open. This information should be available from the show's management. Assuming contact with one-fifth of the passers-by for three to five minutes each, you can assess staffing needs as follows for a show with five thousand attendees that runs for three days: 20 percent of five thousand equals one thousand attendees who will visit your booth. One thousand attendees times three minutes per visit equals fifty hours of visits. Fifty hours divided by the twenty-one hours the exhibit is open equals two or three staff members. Based on personal past experience or information from show management, adjust the formula accordingly.

- Brainstorm ways to attract attendees to the exhibit booth. Unique or popular raffle prizes such as digital cameras, gift certificates to popular restaurants, or high-tech gadgetry work well. Some exhibitors use food to draw people—the smell of popcorn popping or coffee brewing can be a powerful attraction. Chemical Bank, now part of J.P. Morgan Chase, once sponsored a trade booth at a business show in New Orleans and was very successful in drawing visitors by creating a custom newsletter that included a map of the area, favorite restaurants, and sights, along with sales information.

- Determine the quantity and type of literature that will be available at the booth. Make sure the material is relevant. For example, literature on investment alternatives is not appropriate for a home improvement show. Typically, these attendees are interested in information on home equity loans, mortgage refinancing, and credit products. One rule of thumb is to plan for 15 to 20 percent of attendees to take relevant literature.

- Order give-away items at least four to six weeks in advance, particularly if they are custom-made or display a company logo. Compared with printed brochures, premiums have a much higher "take" rate. When ordering premiums, assume that 60 to 70 percent of attendees will take at least one of whatever it is being offered. It may be advisable to "tier" premiums. Good prospects, who have been qualified by booth staff, may get higher-value items than passers-by. The cost of premiums should be related to the value of the potential business. For an international treasury conference, a crystal item with an engraved logo, worth $30 or more, might be appropriate for "A" prospects. For a consumer show, a key chain or pen costing less than $0.50 would make more sense.

Breaking through Booth Clutter

Getting the attention of trade show attendees is always challenging. To help differentiate your exhibit and drive traffic to your booth, conducting pre-exhibit promotions will increase your odds of being noticed. It will take time, effort, and some expense, but it is generally worth the investment. One way to increase traffic is to let attendees know your company is exhibiting. Some shows will provide complimentary or deeply discounted tickets to exhibitors. For consumer shows, send key customers and prospects a show invitation with a pair of tickets three weeks prior to the show. For institutional shows, send a letter letting likely attendees know you will be exhibiting. Invite recipients to stop by the exhibit and receive a gift. This prepromotion has two advantages: it gets some of your better prospects and customers to the show for face-to-face discussions, and the gift provides a means for tracking and follow-up. Remember to always follow up the mailing to customers with a phone call.

An often-overlooked opportunity to reach potential buyers is through an on-site seminar. If the venue has meeting and conference rooms, as many convention centers and hotels do, rent space and host one or more special seminars over the course of the show for attendees. Provide light refreshments and publicize the seminar by invitation and at the booth. Be sure to have a way to capture the names, addresses, phone numbers, and e-mail addresses of attendees. A raffle usually works. A seminar is also an excellent diversion for show attendees and exhibitors (who may be some of your best prospects). It gives them a break from the noise and the crowds of the exhibit hall. If the event itself includes a conference, another tactic is to sponsor a coffee break, lunch, or cocktail reception. Doing so will put you on the program as a sponsor and may entitle you to other promotional benefits.

The appearance of the exhibit booth is a direct reflection on the company. Although size may not matter, appearance does. Always maintain an inviting and professional space. Companies spend huge amounts to create a professional atmosphere within their booth space and don't wish attendees to see an exhibitor slouched in a chair or eating lunch. Booth staffers will not win new business by extending a greasy hand to a prospect.

Following Up Leads

Getting solid sales leads from a trade show or even getting an attendee to stop by an exhibit booth is hard work and takes careful thought and planning. Since

Trade Show Errors

At one time or another everyone makes a mistake. Knowing the most common pit-falls can make the trade show more cost-effective, create a better experience for the exhibitor, and generate more of those all-important leads. When planning for the next trade show, keep the following "don'ts" in mind:

- Don't assume you know the composition of attendees and exhibitors based on the show's name. Be sure the show organizer provides attendee demographics and lists of current and previous exhibitors.
- Don't underestimate the need and value of assigning measurable show goals to each staff member, such as number of contacts per hour, number of leads per day, and number of show-related sales.
- Don't underestimate staffing needs at the booth. Staffers who are overworked, tired, and hungry can't be effective. Plan for exhibit booth staff to take a thirty- to sixty-minute break every two to three hours.
- Don't send staff who have insufficient product knowledge. Make sure all staff are well versed in the company's products and services. It may mean holding a training or refresher class prior to the trade show.
- Don't forget to review the list of exhibitors for prospects. Take time to "walk the show" and visit with other exhibitors.
- Don't establish physical barriers between yourself and attendees. Avoid placing tables, counters, or chairs across the front of the exhibit space. Doing so restricts access to the exhibit and places a barrier between the exhibitor and prospect. Even small spaces should be made inviting to potential prospects.
- Don't distribute expensive literature. Half or more of the literature distributed at a trade show almost immediately finds its way into the trash.
- Don't allow staff to eat or make personal phone calls while in the booth. They should look interested and available to speak with attendees at all times.
- Don't let staff close the exhibit earlier then the published show times and dates. There is a tendency to wind down early at the end of a long day and to begin packing up hours before the official close on the final day. Research has shown that many attendees use the end of the show to revisit exhibitors they are interested in doing business with.
- Don't let sales leads go stale. Follow-up within the first forty-eight hours is key to success.

lead generation is usually the reason companies dedicate resources to exhibiting, the No. 1 priority following the show must be to follow up on the leads that were obtained.

Know what needs to be tracked. Decide in advance what information you want to capture beyond name and contact information. For consumer shows, design forms for visitors to fill out in connection with a raffle. Provide ample space for attendees to write in their names, addresses, phone numbers, and e-mail addresses. Many forms also ask for age, household income, occupation, and other personal information. The form should also ask visitors to mark the products or services they are interested in learning more about. The attendee's signature indicating permission to follow-up with a phone call or e-mail is also a good idea.

Many business shows provide attendees with registration cards that have magnetic strips containing all relevant information. Or you may collect business cards. Try to supplement these with other useful tracking data, such as size of company and product interest, for lead follow-ups. To minimize lapse time, a letter should be prepared prior to the show and then personalized and mailed to every lead within forty-eight hours of the show's close. The letter should thank prospects for visiting the exhibit booth and inform them to expect a phone call following up on their interest in the company's product or service. Also send thank-you notes to clients who stopped by the exhibit booth. If a seminar was held, a similar letter should be sent to those attendees, thanking them for attending and alerting them to expect a follow-up phone call.

Under do-not-call rules, it is legitimate to call prospects who have spoken to a staff member and requested information. If you are collecting phone numbers from a raffle form, on the other hand, you will need to get legal clarification about following up by phone. The same gray area exists about e-mail. If it was not specifically requested, it could be regarded as spam under the "CAN-SPAM" law. Since a letter is more personal, it is usually more effective to follow up by regular mail and phone.

Measuring Results

Implement the following checklist to insure lead follow-up and accurate reporting:

- Within forty-eight hours after the show, enter all attendee data into a spreadsheet.

- Assign leads and make salespeople accountable. Determine prior to the event the number of leads an individual salesperson can reasonably respond to. Have salespeople ready to handle the excess leads or those leads in which an individual salesperson's particular expertise or territory makes it a logical hand-off.
- Assign one or more lead coordinators. A lead coordinator manages the flow of leads to the sales force, the follow-up, and the input of information into the database.
- Track appointments scheduled, appointments completed, referrals, sales by product type, dollar amounts of the sales, and whatever other information is relevant to your measurements.
- After the leads have been pursued by the sales force, you can arrive at an approximate ROI by dividing new business generated from exhibit visitors by the expense of the show. Be sure to include any new sales to your own invited clients. If new sales outweigh the expense of the event, the event can be considered successful. Some companies may look for a 2-to-1 return to consider an event a success, whereas others may look for a larger or smaller multiplier.

Seminars

In many ways, coordinating seminars is similar to preparing for trade shows. The big difference is that the roles of organizer, sponsor, marketer, operations director, and salesperson all belong to the host. From the selection of the topic, attendee mailing list, and venue selection to filling the seats and planning follow-up activities, all of the steps need to be carefully coordinated. Seminars can be highly successful or dismal failures. Although no one can control all of the factors that will attract prospective customers, there are ways to improve the odds of success.

Planning

Identify the target markets and their needs (for example, retirement planning or regulatory changes), and select the seminar topic that is important to them. In planning the presentation, determine if partners or additional experts are needed to speak on complicated or multifaceted topics. For example, a financial planner might invite an estate lawyer to participate in a seminar on estate planning.

Seminars for institutional clients are sometimes expensive, several-day affairs. Bankers Trust (now part of Deutsche Bank) held client seminars at top-of-the-line resorts, such as Pebble Beach. Product experts and analysts, along with well-known outside speakers, conducted morning sessions, then guests played golf or enjoyed wine tastings in the afternoons. High-net-worth clients also require special handling. A leading private client insurer held a successful event for directors of family offices at a private, terraced suite in the Stanhope Hotel in New York City. Clients sipped cocktails and gazed at the view of the Metropolitan Museum and Central Park while listening to speakers talk about art collecting—and insuring collections.

The larger the event and the more speakers and guests, the longer and more complex the planning process. Outside speakers should be invited at least two to four months before the event in order to ensure firm commitments. If you're planning a panel presentation, the ideal number of panelists is three. But invite four—or have a backup speaker—in case one of them must cancel at the last minute. Ideally, your speakers will confer with the organizer and one another at least a week before the event to make sure the material covered is relevant. Make it clear that speakers are there to educate the audience—not give a sales presentation. Offer speakers the ability to leave sales literature for attendees to take with them. It is polite to give your speakers a token gift usually worth less than $100. Obviously, you do not need to give a gift if you are paying for a speaker's services.

Once the topic is established, the next step is to select a date for the seminar. This is not as easy as it sounds. In choosing a date and time, there are a number of things that need to be kept in mind:

- Are other high-profile events planned for the date being considered? This could adversely affect attendance.
- Typically July and August are not good months for seminars because of summer vacation plans, although some practitioners disagree and focus on these summer months because schedules tend to be less hectic.
- Avoid mid-December to early January because of the crush of holiday obligations.
- Avoid Sundays, Mondays, and major holidays. Some feel Friday nights can be effective if a reception is built into the evening.
- Select a time and venue that will be convenient for the target audience. Breakfast or immediately after the workday are generally good times to reach working people. Saturday mornings may be best for couples. Consider providing on-site babysitting services for couples with young children.

Choose a Co-sponsor

A Chicago branch of a major financial services company sent out five thousand seminar invitations to a targeted subscriber list of a well-known national magazine. The seminar was co-branded with the name of the publication in order to draw additional attention. There were 200 positive responses to the invitation, and 110 of those showed up—a respectable 2 percent response rate.

When selecting a venue, try to be creative. Look for locations that are unique, such as museums, art galleries, or new restaurants. This gives invitees another reason to attend. If a meal or refreshments will be served, be sure the venue can accommodate the need. There is a growing trend to host seminars in restaurants, where attendees enjoy a free meal along with the seminar. This will dramatically add to the cost of the seminar, so it should be factored in early on. If providing a meal, it is important to work closely with the restaurant owner or manager to understand all of the expenses that could be incurred.

Marketing the Seminar

There is always a worry that "confirmed" attendees will fail to show up. There are several ways to improve the odds of filling the seats:

- Invitations must be sent out early enough (generally three to four weeks in advance). Make sure the invitation specifies where and how to RSVP—by phone, e-mail, or reply card.
- Phone follow-up within a week of mailing is optimal, but not always possible under do-not-call rules, unless you have a prior relationship. Consider, instead, inviting clients (whom you may call) and ask them to bring a friend.
- Reconfirm with those who have said they will be attending. This should be done two to three days prior to the seminar and should serve as a reminder and to let guests know that you look forward to seeing them at the seminar.

Even with this approach, plan on at least 25 percent of "confirmed" attendees not showing up. If it rains or snows on the day of the event, attendance will drop even more.

The Magic Word "Free"

A local office of a financial services company held a financial planning workshop that was advertised in the local paper. The number of attendees—zero! Why? The ad did not specifically say that the seminar was free. "Free" is one of the most important words to use when inviting people to a seminar, whether through advertising or invitation.

As with any piece of direct mail, make sure the list is targeted and the communication addresses the audience's needs. Response to your invitation will vary, depending on the topic, speaker, venue, list quality, and whether the invitees are customers or prospects. For a purchased prospect list and a run-of-the-mill topic, estimate a 1 to 2 percent response. This means that you will have to send five thousand pieces to fill a fifty-seat room. If you are mailing to your own customers, or have a big-name speaker, you could draw 10 percent or more. If you get lucky and are oversubscribed, you can always set up a second session.

If the seminar will be marketed through newspaper or radio advertising, be sure to include a call to action—a phone number or Web address for reservations. This will provide a gauge as to the number of attendees that can be expected. Because these individuals are responding to a nameless and faceless ad, there may be less commitment on their part to attend, so no-show percentages will be higher.

During the Seminar

Determining how many people you will need to work the event and who they should be is vitally important. The presenters themselves will be kept busy on the day of the event, so staff will need to sign-in and greet attendees, answer questions from venue staff and guests, say hello to clients and special guests, make sure the refreshments are ready, and confirm that everything is running smoothly.

When selecting seminar staff, make sure they are comfortable and conversant with the subject being covered so they can handle general questions. Pick people who are outgoing and approachable. Also be certain that the staff know the layout of the venue, including locations of restrooms, phones, coat check, and other amenities. Conduct a walk-through at least an hour before the start of the seminar. Assign someone to handle the audio/visual needs, including setting up the laptop and projector, raising and lowering the lights, and cueing slides and videos. When handled properly these details let the audience know that thought and preparation went into all aspects of the presentation. Conversely, lack of preparation—for instance, if the speaker needs to walk to the back of the room to lower and raise the lights—reflects poorly. Make sure all support staff are on-site at least sixty to ninety minutes prior to the start of the seminar.

Depending on the room configuration and the number of attendees, there are several options for the most appropriate seating arrangements:

- Small tables for four. This seating arrangement has proven effective in seminars where clients are invited to bring friends. The client couple can enjoy private conversation with their friends before the seminar begins.
- Tables of six or eight (preferably round tables) for seating people who do not necessarily know one another.
- U-shaped arrangement of tables
- Auditorium or classroom style

Regardless of the style chosen, make sure there is ample walking space and room for display tables, refreshments, and a speakers' area.

The Presentation

The room looks great. The staff is getting attendees into their seats. Now it is up to the presenter to pull it all together and make the attendees grateful they came. The presentation should be delivered in a clear and understandable manner. If slides, overheads, or computer images are used, be sure they are clear and readable from every corner of the room. It is unprofessional to apologize for the readability of a presentation slide. The following guidelines will help ensure a successful talk:

- If you are the one presenting, write out the main points of the presentation in advance and rehearse them with your colleagues. Do not read from a script—you'll put everyone to sleep—but feel free to refer to notes.
- The presentation and the information provided should be genuinely educational. The audience is there to learn—not for a sales pitch.
- The presentation should be made as interactive as possible. Create opportunities for audience participation and encourage questions.

- Limit each slide to one key point. Don't crowd too much information onto one slide. Break up complex information into multiple slides. Estimate one to two slides per minute.
- An audience's attention span is thirty to forty-five minutes. Keep presentations within a reasonable time frame.
- Provide attendees with handouts of material related to the seminar topic or a summary of the presentation itself.

Follow-up: The Key to Success

It is startling how many seminar leads are never pursued. As with trade shows, some people think that once the event is over, the job is done. Not following up is akin to training for a marathon, running the race of a lifetime, and just before the finish line, pulling up short and walking away. The end of the seminar signals the start of the real work, the stage at which follow-up and selling begins. Initiating a few simple practices will keep the lines of communication open:

- Create a follow-up letter that can be sent to attendees immediately after the seminar.
- Invitees who requested an appointment or additional material should be the highest priority and be contacted within forty-eight hours of the seminar.
- Confirmed invitees who were unable to attend should be sent a letter indicating that a follow-up call will be made to answer any questions. Also, send a copy of the presentation or other relevant material.

Measuring Results

Return on investment in a seminar is relatively easy to assess. These are the important measurements:

- Cost-per-qualified lead. Divide the overall costs of the seminar (invitations, space, refreshments, staff time, speakers' gifts, handouts) by the number of those who responded (even if they didn't attend). The cost-per-lead should be a metric that you will use to measure other seminar efforts.
- New business. After following up with both attendees and no-shows at least once and preferably three to four times, total the new or additional business generated by these leads. If possible, project this business forward for one to three years.
- ROI: Determine this figure by dividing new business by total cost.

Resources

Organizations: National Association of Consumer Shows (http://www.publicshow .com), Center for Exhibition Industry Research (http://www.ceir.org), Sales Marketing Network (http://info-now.com), and Promotion Marketing Association (http://www .pmalink.org).

Publications: *Association Meetings* (http://www.primedia.com), *Corporate Meetings and Incentives* (http://www.primedia.com), *Insurance Conference Planner* (http://www .primedia.com), *Tradeshow Week* (http://www.tradeshowweek.com), and *PROMO* (http:// www.promomagazine.com).

Relationship Marketing

11

It is far cheaper to retain current customers than to acquire new ones. Relationship marketing not only helps increase customer longevity but also builds customer wallet share. That, in turn, increases loyalty and profitability.

In October 1997, twenty lucky co-workers won $55 million in the Texas Lottery. By the time they had verified their win, it was 2 a.m., but the group decided they did not want to risk losing the ticket. So they called up the president of Texas First Bank, who met them in downtown Texas City along with a lawyer and a justice of the peace. On the hood of a pickup, they drew up an official contract agreement, signed it, and stuffed it with the lottery ticket into the bank's night deposit box.[1]

It's not likely that similar winners could get hold of the president or anyone else at Bank of America or Wachovia in the middle of the night. That kind of customized, small-town service doesn't exist much anymore. And yet, the country's largest financial institutions are attempting to reintroduce something like it. Today, it gets fancy names—service marketing or relationship marketing or retention marketing or loyalty marketing or customer relationship management (CRM)—but it all means the same thing: finding a way to keep customers happy so they will stay and grow as customers.

In a saturated market like financial services, it is extremely important to focus marketing efforts on retaining, cross-selling, and up-selling current customers, in both consumer and institutional markets. Estimates of the cost of retaining customers versus acquiring them vary by factors of 5 to 10 times or more. Clearly, it is cheaper by orders of magnitude to retain current customers than it is to acquire new ones. Successful cross-sales can help build customer loyalty: the more products customers have, the more likely they will stay with the provider. Up-selling is important because the greater the percentage of assets a customer has with a given institution (known as "share of wallet"), the greater the profitability of the customer.

> ### Financial Institutions Need to Shift Marketing Priorities
>
> A 2002 Gartner survey of large financial services providers, including banking, investment firms, insurance, and credit cards, asked respondents: Which strategy is most important in terms of driving your retail marketing initiatives? Customer retention was mentioned by only 9 percent of financial institutions, whereas acquiring new customers was the first priority for 43 percent. Given that new customers are the most expensive to acquire and service and have the least loyalty, these priorities are clearly misplaced. Gartner estimates that retaining one high-profit customer or up-selling a mid-level to become a high-profit customer can cost one-tenth of acquiring a new mid-level customer.[2]

Why Customer Retention Matters

Before you can grow customer assets, you have to make sure you keep the customers you have. In some subsegments of the industry, this is not difficult, because customers are virtually locked in. For example, holders of commercial mortgages are hemmed in by prepayment penalties; annuity policyholders generally pay a substantial penalty for early withdrawals. Even in situations where customers can move freely, they generally don't. A private banking client has too much tied up in his banking relationship to change banks because someone offers a better deal. A corporate retirement plan sponsor may put millions of dollars at risk if it changes plan providers. In many cases, the rewards of moving just aren't worth the costs—psychologically or financially.

But that doesn't mean financial marketers can afford to ignore current customers. In some subsegments of financial services, customer turnover is relatively high. Credit card consumers who carry balances routinely switch to better interest rate offers. In mutual funds, many investors chase returns. By one estimate, defection of retail shareholders is more than 15 percent annually, and for retirement plans, annual asset outflow is 10 percent.[3] Turnover on checking accounts can range from 10 percent to 17 percent or more in a competitive market—close to the national norm of 20 percent for service providers as a whole.[4]

There are also high-risk moments or trigger events that can cause loss of clients. A merger presents one such risk. If clients are going to have to adapt to new systems and new personnel anyway, they figure they might as well examine some of the alternatives. Similarly, an adviser or broker who is changing firms may bring many of her clients along with her. Or a trigger event may occur, such as a customer move to another locality or a need for a financial product not offered by the current provider.

The advantages of retaining current customers go beyond just having one more customer.

The longer the customer's tenure, the more profitable the customer. One study found customer profitability increased substantially in the second year and thereafter, as purchases rose and expenses associated with servicing new customers declined. In mutual funds, a $10 billion manager can earn the equivalent of $1 million in annual revenue by lowering outflow by 10 percent.[5]

Current customers are the best potential new customers. Cross-selling (selling a new product or service) and up-selling (increasing the investment in the customer's current service) are the most cost-effective ways of generating new business. A happy customer who already does business with you is far more likely to buy more products and services in the future.

Existing customers tell their friends. In some businesses—retail brokerage, for example—33 percent of new business may come from referrals by customers.[6] Willingness to recommend is also a marker for client longevity.

The loyalty cycle is important. The more business that customers do with you, the more they are likely to remain customers, the more profitable they are

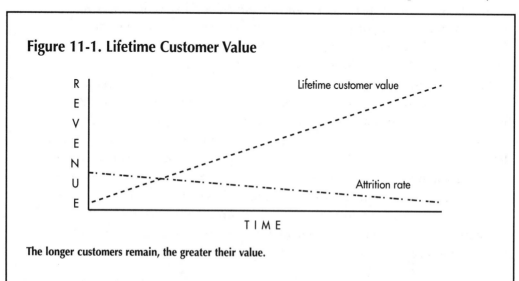

Figure 11-1. Lifetime Customer Value

The longer customers remain, the greater their value.

How Not to Keep Mortgage Customers

When interest rates started to drop in 2001, most mortgage lenders were so busy processing paperwork for new customers that they didn't bother trying to keep the refinancing business of their current mortgage customers. According to a 2002 report, "many lenders are letting a great chance to cement long-term relationships pass them by." With increasing competition for mortgage business from online and offline lenders, and "very little loyalty" among borrowers seeking only the best rate, lenders were losing borrowers "and the subsequent chance to cross-sell other products."

One exception cited was Countrywide, the largest independent mortgage lender. Successfully using one-on-one marketing, it gave customers the opportunity to set up a personal rate watch on Countrywide's website. When rates dropped to the level specified by the customer, the bank sent an e-mail. In addition, the bank sent personalized e-mails to other, selected customers, showing how much they could save on their current mortgage by refinancing at the current rate. The result: huge increases in customers retained.[7]

---

likely to be. Lifetime value of customers increases with each product they purchase and each year they remain customers. One analysis showed that a 5 percent increase in retention could raise profitability on bank deposits by 25 percent.[8]

Methods of Relationship Building

Building customer relationships involves both customer service and marketing. Unfortunately, in most organizations, the marketing function does not have a great deal of authority over the service side of the equation. (The exception is situations in which sales and service are combined in one function, such as an independent financial adviser.) But even though service quality may be outside the control of marketing, there are proactive tools marketers can use to improve retention levels.

Special care for newcomers. Like most companies, American Express has found that attrition rates are highest during the first twelve to eighteen months after a cardholder has signed on. The company therefore assigns new customers to a special service team. New customers also receive more special offers and attention, especially around the time of the first renewal. Other ways that financial marketers can give new customers special attention is through welcome packages that may include special value-added offers, direct contact information, and a phone call to ensure that the client is satisfied with the activation of the service.

Pre-emptive intervention. One of the most important proactive tools is to create a structured program to intervene when (or even before) there is a risk of customer attrition resulting from a service problem. In some cases, this is done very simply by creating templates for letters of apology or explanation that are used by the field. Chase Manhattan Bank, for example, at one time offered branch managers an online letter library with numerous options—from a simple apology to a gift basket. By making amends for inconvenience, financial institutions can actually turn service failures into relationship-building experiences. Satisfying the customer after a service problem actually looms larger than the problem itself in influencing overall customer satisfaction, future purchase intentions, and positive word-of-mouth communications.[9]

Many CRM systems can anticipate "at risk" clients through metrics that identify anomalous behavior patterns (such as a large withdrawal). Where there is an account representative, that person can intervene through a phone call or personal letter. For example, Fifth Third Bank uses its at-risk modeling capacity to send alerts within 24 hours to either its contact center, or for the highest-value customers, to the branch. By rapidly taking proactive steps to keep the customer, new account attrition was reduced by 50 percent in six months.[10]

Maintaining ongoing contact. Of course, it is best not to wait until there is a problem before contacting the customer. Merrill Lynch has successfully improved customer value (both retention and up-sell) by having its financial advisers schedule monthly phone conferences with their high-value clients. Not only do clients feel they are getting more personal attention, but they often save up their questions for the appointed phone conference, thus saving their own and the adviser's time.

Another brokerage firm creates "personalized, hand-written" notes that are actually computer-generated. These are "signed" by the individual's financial adviser and are sent after certain events, such as a "thank you for your business" when a client buys a new product. This firm's metrics have shown that one-to-one contact is the most important factor in retaining a client's business and that the primary reason clients leave is that they haven't been contacted.[11]

Effective Merger Communications

In 1997, the then Bankers Trust (BT) acquired the corporate trust business of what was then NationsBank. The success of the transition resulted from BT's proactive efforts to keep clients and staff informed every step of the way. The following practices were key:

Laying out the steps of the merger transition in advance alleviates the anxiety of institutional clients and enables them to plan.

- Communications were integrated into transition management. By including the marketing department in weekly transition team meetings, the marketing representative had the information as soon as decisions were made and could then create materials to inform internal staff and clients.
- Internal staff were informed well ahead of public announcements. Management quickly decided which office locations would be retained and communicated this information so that staff were not left in the dark about their future.
- Client representatives were given as much information as was available, which they were encouraged to share with clients.
- Both clients and staff received regular communications throughout the process. Personalized letters were written from senior management to clients announcing the deal and explaining how and when each client's account would be changed over. In addition, clients and staff received regular newsletters outlining the process, reporting on progress to date, and answering common questions.

Honest, frequent, and timely communications are important, whether the customers are individuals or institutions. Examples might include newsletters, regularly scheduled personal letters and phone calls, targeted direct mailers, field salespeople calling on clients, open houses, seminars, and other client functions, such as meetings with clients at trade shows and conferences. Even something as basic as an account statement can affect customer loyalty. Upgrading its

---

Improving Cross-Sell

After implementing CRM in the 1990s, the Bank of Oklahoma found itself "data rich and action poor." The technology "had been more of a segmentation and pricing tool than a relationship-building tool," according to Steven G. Bradshaw, head of consumer banking. To focus on the customer's individual needs, staff were given training and a profile questionnaire designed to elicit information about current and future financial plans. Sophisticated tickler systems ensured appropriate follow-up calls. The results: Referrals from one bank area to another were up 400 percent in the first six months over the same period a year earlier. Sales were up 40 percent, and customer satisfaction had risen by 10 percent.[12]

---

format to make it easier to understand is a prime retention device.

Personalization. High-value clients should get personal phone calls or letters whenever there are appropriate occasions, such as following up on past sales to ensure satisfaction, checking to see if their needs have changed, recognizing important events in their lives (marriages, birthdays, children going off to college, retirement), passing along helpful information, and just saying hello. CRM systems attempt to create this kind of personal knowledge on a large scale. Although systems-based analytical tools are not yet a match for one-on-one human relationships, financial firms are developing ways to exploit event-based opportunities to retain, cross-sell, and up-sell customers. For example, predictive modeling can help marketers anticipate customer events, future financial needs, and demands for products on an individual-customer basis. Individualized marketing campaigns can then be developed that correspond with specific events.

Cross-sell and up-sell. Although it may be self-evident that it is profitable to sell more to your customers, what may not be self-evident is that doing so also strengthens the relationship. Each additional service encourages the customer to invest more resources, more time, or more trust in the relationship. One study found a 15 percent likelihood that banking customers who used only one bank product would remain in the relationship for five years. In contrast, there was a 45 percent likelihood of a five-year relationship for customers who had two products, and 80 percent for customers with three.[13]

Customer rewards. For direct marketing companies without a sales force, such as credit cards and no-load mutual funds, building a one-to-one relationship with customers is more difficult. Credit card marketers were among the first to come up with rewards programs, such as those that award frequent-flyer miles or other prizes for each dollar spent on a particular card. More recently, issuers have come up with the affinity card, such as those tied to college alumni associations. With this type of program, for

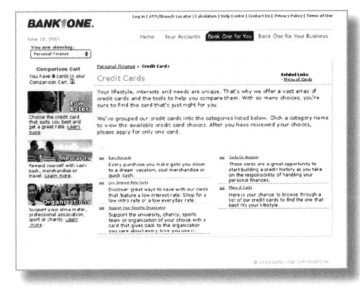

A "do-it-yourself" loyalty program. Customers decide whether they want lower interest rates, a choice of rewards, or a choice of nonprofit contributions.

every dollar spent, your school gets a contribution. A new wrinkle is to offer a "do-it-yourself" loyalty program that lets customers decide which rewards they want—whether lower interest rates, broader rewards, or more money to a favorite cause. Bank One's website features a particularly wide selection, offering hundreds of cards with different affinities (colleges, charities, professional associations), terms, and rewards.

Although not formal loyalty programs, special benefits are often offered to more valuable customers. For example, many mutual fund companies offer a different fund class, with lower fees, to large shareholders (generally with assets of more than $100,000). Many banks offer a preferred customer account relationship (such as the Chase Select Banking Account) that offers benefits such as a special number to call for service, a dedicated teller window, or free travelers checks. Institutional clients may be invited to client seminars or training sessions at high-end resorts.

Formal Loyalty Programs

One of the most brilliant marketing ideas ever dreamed up was to emboss a year after the words "Member since…" onto the American Express card. Membership is central to the American Express brand, and that message is reinforced by its taglines ("Membership has its Privileges," "Membership Rewards®"), its advertising, its merchandising, and special events. AmEx has created such a sense of loyalty that customers are willing to pay more for the privilege of being higher-level members. There are several tiers of American Express cards, each charging different annual "dues," with a corresponding increase in benefits and a perceived elevation in personal status for the cardholder.

AmEx members are so loyal, in fact, that members were willing to join a card level that didn't even exist. For years, there were stories about the mysterious (and nonexistent) American Express "black" card, reserved for the upper-most tier. Since AmEx couldn't quash the rumors, it decided to make them true—and issued a black Centurion card in 1999. The company found that many of its most loyal customers wanted the card—and were willing to pay $1,000 per year for the privilege.

Few companies have developed the level of customer loyalty that AmEx and its long-time agency, Ogilvy & Mather, managed to cultivate over many years. But many try. Credit card issuers, in particular, have developed loyalty programs that involve rewards for purchases. Once the customer has built up a certain level of rewards, the cost of leaving is high. If your customer has 50,000 points saved up, she will be reluctant to give up your card, even if she has to pay a higher annual fee. The downside with any loyalty program is that competitors soon match whatever you're offering. And then you're back to square one—no differentiation.

Loyalty programs are expensive to set up and manage. Formal programs make the most sense when a product or service is essentially a commodity—for example, securities trading. Soft-dollar services are essentially a kind of loyalty marketing, as investors get "credits" toward free research or other services in exchange for trading commissions. Another example is prime brokerage, where a hedge fund manager gets low-cost or free office space and other services in exchange for its trading business. Whether on the consumer or institutional side, there are several steps to creating and managing a useful loyalty program.

Branding the program. The program should conform to the company's overall brand image but create a sense of a separate, more privileged "club" of special clients. This may involve a separate logo and/or tagline.

Membership package. You need to let your customers know that they are now members of the "club." A welcome letter is a must—a welcome kit is even better. The kit can contain information about "club" benefits, a copy of the newsletter, perhaps a membership card, and a premium designed to reinforce the brand message. For example, a mortgage development program directed to realtors could offer information on a CD-ROM to help them prequalify home buyers. Unless your members have specifically asked to join, they probably won't realize they're members of the club unless there is a strong welcome package and ongoing follow-up.

Teaming up for added awareness and benefits. Gain the goodwill of clients by aligning with charitable partners. If your card supports the Audubon Society, include Audubon information, a bird-themed calendar, and other related items. A small-business–oriented program, for example, might benefit the local chamber of commerce or offer scholarships to community college students aiming for business careers.

Teaming up with a for-profit company in a noncompetitive industry can also be effective. A bank that sought to establish a loyalty program for college savers teamed up with a computer retailer. Those joining the program were entered into a sweepstakes with computer hardware and software as prizes. Both parties benefited from the promotion.

Referral rewards. Referrals are your best source of high-value new customers, and who better to give a referral than a satisfied, current customer? Referral rewards should be built into the program. For example, if the program involves donations to charity, a referral would generate an additional donation, perhaps with an acknowledging gift from the charity in return (for example, a baseball cap with a logo). Or a referral program could offer better pricing on products or fees, or additional services. A financial adviser who receives a referral could offer the referring customer a free retirement planning analysis or other program that normally would involve a fee.

Special events. Another way to make loyal customers feel special is to invite them to special events. Fleet Bank, for example, invited entrepreneurial women to monthly breakfast meetings at an upscale hotel that featured successful women entrepreneurs. Neuberger Berman created The Women's Partnership, which offered seminars where members met and a website that also fostered communication among members. At one time, Chase's Small Business area had a special program for accountants. Among other benefits, accountants were invited to bring their clients to seminars of special interest to small-business owners. Not only did this allow the accountants to build stronger relationships with their own clients, but it also introduced new prospects to Chase in a low-key way, with an implied endorsement from their accountant. On the institutional side, special events to entertain top clients are commonplace and range from corporate skyboxes at the Super Bowl to lunch at one's club. More on event marketing can be found in chapter 6.

Client feedback. A loyalty program should provide two-way communications—learn as much as you can from your clients. For example, ask members to fill out a questionnaire when they join or call them at intervals to determine if their needs are being met. Set up an online chat group and use it to test market new ideas. One European bank set up a loyalty program specifically to find out as much as possible about customer's financial behavior. In order to join and get special pricing and exclusive offers, members filled out a questionnaire. The bank then used this data to refine its direct mailing efforts to these customers, in some cases improving response by 400 percent.

Client Publications

A loyalty program almost always includes some sort of regular communication, such as a newsletter or magazine. A newsletter is generally from two to eight pages long and may be sent as a statement stuffer, a stand-alone mailing, or an e-mailing. A magazine (such as Schwab's *On Investing* or Fidelity's *Fidelity Focus*) is a more expensive option. It looks like a "real" magazine, with long, thoughtful articles written by professionals. It is usually printed on slick paper, in four colors, and can run thirty-two pages or more.

Even without a formal loyalty program, newsletters and other client publications are valuable for relationship building, as one of their main benefits is to get your company's name in front of the client regularly.

It is a mistake to try to cost-justify a publications by looking for sales increases directly tied to them. Newsletters are not direct sales vehicles. Rather, they should be seen as retention tools and brand builders. If done well, they help build a more positive image of your company or your products. Measurement of a successful newsletter will be a matter of increased brand recognition and improved attitudes toward the brand.

Frequency. There is no point in creating a newsletter unless you send it often enough to be noticed. Until customers have received four issues in the course of a year, they probably won't even realize they're receiving a newsletter. Bimonthly publication is even better for a mailed newsletter. For an e-mail newsletter, monthly is generally sufficient, although some successful e-newsletters—such as Fierce Finance.com—are e-mailed daily. Since you will want to get permission to send an e-mail newsletter (see chapter 8), you might ask the intended recipients how often they prefer to receive one.

Costs. Many variables enter into cost. First, is the newsletter going to be distributed by mail or online? Clearly, online is cheaper—there are no printing, lettershop, or postage charges. But online is not always appropriate. A paper newsletter is something a client can read at his leisure. He can hold onto an article of special interest. He can call you if he wants more information. Bottom line: Paper carries more weight.

Whether paper or online, there will be creative costs. You will probably need a writer, a designer, and possibly a programmer. You may also want original photographs or illustrations, which will add substantially to your costs. For most purposes, stock images will be adequate and less expensive. Printing costs will depend on the number of pages, the number of copies, the newsletter's size (flat and folded), the type of paper, the binding, and the number of colors. If you have fewer than 1,000 copies, there are digital short-run presses that do not carry the set-up charges of larger print runs. Go for the highest quality printing and paper you can afford; it will be noticeable to the recipient. Also, make sure you have the grammar and spelling checked—you might not think a typo will impact badly on your image, but it will. If all this seems like too much effort, there are also "canned" newsletters that you can purchase and overprint with your name, photo, and sometimes a column.

Before you begin planning your newsletter, make sure you have a commitment to keep it going. Many newsletters run out of steam within the first few issues because people exhaust what they have to say or lack time to produce it. The first issue is the most expensive, since it involves creating a template for both art and content. There is no point in spending the money if you are not going to continue.

Table 11-1. Do's and Don'ts for Newsletters

DO'S	DON'TS
Plan the contents of each issue in advance. Include a time line for completion. Get agreement on the topics and the schedule from everyone involved.	Ask low-level managers to make decisions only to overrule them later.
Make sure contents are appropriate for the audience in subject matter, tone (informal vs. formal), and level of readability (e.g., mass audience, professional, age-specific).	Talk down to your readers or use insider jargon if you are trying to reach a general audience. Don't make your newsletter sound like a business report. Use a journalistic model, with a compelling lead paragraph, lots of quotes, and informative examples.
Feature anyone in your organization who can provide information of value to your readers, such as economists, analysts, and other industry experts.	Include a letter from your president unless he or she is a well-known industry expert.
Read the contents in manuscript, before the issue has been laid out.	Decide after the issue has been laid out to omit a story or make other changes that will require a new layout.
Use call-outs, sidebars, captions, and other visual elements to direct the reader's attention to important subject matter.	Assume that the reader will find the "meat" of the story in the fourth paragraph.
Proofread carefully before the issue goes to the printer or up on the website. Pay particular attention to headlines, call-outs, etc., which are generally not spell-checked. And remember that spell-checking won't catch words that are used incorrectly, like "site" for "cite."	Wait until you see the bluelines (printer's proofs) to proofread—you will incur sizable charges for changes at this stage.

Tone and content. To whom are you directing the newsletter? The content should match the target audience's interests and level of sophistication. Think about what other publications your target audience reads. If they are business clients, they are probably readers of the *Wall Street Journal,* so that should be your model for tone and language. One internal publication for Chase used *Business Week* as a visual model—lively, but professional.

When planning your first issue, aim for regularly scheduled features. This makes it easier to come up with story ideas. For example, a newsletter for Neuberger Berman's Prime Brokerage area had regular updates on operations, technology, and legal issues, and a Q&A explaining electronic features. A newsletter for high-net-worth property insurance clients of Marsh featured a regular column on antiques and collectibles, another on insurance news items, and another on how to mitigate risks.

A newsletter directed to clients (as opposed to newsletters to staff or the sales force) should not be entirely devoted to selling products and services. If the newsletter is perceived only as advertising, it will not be read. There should be editorial content that is of benefit to the reader. For example, a newsletter for small-business clients of Chase offered a service feature in each issue on topics such as time management, simple marketing ideas, or reducing employee theft. Ideally, the client should regard at least half the content as editorial, not advertising. Offering charts, checklists, how-to information, important dates, and similar material may inspire the reader to save the issue and refer to it later.

An internal newsletter designed in the style of *BusinessWeek*—a familiar model for corporate readers.

The design should give visual variety to engage the reader. Long blocks of text look uninviting.

For internal audiences, good subject matter includes case studies of successes. Not only can sales reps and others learn from their colleagues' success, but the person featured in the story also receives the reward of recognition—a powerful motivator. Sales contest results, photographs of events, profiles of heads of the various departments, and close-ups of individuals with unusual hobbies or charitable interests can also be good regular content. If you want to make sure internal staff reads the newsletter, here is a clever trick. One newsletter editor ran a contest in which an employee who spotted his or her own Social Security number won a prize. The numbers were scattered randomly through the text—to spot the number, one generally had to read the story.

Conclusion

Large financial companies spend tens of millions of dollars on automated CRM systems that they hope will give them a competitive edge. Yet, in many cases, as institutions get large enough to afford these massive data-manipulation systems, they get further from their customers. As the banking industry, for example, becomes more and more concentrated, the megabanks are losing market share to smaller banks. Why? Because smaller banks can offer personalized service that the megabanks can only approximate. In the University of Michigan's 2003 American Customer Satisfaction Index, only Wachovia equaled the average score for "all other banks" (made up of regional and community banks). All the other major banks scored lower.[14]

Relationship marketing can work for big companies—just look at American Express. But it will take more than "event-triggering" or "loss-based predictive modeling" to create a company that customers love. It requires staff training up and down the corporate ladder, solid and sustained management commitment, the ability to track and measure service performance, and rewards for service excellence. Lots of financial companies give lip service to these factors, but ask yourself this: Which bank would you choose if you had won the lottery?

CHAPTER NOTES

1. Glen Fest, "Doyle Town," *US Banker,* February 2003.

2. Gartner Group, "Financial Services Marketing: Moving from Push to Pull," presentation by Kimberly Collins Ph.D. to the American Marketing Association, March 2003.

3. Howard Schneider presentation, "Practical Perspectives," at the Investment Company Institute annual meeting, May 22, 2003.

4. F. F. Reichheld and W. E. Sasser Jr., "Zero Defections: Quality Comes to Services," *Harvard Business Review,* September–October 1990, 105-111. Cited in Cindy Claycomb and Charles L. Martin, "Building Customer Relationships: An Inventory of Service Providers' Objectives and Practices," *Journal of Services Marketing,* 16, 7, 2002, 615-635.

5. Schneider, "Practical Perspectives," see note 3.

6. Presentation by William Craeger, director of research and analytical marketing at Merrill Lynch, to Columbia Business School Alumni Club, January 15, 2003. Frederick Reichheld of Bain & Co. has determined a strong correlation between willingness to recommend and re-purchase rates. See Reichheld, "The One Number You Need to Grow," *Harvard Business Review,* December 2003.

7. Randall Foster, "Has Customer Understanding Finally Become an Attainable Commodity?" *American Banker's Financial Services Marketing,* January–February 2002, 31.

8. Bain & Company study, published by F. F. Reichheld and W. E. Sasser Jr., "Zero Defections: Quality Comes to Services," *Harvard Business Review,* September/October 1990, 105-111.

9. R. A. Spreng et al., "Service Recovery: Impact on Satisfaction and Intentions," *Journal of Services Marketing,* 1995, 15-23. Cited in Claycomb, "Building Customer Relationships."

10. Gartner Group, see note 2, 16.

11. Presentation by Lou Schwarz, senior database marketing specialist at Fletcher Knight, to Columbia Business School Alumni Club, January 15, 2003.

12. Steve Bills, "Successful CRM Projects Stress Quantifiable Results," *American Banker's Financial Services Marketing,* August 28, 2002, 4A.

13. C. B. Furlong, "Twelve Rules for Customer Retention," *Bank Marketing,* 1993, 14-18. Cited in Claycomb, "Building Customer Relationships."

14. American Customer Satisfaction Index, "Recent ACSI Scores for Q4 2003: Retail, Finance/Insurance, E-Commerce," http://www.theasci.org, February 2004.

Conclusion

Until recently, the financial services industry was a backwater in terms of marketing sophistication. When Lorenzo de Medici conducted banking business with the pope, he used his personal contacts and reputation to generate deals. The investment banking industry still operates pretty much the same way. Yet today, certain segments of the financial industry are marketing innovators; banks, for example, were among the first to adopt customer relationship management. Nevertheless, a large portion of the industry is just now beginning to move from a sales model to a marketing model—a move consumer products manufacturers made in the 1950s.

Ironically, as the "old-fashioned" relationship-driven businesses, such as investment bankers, wholesale bankers, and brokers and financial advisers, adopt technology and centralized management, "sophisticated" direct marketers, such as credit card issuers and direct life insurers, are going the other way. The hottest concepts in marketing today are "one-to-one" marketing and relationship management. Today's state-of-the-art marketing organizations are using statistical modeling and other technology-based processes to replicate the old-fashioned one-to-one, relationship-based methods.

Relationship marketing is not the only thing that's regaining popularity. Banks, which started out as retailers, are rediscovering merchandising and display. Institutions like Washington Mutual and Commerce Bank are successfully modeling their branches along the lines of Starbucks and Wal-Mart to lure customers inside. Word-of-mouth—now, trendily, called viral marketing—is what all businesses are founded on: doing a good job so people will say good things about you to other people. In the Internet age, the process can perhaps be accelerated, but Wall Street has always been a rumor mill. No doubt buyers and sellers were gossiping about who was doing what back in the days when the New York Stock Exchange met under a buttonwood tree.

The issues of most pressing concern to financial marketers today are not

What Goes Around, Comes Around

The financial services category encompasses a range of marketing methods and levels of sophistication. One-to-one selling, which many would regard as "old-fashioned," is still the marketing method of choice for most institutional sales, such as pension plan providers and investment bankers. If one looks at the financial services marketplace as a continuum, with personal relationship selling at one end and the use of technology at the other, then institutional sales would be the most personal and least technological.

Independent investment advisers tend to be almost as personal as institutional sales-people, though they may use some technology, for example, to create large mailings. Wire house salespeople who make commission-based sales occupy a middle range on the continuum. Many brokerages have instituted sophisticated systems that are designed to improve broker productivity. Some of these systems can even "hand-write" a "personal note" from the broker to the client.

Banks and other top-down marketers moved away from the one-to-one personal relationship model as they pushed clients to non-branch channels such as ATMs and the Internet. But now, using technology, they are moving toward "virtual personal relationships" through such means as online customer service that can be activated during online transactions to connect customers with real people. Finally, at the other end of

really new; they're just appearing in new guises. Branding, for example, is the updated version of building a quality reputation. Attempts to build bridges between sales and marketing have been practiced since the days when managers in the home office visited regional branches to "buck up the troops." Concerns about "metrics"—or how to quantify return on marketing investment—date back at least to nineteenth-century merchant John Wanamaker's quip about not knowing which half of his advertising dollars was being wasted. Even the latest rounds of financial market scandals are mere echoes of the past. Let us not forget that the Glass-Steagall Act, repealed in 1999, was first imposed in 1933 because of the scandals of that day.

None of this is meant to suggest that financial professionals have little to learn about marketing. Unlike marketers in many other industries, many financial services marketers come from elsewhere—either a different industry or a different position in financial services. When one moves from the trad-

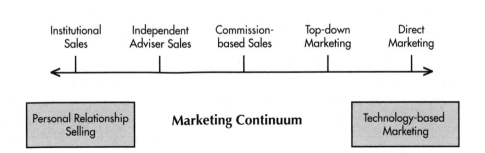

| Institutional Sales | Independent Adviser Sales | Commission-based Sales | Top-down Marketing | Direct Marketing |

Personal Relationship Selling — **Marketing Continuum** — **Technology-based Marketing**

the spectrum, credit card issuers and other direct marketers use the most sophisticated, modeling-based methods. Most direct marketers never interact personally with their customers; instead, they are attempting to emulate personal relationships through CRM and machine-created personalization. For example, a website might use programming that recognizes a customer, greets her by name, and offers suggestions based on past behavior. The paradox is that as marketers move further from the actual customers, they are at the same time attempting to recapture the type of one-to-one relationship that institutional salespeople still maintain with their clients.

ing floor or sales force to a marketing position, the product knowledge is there, but there may not be a lot of marketing know-how. On the other hand, the increasingly common career route that leads from a consumer products company to a financial services company is not sufficient preparation for the industry-specific challenges that must be faced. Even moving from managing local marketing initiatives for a consumer bank to handling local marketing initiatives for a consumer diversified financial company—as one of the coauthors did—involves a thorough change in perspective. They may all be called "banks," but investment banks, merchant banks, mortgage banks, and commercial banks all require different skills and knowledge on the part of people charged with marketing their products and services.

Large financial organizations are often accused of not communicating across the "silos" represented by their various operations and departments, and there are even greater apparent gulfs between banking and brokerage, money management and trading, insurance and credit cards, and all the rest. Despite these differences within the financial subsegments, financial marketers can learn from one another. A successful e-marketing campaign by a mutual fund company can inspire a personal financial planner or a wholesale banker.

The reader will have noticed that there is very little in this book about financial services practices outside the United States. Americans can learn much from other business cultures and, in fact, financial marketing theory and practice often appear to be more advanced in Europe than in the United States. But given the size of the U.S. financial industry and its international prominence, it seemed sensible to start here. Writing the first book devoted to financial marketing in the U.S. since the 1980s, we have attempted to give an overview of current practice, provide a guide for students and practitioners, and start a conversation about next steps. We welcome your comments and suggestions, case studies, and questions. Our website, The Financial Services Marketing Handbook (http://www.fsmhandbook.com), will be continually updated with new case studies and more information on subjects that could only be touched on here. We look forward to engaging with our professional colleagues.

APPLYING MARKETING PRINCIPLES TO SALES PRACTICE

Appendix Contents

Appendix

This appendix is devoted exclusively to the sales professional—whether you sell to consumers or institutions, whether you are independent or receive compensation from a brokerage, insurance company, or other financial services organization. This special section is designed to help you focus on how the marketing strategies and tactics described elsewhere in this book can improve your sales effectiveness.

To help you translate the principles of marketing into sales practice, we have provided four examples of real-life sales situations that are threaded throughout the rest of the appendix.

Anyone who makes a living by persuading other people to buy something needs to understand what marketing is. Marketing is the process of planning who you are selling to, what you are selling them, and then choosing the tactics that will best achieve your goals—from personal sales calls, seminar selling, or inviting clients to a golf outing to direct mail, public relations, and the Internet.

Many sales professionals are great champions of planning—for their clients. If you sell financial advisory or consulting services, you've no doubt talked to your clients about the importance of having a road map to achieve financial goals. But do you have as good a map for your own business goals?

Market planning takes time—something most sales professionals cannot spare. But consider whether it is worth taking a few hours to ensure a steady stream of new prospects, month after month, in all markets. A market plan doesn't have to be elaborate. Even the most basic market plan can help improve your sales success in numerous ways:

- **Increase profitability.** Like most businesses, you probably derive 80 percent of your profit from 20 percent of your clients. But are you allocating your time to reflect that? Are you getting the most from your best clients? Could you get more—share of wallet, referrals, longer retention? How do you get more clients who resemble that highly profitable 20 percent? A marketing plan helps you apportion your time and budget to make sure you are targeting the highest-value clients and prospects.

- **Save time and money.** "Seat of the pants" marketing is inefficient. If you respond to opportunities as they come up—buying an ad in the journal of an organization because a friend is a member, or joining a chamber of commerce to develop contacts—you may or may not achieve results. But even if you do get new business, how do the results compare to other tactics you might have chosen? Your marketing plan sets your objectives, provides a road map, and lets you measure results. A plan doesn't prevent you from taking advantage of one-off opportunities, but it will tell you at every stage whether these opportunities are suitable for your goals.

- **Work better as a team.** As more companies create a team-based approach to selling, market planning is a way to get input and buy-in from everyone on the team, to make sure each person knows what is expected, and to align all sales efforts against a common set of objectives.

- **Build better relationships with clients.** Most financial sales organizations have shifted focus away from generating transactions toward building relationships. Selling is no longer about "eating what you kill." It's about understanding client needs and finding appropriate ways to meet those needs. From a marketing perspective, relationship-building is less about acquiring new customers and more about retaining and increasing business with the clients you already have. Better relationships generate more referral business.

- **Determine what works.** Many salespeople use the same tactics repeatedly: a client lunch at the country club, trade shows, building alliances with other professionals. While these approaches may work, there may be others that could bring bigger results with fewer resources. Successful marketing depends on measuring the results of every campaign and using those metrics to make every dollar work harder.

Building Your Plan

A formal market plan can be a twenty-page document or a two-page spreadsheet. There are many extras that can strengthen a plan, but there are only four essential elements for a successful plan.

1 Segment Your Markets

Every plan should focus on a few well-defined segments, including the following:

- Your current clients. Your current clients are always your best prospects. You need to identify specific goals, such as generating more income per client, increasing the percentage of clients' assets, or increasing the number of clients who contribute the most to your bottom line.
- Those who resemble your top clients. For example, the top 20 percent of your clients may be mostly entrepreneurs, or golfers, or people who drive Mercedes—or all three. Find as many common elements among your top group as you can. This will help you develop specific marketing tactics (such as a joint program with your local Mercedes dealership).
- Expand your client base. If your client base is maturing or you're in a competitive market, explore the potential of a new target segment. Is everyone pursuing doctors? How about hospital administrators or pharmaceutical sales executives?

2 Set Goals

For each of your target market segments, you need to set measurable goals that are meaningful for your practice. For example, for a new target segment, a set of objective goals might look like this:

Segment: Pharmaceutical Sales Executives with Incomes over $250,000

	1-YEAR GOAL	2-YEAR GOAL
Number of new clients from segment	4	12
Average account size	$150,000	$350,000
"Wallet share" per account	40%	60%

3 Prioritize Tactics against Goals and Resources

There are many marketing tactics—from advertising to the Internet, from seminars to referral-building techniques. Go back to your goals and list all of the tactics that might be effective in reaching them. For example, penetrating a new market segment can be accomplished through advertising, seminars, or professional contacts.

Brainstorming potential acquisition and expansion tactics can be fun and creative, and should include your whole team. When you've finished, list all the potential tactics you've come up with. Assign each a score, based on its cost, the human resources required, and the likelihood that the tactic will result in a positive return. The chart below shows an example of the results of such a brainstorming session, based on pharmaceutical sales executives.

	OUT-OF-POCKET COST	TOTAL STAFF HOURS/YEAR	ESTIMATED RETURN*	SCORE
Join their professional organizations	$500	30	5:1	A
Develop opportunities to speak to their groups	$0	20	N.A.	A
Sponsor charitable event	$5,000	30	4:1	B
Seminars	$20,000	120	5:1	B
Advertise in their group publication	$15,000	15	<1:1	C

* Estimated return can be a ratio (i.e., 2:1 = $2 in potential new business for every dollar spent) or another metric meaningful to your business.

This example demonstrates that a rather simple tactical plan can clearly show where you are most likely to get the best return for your marketing dollars and staff resources. Allocating your budget against your priorities will help you avoid wasting money on items that have low potential.

4 Measure Results

The first time you lay out your plan, there will be some guesswork involved. Will tactic "X" really return 5:1 on your investment? How much new money is that anyway? How many new accounts? Did that match your estimates?

To answer such questions, you must measure your results against your expectations. Tactic "X" didn't work as planned? Don't do it again. Or try doing it a different way. Tactic "Y" took longer and cost more, but still performed well. Perhaps you should re-prioritize.

Measuring the results of your marketing plan is no different than evaluating a portfolio strategy. If your plan didn't help you reach your goals, change it.

Practice Examples

The four examples that follow are meant to cover a range of financial sales situations. Inez G. (IG) runs an Insurance Group. She's a top producer and sales manager of her own agency. Her group is affiliated with a national insurance company, but Inez and her employees have a good degree of autonomy in marketing matters, with complete responsibility for their own profitability.

Ron W. (RW) is a Retirement Wholesaler who works for a mutual fund company and is a wholesaler of defined contribution plans. His market is wire house financial advisers, so his marketing mission is twofold: selling these advisers on his own product, and helping the advisers sell to their clients.

Bonnie-Dee M. (BDM) is a Bank District Manager. Bonnie-Dee's markets are her branch managers, their staff, and their customers. While Bonnie-Dee must work within the bank's overall marketing structure, she can authorize marketing initiatives that will drive more business to the branches.

Frank A. (FA) is just starting an independent Financial Advisory practice after working for many years as a commissioned broker. His example is designed to mirror the issues faced by those who are relatively new to marketing, but it should prove helpful to anyone who is dealing with a particular business situation (such as creating a direct mail campaign) for the first time.

Each example illustrates how the lessons learned in the body of the book are applied in the real world. It may be helpful to refer to the corresponding chapter when reviewing the sales examples.

Key:
IG = Inez G. = Insurance Group
RW = Ron W. = Retirement Wholesaler
BDM = Bonnie-Dee M. = Bank District Manager
FA = Frank A. = Financial Adviser

Segmentation in Practice

This section refers to material discussed in chapter 1.

IG   Segmentation Expands a Salesperson's Practice

Inez G., a top producer for a major insurance company, has grown her practice in Chicago over the years, and she now has five agents on her team. Her group focuses primarily on women business owners. Two members of her group, who were formerly in pharmaceutical sales, concentrate on the planning needs of nurses, nurse practitioners, and physician's assistants. Further, through market research and her own experience, Inez knows that a growing number of Hispanic women are starting their own businesses. Inez reached out to the local Hispanic chamber of commerce and began reading the local and national Hispanic business publications. Through word-of-mouth and networking, Inez initiated an aggressive campaign to recruit Hispanic agents who could devote their efforts exclusively to this growing and valuable market.

RW   A Wholesaler Prioritizes Segments

Ron W. is a wholesaler for a national mutual fund company, specializing in defined contribution retirement plans. His market consists of wire house brokers in six states in the Southwest. His employer provides marketing, sales, and product support, but Ron is the primary driver of business initiatives in his region.

Ron's territory includes more than 3,000 individuals who are potential retailers of National Mutual Fund Company's product. Ron has prioritized his total market into several subsegments, as outlined below:

- By current status. Because he has limited time to sell and service his clients, Ron has assigned one of two status levels to each current and prospective account: "A" status includes the top 20 percent of current accounts and "hot" prospects. These are individuals who have large books of business with Ron's competitors and who have indicated an interest in adding NMFC's product to their offerings. Ron devotes 80 percent of his time to his "A" list.

- By sales potential. Although 80 percent of his current clients are therefore in the "B" category, some have more potential value than others. Ron is attempting to analyze the potential for sales among those "B" clients who may be doing business with competitors. Another "B" group includes "warm" prospects who have indicated interest in NMFC's product but whose potential value is unknown.

Key: IG = Inez G., Insurance Group; RW = Ron W., Retirement Wholesaler; BDM = Bonnie-Dee M., Bank District Manager; FA = Frank A., Financial Adviser

- By strength of relationship. Ron is well known among his "A" list clients and well regarded by most of them. However, he has to compete for recognition with "B" list clients and "A" and "B" list prospects. So he will need to develop relationship-building tactics that will highlight his retirement services expertise and his ability to help his target brokers increase their sales.

BDM Additional Segmentation by Bank District

Bonnie-Dee M. is the district manager for the Alligator Banking Corporation Bank (ABC Bank), a mid-size bank with branches throughout Florida and Georgia. Bonnie-Dee is responsible for forty branches in southeastern Florida.

Even though ABC Bank has sophisticated segmentation metrics, derived from its CRM data, it encourages local districts to customize programs for their particular demographic segments. In South Florida, that means the elderly. Nearly 40 percent of ABC Bank's customers in Dade, Broward, and Palm Beach counties are 65 or older.

FA A Start-Up Independent Financial Adviser Selects Target Segments

Frank A. is 33 years old, married, with a 3-year-old child and another on the way. He lives in a leafy suburb outside of Philadelphia. After receiving a BA in economics and an MBA in finance, he joined a large brokerage firm as an account executive, where he built a sizable book of business. But changes in the firm's commission structure and centralization of client records made him realize his prospects for growth at the firm were limited. With a small nest egg that he hoped would carry him through, Frank left his commissioned sales position and became an independent financial adviser.

Although several of Frank's best clients made the move with him, Frank knew that he needed to start more prospects down his pipeline. It can take months, or even years, to convert prospects into clients, so Frank needed to continually develop new leads.

Instead of looking for "everyone" to target, Frank realized he needed to focus on specific client segments. By taking a narrow focus, he was not eliminating prospects—he was putting his limited resources behind the most viable prospects.

Many of Frank's clients from his former job had been families in his town. Several of them had come from his church and his country club. In fact, Frank's clients very much resembled Frank.

Therefore, Frank thought it made sense to begin with his own geo-demographics and those of his former clients. Typically they were married couples, 30–45 years old, living within twenty miles of his town, who owned a home and had at least one child. They would belong to organizations similar to his church and country club.

Targeting a market segment he knew well was a real advantage for Frank, because he already had a lot of information about his chosen segment. Because he travels in these circles, he knows which local publications these potential clients read, where to find them on Sunday afternoons (on the golf course or at the mall). He knows, with a pretty high degree of accuracy, their incomes, education, and the value of their homes. He knows their aspirations for their future and for their children's future.

Frank bolstered this knowledge with solid research. At the library and online, he found census data about his community and identified the zip codes with the highest potential. He researched the names of business and social organizations, church groups, and civic groups, and he contacted friends and business associates to provide him with company and organizational lists that might be useful in his prospecting efforts.

Looking for parents with elementary-school-age children, he compiled lists from PTA directories of elementary schools in the target zip codes, and even used online access to old issues of the newspaper to find old birth announcements. From all this research, Frank compiled a list of names of families in his targeted demographics. He would use these, along with purchased lists, for direct mail campaigns (see the section on "Direct Marketing in Practice" later in this appendix).

His best prospecting tools, he felt, were his church and country club membership directories. Since he knew many of the members by name, he could judge whether they fit into his target segments and whether they lived in his targeted zip codes. Based on his chosen demographics, he winnowed these two lists down to the families who best fit his target segment. Frank would focus on getting referrals to these names first.

Positioning in Practice

This section refers to material discussed in chapter 2.

IG Establishing a Reputation and Differentiating a Practice

Early in her career Inez G. realized that she couldn't be all things to all people, so she focused on meeting the insurance and financial planning needs of women business owners. She established and began marketing herself under her own "doing-business-as" name, or DBA, which she named the Women's Planning Group (WPG). She created brochures geared specifically toward women, held seminars on topics important to women business owners, and coordinated business card exchanges to help women network and meet other female business owners. She also became active in local chapters of women's organizations, including the National Association for Female Executives (NAFE) and the National Association of Women Business Owners (NAWBO). Her involvement helped her grow her business, and at the same time positioned her and her agents as positive forces and role models among women business owners. Inez now has three agents supporting the women's business market and two agents focused on female medical practitioners. She and her team are now exploring opportunities among female Hispanic business owners that she identified in her segmentation process.

RW Positioning within a Larger Firm

Because Ron works for a nationally recognized mutual fund wholesaler, he does not need to develop a look or image of his own. However, he does have to position himself and his firm within his broker market. Some of the brokers he works with have complained that Ron's home office is bureaucratic and takes too long to answer inquiries or create proposals. Therefore, Ron's positioning strategy will involve countering the negatives of his parent company with his own exceptional level of service. He has developed a mission statement that states:

– I am reachable by cell phone or pager 24/7

– Every call or e-mail will be returned within 24 hours or less

– Every open inquiry will get a weekly status update

Most important, Ron is faithful to these statements. His client brokers know that they can rely on him to service their accounts, resolve issues with the home office, and make sure that sales are credited promptly.

Key: IG = *Inez G., Insurance Group;* RW = *Ron W., Retirement Wholesaler;* BDM = *Bonnie-Dee M., Bank District Manager;* FA = *Frank A., Financial Adviser*

BDM Sub-Branding and Co-Branding a Local Market Initiative

ABC Bank had developed a Silver Assets program for its customers over age 50. It included free checking, free MasterCard or Visa, preferred rates on home equity loans, preferred rates on certificates of deposit, and a special reverse mortgage program. The Silver Assets program was widely advertised in newspapers in Miami, Fort Lauderdale, Boca Raton, and West Palm Beach.

Bonnie-Dee decided that her district would go one step beyond the Silver Assets program and institute a breakfast seminar series on investing for retirees. She decided, with corporate approval, to sub-brand the new initiative, and she held a contest among the branches to come up with a name. The winner was Silver Assets Investment Focus—SAIF—pronounced "safe." The name was easy to remember, lent itself to brand extensions (see the discussion on SAIF Harbor in the "Relationship Marketing in Practice" section), and conveyed the positive attribute of safety.

There were several advantages to creating these seminars: 1) They would bring prospects and customers into the branches, along with friends and family (possible referrals). 2) ABC Bank branches in the South Florida district had a very low level of market share in investment products. The bank's primary rivals for investment assets were national and local brokerage and financial advisory firms. The seminars would position the bank as a source of financial planning expertise. 3) The program could be co-branded with community organizations. This would be a win-win, because the bank would get recognition for its support, and the organizations would get financial backing for their activities. It could also boost ABC Bank's commercial business with these local nonprofit organizations.

FA Positioning a Start-Up

When Frank started his business, the first thing he did after filing the necessary business papers was to order personalized business cards, letterheads, and envelopes. His card read "Frank Aldrich, Financial Adviser." He went for an upscale look, black and dark-red inks on cream-colored paper.

To establish his company's image, Frank needed to answer these four questions:

1 What values and attitudes about your company would you want to convey to your constituencies? Think of three adjectives that describe your most important qualities.

2 What are your major strengths?

3 Who are your major competitors?

4 What factors differentiate you from your competition?

Key: IG = *Inez G., Insurance Group;* RW = *Ron W., Retirement Wholesaler;* BDM = *Bonnie-Dee M., Bank District Manager;* FA = *Frank A., Financial Adviser*

For his three adjectives, Frank chose knowledgeable, empathetic, and high-quality. What he hoped to convey by the word "knowledgeable" was that he had been in the financial advisory business for many years, kept up with changes and new ideas, and offered a high level of expertise. By "empathetic," he meant he listened to his clients and explored their situations and needs with them to help them find suitable solutions. By "high-quality," Frank was referring not just to the quality of his advice, but also to the quality of his service, his employees (when he had some), and everything else concerning his business.

For his strengths, Frank identified:

- experience—years in business, advanced degrees
- particular knowledge and interest in college funding
- personality traits—finds it easy to talk and meet people, good listener
- high standards of performance and integrity

There were two other independent advisers in his geographic region, along with the offices of several national brokerage firms. Frank outlined his strengths and weaknesses by evaluating himself against his competitors. Frank began by listing his strengths—the areas where he thought he was superior in knowledge, communications skills, and professionalism.

FRANK'S STRENGTHS	ADVISER 1	ADVISER 2	NATIONAL FIRMS
Experience	= to Frank	> Frank	< Frank
College funding expertise	No experience	No experience	< Frank
Communications skills	= Frank	< Frank	= Frank
Professionalism	= Frank	= Frank	= or < Frank

He then evaluated his competitors on these variables. For example, Adviser 1 had as much experience as Frank but had no particular knowledge of college funding. Adviser 2 had more experience, but poor communications skills. This exercise made it plain to Frank that he had qualities that differentiated him from the competition. In particular, he had no peer in college funding expertise and would emphasize this and his other strengths in his communications material.

The Market Plan in Practice

This section refers to material discussed in chapter 3.

IG   Building a Plan

Until recently, Inez did not have a formal market plan. Nevertheless, she had built her business systematically by gathering demographic information and conducting research concerning female business owners in Chicago. She contacted leading women's business organizations and created lists of leading women in the community with whom she hoped to cultivate relationships. Most of her marketing efforts were focused on networking. Occasionally, she would try something new—for example, a public relations agency contacted her about sending out press releases on her behalf. She agreed to a three-month trial for $2,000 and did get one local television interview as a result. But she did not get any new business from the news appearance, so she decided not to renew.

Now that she has five salespeople working for her, Inez needs a more formal approach to market planning so that everyone knows what their assigned tasks are and everyone is working toward common goals. She meets with her group four times a year to brainstorm tactics. Inez determines her budget based on a percentage of her sales and then prioritizes sales tactics based on cost and potential return. Staff members volunteer to carry out initiatives, or Inez assigns tasks to the most appropriate person. For example, Carla, who was in pharmaceutical sales, wants to set up in-hospital seminars for her target health-care clients. Carla will contact the hospital administration to make the arrangements and be responsible for creating the event and tracking the results, but everyone on Inez's staff will participate in making the seminar a success.

Other tactics that Inez has decided to try out in the coming quarter include some limited advertising, some co-op arrangements with her home office, and possibly a local sponsorship.

RW   A Formal Plan

Unlike Inez and Frank, Ron works for a large corporation, so he does not have total control over his plan. Once a year, in September, National Mutual Fund Company requires Ron to submit results from his current year and estimate next year's goals. These are the data that Ron is asked to provide for his sales territory.

Key: IG = *Inez G., Insurance Group;* RW = *Ron W., Retirement Wholesaler;* BDM = *Bonnie-Dee M., Bank District Manager;* FA = *Frank A., Financial Adviser*

TOTAL NUMBER OF BROKERS SELLING NMFC 401(K) PLANS

- % change for each of the previous three years
- Projected number for the next three years

$ REVENUES OF NMFC PRODUCTS IN CURRENT YEAR

- % revenue change for each of the previous three years
- Projected revenues for the next three years

ESTIMATED MARKET SHARE IN CURRENT YEAR

- Increase/decrease in market share for each of the previous three years
- Projected increase/decrease over next three years

Ron also has to indicate any local factors that may affect his projections, such as new competitors entering his territory, the impact of national initiatives, and business conditions in the territory.

In addition, Ron must create a budget for the forthcoming year. Using his current year's budget, Ron estimates how much of his revenue was attributable to a given tactic (such as trade advertising, trade shows, and relationship-building). For example, he spent $50,000 on seminars and can trace $1.5 million in product sales to these seminars, a return of 30:1.

To propose next year's budget, Ron allocates his prior year's budget according to the return on last year's investment. Since seminars were a big success, he allocates a larger portion of his budget for them in the coming year.

After he has submitted his plan, the home office will assign new goals and budget. In past years, these have been pretty close to what Ron requested.

BDM   Buy-In on the Market Plan

Bonnie-Dee asked each of the forty branch managers in her district to create a market plan for the Silver Assets Investment Focus (SAIF) program. She asked them to report on the following for their branches:

Customers

– Current investment assets among customers age 60 or older
– Estimate of ABC Bank's market share of investment assets in this group
– Total investment assets held by this group

Non-customers

– Total market potential in number of customers and dollar size of assets

From these data, Bonnie-Dee will establish sales goals for the district. She also asked the branch managers to supply her with information she needed to establish a budget:

- Number of registered investment sales reps in each branch (some branches share reps)
- Suggestions for locations to hold monthly breakfast meetings and estimated costs, including room rental, food, and service
- Estimate of number who would attend each breakfast meeting
- Other expenses to make the seminars a success, including advertising, direct mail, signage, possible gifts, and staff resources.

In addition, Bonnie-Dee asked for a SWOT analysis (conditions in each branch that could influence the success of the program) and a competitive assessment (what were competitors doing that was similar, and how could ABC Bank do it better).

Once Bonnie-Dee had all the data, she put together a preliminary plan, setting out budget and goals for each branch. She reserved a portion of the budget for the branches to allocate as they chose, with her approval. At a regularly scheduled meeting of all branch managers, Bonnie-Dee presented the preliminary plan and opened it to discussion. After the plan was revised, the branch managers presented it to their sales staff for comments and additional revisions. Once Bonnie-Dee received the final plans back from the branches, she submitted them to her senior management for approval.

FA   A Plan for an Independent

Before creating a formal market plan, Frank had already identified his target market as people like himself—married couples, aged 30–45, homeowners, with at least one child. He also decided to position himself as an expert in two areas: education funding and financial planning. He was passionate about the need to plan ahead for financing education since he had had to work nights and weekends to pay his way through college and graduate school. He also believed that almost everyone needed to take the time to develop a financial plan. People needed a road map, he thought, not unlike his own marketing plan.

For his market plan, Frank evaluated his own strengths and weaknesses, his competition, and the opportunities and threats in his environment.

Key: IG = Inez G., Insurance Group; RW = Ron W., Retirement Wholesaler; BDM = Bonnie-Dee M., Bank District Manager; FA = Frank A., Financial Adviser

Frank's SWOT analysis

Strengths

– Well known and respected in his community

– Strong sales and customer relations experience

– Subject expertise (college planning)

– Active in church group and country club

– Base of clients

– Marketing support available through wholesalers

Weaknesses

– Start-up—not yet known in community

– Well-established competition

– Identified with his former firm

– Limited budget for promotion

Opportunities

– Demographic: mini–baby boom in community

– Technology: ability to perform sophisticated financial analysis on his laptop

– Regulatory: licensing requirements a barrier to entry for new competitors

– Economy: market downturn—people are looking for safe investments

– Political: Wall Street scandals making independent advisers more attractive

Threats

– Economy: market downturn—people afraid to invest

– Economy: layoffs may lead to more brokers becoming independent competition

Frank's Competitive Analysis

	FRANK	LOCAL INDEPENDENTS	NATIONAL BROKERS
Size of marketing budget	Small	Moderate	Large
Target segments (asset size)	$150,000+	$250,000+	$500,000+
Target demographics	30-something	50+	50+
Unique selling advantage	Focus on college funding	Established	National reputation
Key marketing tactics	Public relations	Seminars	National advertising

Key: IG = *Inez G., Insurance Group;* RW = *Ron W., Retirement Wholesaler;* BDM = *Bonnie-Dee M., Bank District Manager;* FA = *Frank A., Financial Adviser*

Marketing Objectives

	MONTHS 1—6	MONTHS 7—12	YEAR 2
Number of qualified new prospects	12	24	75
Number of new clients	4	10	35
Number of retained clients*	0	4	13
Management fees**	$9,000	$54,000	$216,000

* Frank is not including clients he brought from his previous firm, until pending lawsuits are settled.

**Frank assumes that the average portfolio will be $150,000 and his average fee 3 percent, for an annual total of $4,500 per client.

Marketing Budget

Value of co-op advertising from wholesalers $15,000

Out-of-pocket expenses for marketing $15,000

Other resources:

  Part-time intern from local college

  Exchanging services with a printer (financial plan for printing)

Advertising in Practice

This section refers to material discussed in chapter 4.

IG   Determining When Advertising Is Appropriate

As Inez's business grew, she needed to keep the pipeline filled for her sales staff. She decided it was time to advertise the "Women's Planning Group" (WPG). She identified a local women's business magazine and a women's association publication that reached a fair percentage of her target audience. Inez wanted the advertising message to convey urgency and address the importance of planning for both individual and business success. Inez hired a client who owned a small advertising agency to create two ads—one offering a free planning session with WPG and the other an invitation to a seminar. Inez assigned one of her staff to work directly with the publications on placement and deadlines.

Her ads were successful in bringing in new prospects. Once she began advertising, she started receiving phone calls from ad sales reps at other publications.

Every neighborhood weekly tried to solicit her ad business and she got calls from both Chicago daily newspapers, which publish special supplements for the small-business market. Since she was also running regular recruiting ads and would need to begin advertising in Spanish when she added Hispanic sales associates, Inez decided to hire the ad agency to handle her account.

RW Advertising for Corporate Buyers

While Ron doesn't have to worry about consumer advertising, which is handled by the home office, he does offer co-op advertising opportunities to interested brokers. For example, if a broker wishes to offer a seminar to potential business clients about retirement planning for their employees, Ron's company will provide the brokers with all the necessary seminar materials, including ads for their local publications. A local advertising manager at the home office helps the brokers with placement and ensures that any advertising is in compliance with all applicable laws and regulations.

BDM Local Advertising

As a first tactic, Bonnie-Dee asked the branch managers to prepare a list of local nonprofit community organizations that served wealthy seniors. These included assisted living and senior homeowner organizations, recreational and cultural centers (including golf clubs, music groups, and museums), religious organizations, and health-care providers (including hospitals and rehab centers). The branch managers were asked to approach the managers of these organizations to gauge interest in working with ABC Bank on the SAIF initiative.

Organizations that agreed to participate would be prominently featured as co-sponsors in the SAIF advertising. Customized posters were created for each participating site, advertising a series of breakfast meetings and indicating that the bank would be making a donation to the nonprofit organization on behalf of each attendee. Organizational partners were given other customized materials, including invitation kits for their members/clients.

FA A First Ad

Frank's first advertising opportunity arose when a country club asked him to buy a placement in its annual commemorative edition, held in conjunction with its golf tournament. Since Frank was one of the tournament's sponsors, the ad was included in his package. But what should it say?

Frank looked at the previous year's book and saw that most advertisers used their half pages to congratulate the players or the club. But Frank didn't want to waste the opportunity to market his financial advisory business. After all, the people who would see this were his target markets and they would probably keep the book for a long time. Still, he had to be subtle about the message—it shouldn't appear to be too self-serving.

Frank had a friend who wrote copy for catalogues, and she offered to write his ad. What she came up with was appropriate to the occasion but also fit with Frank's objectives of creating awareness of his services as a financial adviser:

Frank Aldrich, Financial Adviser, Congratulates
the XYZ Club on its 18th Annual Tournament
The children who were born when the tournament got its start
are now ready for college.
Will you be ready for college when your children are?
For a no-cost, no-obligation consultation on college funding, retirement
planning or other financial goals, please call me at 215-555-1234.

The printer who printed the book laid out the ad for Frank according to his guidelines (serif type, black letters on white background). Frank also liked the line "Will you be ready for college when your children are?" so he asked his friend to turn it into an ad for other publications.

Public Relations in Practice

This section refers to material discussed in chapter 5.

IG   Getting Out the Word about the Women's Planning Group

Inez G. recognized the value of the press after she read an article about financial planning and it quoted a competitor. She believed her competitor was well positioned in the article, and the story provided a lot of good information. Her feeling was confirmed when two days later one of her best clients called to ask if she had seen the story and to question why Inez wasn't quoted.

Inez called her team together and set out to develop a PR action plan that included personally building relationships with reporters and editors. She knew

---

this was critical if she wanted reporters to think of the Women's Planning Group when they needed information on financial planning or a quote from a financial planning expert. One of the insurance companies whose products she represented offered her the use of prewritten, compliance-approved articles on financial planning for women business owners. Her team submitted these articles, with Inez's byline, for placement in local business and general market publications. The staff prepared press releases announcing each of the WPG's monthly seminars, and developed the "Financial Planning Tip of the Month." This short, two- or three-sentence piece of financial planning advice included a quote from Inez or one of her agents. It was frequently picked up as filler by the local weeklies and occasionally the big Chicago dailies.

RW Institutional PR

Ron took every opportunity to speak to groups of brokers. If the brokers' parent company was having a training program or seminar on financial planning for entrepreneurs, Ron got in touch with the organizers to see if there was a place on the program for him to talk about retirement plans for small business. Ron was also a frequent speaker at professional organizations and wrote a regular column on retirement planning for a publication read by many of his target brokers. He even helped his clients get publicity—for example, because he knew all the chamber of commerce directors within his territory, he often helped his client brokers get in front of business owners.

BDM Generating Publicity for the SAIF Program

Continuing to operate on a local level as she had done for her advertising, Bonnie-Dee asked her branch bank managers to provide contact names for media outlets, including newspapers and other publications, radio programs favored by the target market, and broadcast and cable television news operations. The bank sent a release offering an interview with one of the bank's top investment advisers, commenting on how recent changes in interest rates would affect seniors' income. Other press releases were created for the branches to send out under their own names, announcing the Silver Assets Investment Focus program, with new releases issued for the announcement of each major co-sponsor. As the breakfast series got under way, members of the press were invited to attend and to follow up directly with the investment adviser if they had questions. The bank's central marketing department also prepared a series of articles, to be offered to the press under the investment advisers' byline.

Key: IG = *Inez G., Insurance Group;* RW = *Ron W., Retirement Wholesaler;* BDM = *Bonnie-Dee M., Bank District Manager;* FA = *Frank A., Financial Adviser*

FA A Public Relations Investment Pays Off

While attending a chamber of commerce luncheon meeting, Frank listened to a speaker discuss the "Power and Importance of Publicity in Building a Practice." He was impressed by what he heard and began to see the value in publicity. His first instinct was to hire the speaker, an independent specialist, to handle his PR. But her price of $900 for a single press release was too steep for Frank's budget.

He did feel that he had picked up a few pointers from the speaker, and Frank began developing his strategy by asking his college intern to research a list of questions.

- What are the media outlets in my area? Specifically, what are the names of community newspapers, business publications, radio stations, broadcast and cable stations, and regional magazines? The intern researched the information online and at the library and made follow-up calls. Frank requested or bought copies of all print publications that he was interested in contacting, and he personally took a look at the programming on the TV and radio outlets that the intern had listed.
- Which editor should I contact? Is there a business editor? Where there was not, Frank's intern called the managing editor and asked her (or her assistant) to whom to address his queries.
- What types of information are most important to the outlet, such as business, lifestyle, politics, social, or general interest? Knowing the editorial focus of the media outlet helped identify stories that were most appropriate to readers.
- What are the deadlines? Press deadlines have little or no flexibility and must be adhered to rigorously.
- What is the outlet's preferred way to receive information (paper or electronically)?

Frank then developed a checklist of how he could use publicity to benefit his business.

Serve as a source for quotes as a financial planning expert. From his listening and reading, he compiled a list of reporters who regularly covered financial planning stories. He contacted each of them and asked if they would be interested in doing an interview or needed help with any stories. Although none of them had interest in the interview, they all said they would put Frank

---

into their contact lists. He followed up with a brief e-mail to each, thanking them for their courtesy and including a brief bio and a list of topics on which he was prepared to speak.

A few weeks later, Frank got a call from Jim Sawyer at the *Bucks County Courier,* who was researching a story on a possible change in plan managers for Pennsylvania's 529 Plan. Frank hadn't heard the rumors but offered to check with some people he knew and call Jim back, which he did within the time frame promised. That week's story quoted Frank. The next day, Frank got a call from a reporter at the *Philadelphia Inquirer* who had read the *Bucks County* piece and wanted more information from Frank. Frank was quoted in that story, too. Then Frank read a story in the *Wall Street Journal* and saw that there was an inaccuracy. He e-mailed a letter to the editor, citing the correct information, which was printed. The next day, Frank received several calls from reporters around the country who were seeking information on 529 Plans. Because Frank was ready with quick and accurate responses, he became a first source for many reporters on issues concerning college financing.

Create bylined articles about specific financial topics. Frank called the editors at several local papers and radio stations to find out if they accepted articles on financial planning subjects. One editor at the *Trenton Times* seemed to be interested, but Frank had trouble getting in touch with her to follow up. He decided to write a story anyway, a general piece on college funding. He asked a friend who was a teacher to review the piece before he sent it to make sure it was interesting to a prospective client, easy to read, and grammatically correct. He then e-mailed it to the editor. When he did not hear back from her, he followed up by phone.

She apologized for being difficult to reach, but noted that she was doing two peoples' jobs while her colleague was out on maternity leave. She said she had read the article he had submitted and was interested in running it, but had no budget to pay him. He assured her that it wasn't necessary—the publicity would be his payment. After the first article ran, he got two calls from interested prospects. He also obtained permission to reprint the article and mailed it to all his current clients, along with a handwritten Post-It note saying "In case you missed this" and giving his name and phone number. He received two additional calls from that mailing and one from a prospect who had been referred to Frank from a current client who was very impressed with his article. By that point, Frank felt that he was beginning to receive a good return on the value of the considerable time he had invested in his PR initiatives.

Find out about doing a regular financial advice column for the local paper or radio (i.e., planning tips, retirement information, college funding, etc.). Eventually, the *Trenton Times* editor asked him to write a regular column for the paper on financial planning, which became a regular source of new prospects.

Other ideas for Frank's promotions:
- Put together a booklet of all his college planning articles and send it to clients and prospects.
- Organize a seminar about college financing at a high school or grammar school.
- Send out a press release about his seminars beforehand.
- Send out an article on the same topic after each presentation.
- Give attendees a copy of the article or booklet.

Sponsorship in Practice

This section refers to material discussed in chapter 6.

IG Fitting Sponsorships to Brand Image

Inez was approached by one of her daughter's coaches about sponsoring the girls' soccer team. Inez was delighted to accept—not only for her daughter's sake, but also because the sponsorship meshed with her business objectives. The association of the Women's Planning Group with girls' sports was exactly on message: encouraging women to be independent, strong, and able to compete. For less than a thousand dollars, "The Women's Planning Group" would be on T-shirts worn by fifteen 10-year-old girls, on signage at the games, and in an acknowledgment in the sports annual published by the school.

In addition to enhancing the brand image of her company, this modest investment helped get her company's name out to parents, teachers, coaches, and spectators. It also demonstrated the company's commitment to the community, thus creating goodwill.

RW Corporate Sponsorships and Personal Charitable Activities

Although the home office made the decisions about national sponsorships at

---

Key: IG = *Inez G., Insurance Group;* RW = *Ron W., Retirement Wholesaler;* BDM = *Bonnie-Dee M., Bank District Manager;* FA = *Frank A., Financial Adviser*

the corporate level, Ron requested that National Mutual Fund Company put its name behind some local events as well. Since many of Ron's client brokers met with their small-business customers on the golf course, Ron asked NMFC to participate as a sponsor of several local golf tournaments, where he entertained his clients and their clients at a hospitality suite. He also asked his firm to contribute to some charity fund drives, especially those that were also underwritten by his clients' employers.

As an African American, Ron was particularly supportive of black business owners and was active in fund-raising and mentoring activities for local chapters of scholarship programs for minority business students. Although these activities were personal, they established Ron as a "player" in his community, and he received honors from several organizations. The contacts he built among both black and white community leaders were enormously helpful in building his career success.

BDM   The Value of Cause Marketing

When one of Bonnie-Dee's branch managers approached the Boca Raton Museum of Art about the SAIF seminar program, she was met with a counterproposal. The museum would be happy to co-sponsor the bank's Silver Assets Investment Focus program to its members (most of whom were in the target age/wealth range) in exchange for ABC Bank's sponsoring an exhibit at the museum. The branch manager passed the request on to Bonnie-Dee, who discussed it with her management. The community affairs department of the bank became involved in the discussions, which ended with the bank's agreeing to sponsor an exhibit featuring pre–twentieth-century architecture in the region. One of the most prominent items on display was to be a cast model of the first bank in South Florida.

ABC Bank not only agreed to pay for the exhibit and its related advertising and publicity costs; it also agreed to pay for the creation of the scaled down model, using original architectural drawings. Because the bank licensed the rights to the model, they were able to use depictions of it as the focal point for their advertising—and to commission a company to create small, piggy bank size versions to distribute to SAIF participants.

The bank was very pleased by the synergy created between the SAIF program and the museum, which resulted in publicity and goodwill far beyond what the SAIF program itself would have generated.

Key: IG = *Inez G., Insurance Group;* RW = *Ron W., Retirement Wholesaler;* BDM = *Bonnie-Dee M., Bank District Manager;* FA = *Frank A., Financial Adviser*

FA Weighting Costs and Benefits

Frank A. had his first taste of what it is like to be an event sponsor when he agreed to become a silver sponsor of a golf outing to support the local college scholarship fund. Frank identified this as an effective opportunity to meet his business objectives for several reasons:

- His practice specialized in college funding, so association with a college scholarship was a natural match.
- His target client base included plenty of golfers. Since the club holding the outing was not Frank's home club, he would get an opportunity to meet new prospects.
- Because players included celebrity guests (some Philadelphia Eagles and 76ers players, among others), the outing was likely to be featured in local newspapers and newscasts. This coverage would enable Frank to extend his name involvement through public relations.

For Frank's $2,500 contribution, he was entitled to a foursome of golf, signage at the first tee, his company name on all communications, a company banner at the awards dinner, an ad in the program book, and recognition from the podium for his contribution and support. Also, he had the opportunity to contribute an item to the gift bag each player would receive.

This sounded great and he thought well worth his $2,500 investment. Like many sponsors, what Frank didn't realize was that his $2,500 investment was just the start. He also needed to activate his sponsorship, and he didn't have much time. He went to a print shop to have the signage for the first tee and banner created, which cost $400. He also decided he would donate a sleeve of golf balls for each gift bag. They had to have his logo on them, so he had to buy twenty boxes of logoed golf balls at a cost of $22 a box, which came to another $440. He also had to figure another $100 for lunch and drinks for the members of his foursome. So his initial $2,500 investment was now nearly $3,500. Frank was finding out the hard way that activation costs generally add between 50 percent and 150 percent to the expense of the sponsorship itself.

Frank was still satisfied that he made the right decision, but now he realized that the sponsorship fee was just the start of the time and money that made an event a success. An additional investment was needed to convey the fact of his sponsorship to his target markets and make the event memorable for guests.

Key: IG = *Inez G., Insurance Group;* RW = *Ron W., Retirement Wholesaler;* BDM = *Bonnie-Dee M., Bank District Manager;* FA = *Frank A., Financial Adviser*

Direct Marketing in Practice

This section refers to material discussed in chapter 7.

IG   Identifying the Need for Direct Marketing

Inez and her team had begun to put together an extensive list of prospects culled from articles about new women-owned businesses, chamber of commerce and National Association of Women Business Owners (NAWBO) membership lists, seminar attendees, word-of-mouth, and networking activities. To reach these potential clients, WPG began conducting monthly mailings. A decision was made not to try to sell through the mailing, but rather to use the mailing to develop sales leads. Each mailing included an article of interest to the woman business owner, with a cover letter from Inez emphasizing the importance of financial planning for business owners.

Because their prospects were businesses, not consumers, the "do not call" regulations did not apply. Within three days of each mailing, the team would make phone calls from 8 a.m. to 10 a.m., introducing themselves to the prospects and setting up appointments to meet. Where possible, coffee meetings were arranged, where a WPG team member would meet the prospect for a cup of coffee before the start of the business day. These mailings and follow-up contacts resulted in a continual stream of new prospects.

RW   Using Purchased Lists for Additional Leads

Since no one in Ron's territory was covering independent brokers and financial advisers, Ron convinced the home office that it would be worthwhile to do a test mailing of unaffiliated brokers for new business proposals.

Ron told the home office direct mail experts what he was looking for—independent brokers within his sales territory who specialized in small- to medium-sized business clients. They came up with a list of 750 names. They prepared a letter in Ron W.'s name, which they sent in a plain #10 business envelope with no message on the outer envelope, mailed first class. The envelope also contained a brochure that NMFC had in stock, titled, "Increasing Your Business with Business Retirement Plans."

The call to action was a request for more information. Recipients could mail back a postage-paid card, addressed to Ron W., or they could e-mail or call him directly—his contact information was included in the letter. Altogether, the mailing cost a little over $1,500.

Key: IG = Inez G., Insurance Group; RW = Ron W., Retirement Wholesaler; BDM = Bonnie-Dee M., Bank District Manager; FA = Frank A., Financial Adviser

From the 750 names mailed, Ron got ten responses, a rate of a little over 1 percent. He eventually converted four of the independent brokers into clients worth hundreds of thousands of dollars. So, clearly, the effort was profitable. Next time, Ron planned to roll out similar mailings in waves of fifty and follow up with a personal phone call.

BDM Direct Marketing for the SAIF Program

As noted in the "Advertising in Practice" section, the branches asked their co-sponsors for lists of potential invitees. The branches then filled in the names on preprinted invitations, which included the name of the co-sponsor. In some cases, the sponsor preferred not to give the branch its membership list and filled in the invitations themselves.

Some branches sought to supplement the co-sponsors' lists with purchased lists. Bonnie-Dee gave permission for each branch to spend up to $1,500 for purchase of names meeting certain requirements: within a given zip code, age 60 and above, investable assets of $250,000 or more.

Each branch was to sponsor one breakfast every three months. By inviting one hundred attendees to each breakfast, they hoped to draw at least fifty people (including guests). Although the projected response rate was ambitious, the direct mail professionals at the bank thought it was achievable, for several reasons. The target market of retired people had time on their hands. They would be drawn by the subject ("Successful investing tactics in a changing interest rate environment"); by the food catered by local restaurants known for their ample Southern breakfasts; and by the chance to be with other retirees, especially those who belonged to similar community organizations. Since they were invited to bring as many guests as they liked, even a 10 percent response rate could result in fifty attendees, if each brought five guests. In cases where responses to the mailing were disappointing, current clients of the bank were invited by phone and encouraged to bring their own guests. To ensure a good turnout of those who had responded, branch personnel called with a reminder a few days before the breakfast. The response rate exceeded expectations, and in some cases invitees had to be waitlisted for a future breakfast.

FA Making Direct Marketing Effective

When Frank was still working for his old brokerage firm, he often got lists of people to cold call. These might have been names on purchased lists, people who responded to an ad, or people who had attended a seminar or trade show about college financing. The quality of these leads varied greatly and Frank was determined not to waste his time unless he could get a better response rate than he had before. He figured that 10 percent of those he called should be willing to meet with him.

When Frank worked for the brokerage, he also got materials to help him prospect—sales letters, seminar kits, ads for local publications. Now he would have to develop some of these materials on his own.

The list. For Frank's mailing, he began with two lists, made up of members of his country club and his church. There were about 700 households in total. The first thing Frank did was go through both lists, removing any name that appeared twice or appeared on both lists. He also eliminated 120 families he knew well enough to contact in person.

This left about 450 names. To supplement these names, Frank decided to buy a list of people in several zip codes from a mailing list broker. The initial list (minimum of 3,000 names) was $80 per thousand or $240. He made selects (additional selections) for marital status, presence of children, income, and age, which added another $80 to each 1,000 names. So the list of 3,000 married heads of households with children, with incomes above $75,000, ages 30–50, cost him $480.

Frank received the 3,000 names in Excel format and compared them to his original 450 names. (This is formally called a "merge-purge.") In this way, he found that 200 of his original names were also on the purchased list.

The creative. Frank had a friend who was a professional catalogue copywriter who offered to help create his mailing package and arrange for mailing. Because she was a friend, she only charged Frank $1,500 for the job. (An outside agency might have charged $15,000 or more.)

With Frank's help, the writer composed two different letters. To the 450 people who shared his country club or church affiliation, he wrote a very personal letter, which began as follows:

Dear first name, last name,
    As a fellow member of (name of club/church), we have probably shared a locker room (or church pew). Perhaps your children play with my children, Dan (10) and Ella (6). If we haven't met yet, I hope we will soon, because we have a lot of common interests and hopes for the future.
    One of my hopes for the future is that my children will be able to attend the college of their choice, regardless of cost...

To the other 2,800 names, he wrote a little less intimately, but still personally. It began:

> Dear first name, last name:
> Although we both live in (name of town), I don't think we've had the pleasure of meeting. I am writing to introduce myself and to determine whether I might be of assistance to you in helping you plan for your children's college education or other aspects of your financial future.

In both letters, Frank went on to explain who he is and what his credentials are. He included a clipping of an article about college financing that he had written for the local paper.

He closed with an offer: He would be giving a presentation on college saving at the local library on a date about three weeks following the mailing. If the person couldn't make it, he'd be happy to set up an appointment to meet with him or her personally. Frank included his phone number and e-mail address. He also enclosed a self-addressed reply postcard that read:

> ___ Yes, I will attend the seminar on (date)
> ___ I can't make the seminar, but please call me
> (phone number_____)
> ___ I am not interested at this time

The postage-paid reply postcard was personalized with the name and address of the recipient.

The mailing. Frank asked several friends to read the letters to make sure they were understandable and engaging. The writer arranged for the lettershop to print and personalize the letters, envelopes, and reply postcards, to automatically sign the letters using a facsimile of Frank's signature, and to stuff, stamp, and seal them. (If Frank had a smaller quantity, he might have hired a temp and done all this in-house.) Total cost for 3,250 names: Approximately $1,500 for printing and lettershop and another $950 for first-class, pre-sorted postage.

Because it used preprinted indicia, the reply card only cost him postage if it was returned.

The response. Within two days, Frank received four "will attend" postcards, along with one phone call and one e-mail—the last from someone who asked Frank to call him to set up an appointment. By the end of the first week, Frank received thirty more postcards, of which six asked Frank to make an appointment and six answered they were not interested. He also received four more e-mails, for a total of thirty-four positive responses and six negative responses—a total response rate of 1.2 percent.

A few days before the seminar, Frank followed up with a phone reminder to everyone who said they would attend. Of the twenty-three households who were expected at the seminar, only eighteen showed up. However, two people brought friends, so Frank had twenty prospects at the seminar.

The follow-up. Frank prioritized his follow-ups:

1   Respondents who asked him to set up an appointment. He called these people even before the seminar. Of the seven, he set up appointments with six and got two new clients, worth $3,000 annually.
2   Respondents who came to the seminar. Frank planned to follow up with all twenty of them within two weeks. He set up appointments with ten and got new business from seven, for a total value of $15,000 annually.
3   Follow-ups to those in groups 1 and 2 who didn't respond (N=18) as well as the six who responded negatively to the first mailing. Frank could take his time with this group.

Over the course of the following four months, he gained another five appointments and three more new clients (worth $6,000 annually) from this group, including one who had sent back the postcard saying he was not interested.

Final results. Out of forty respondents, Frank got twelve new clients (30 percent). Frank's new clients were worth $24,000 in year one.

Frank spent approximately $4,500 for the mailing. His profit: $19,500 in year one.

Frank made seventy-four phone calls (including repeats) and got twenty-one appointments, for a conversion rate of 28 percent, far better than the benchmark 10 percent telemarketing rate he had hoped for.

Key: IG = Inez G., Insurance Group; RW = Ron W., Retirement Wholesaler; BDM = Bonnie-Dee M., Bank District Manager; FA = Frank A., Financial Adviser

The Internet in Practice

This section refers to material discussed in chapter 8.

IG Using the Online Channel

As Inez's insurance group grew, she found that the online channel was becoming more and more important for communications among her staff and with her home office. At the beginning of each day, Inez checked the parent company's intranet, to learn about any updates in products, marketing initiatives, and other issues of importance. Inez had purchased a specialized sales package that enabled everyone in her Women's Planning Group to manage their accounts online, with a direct, real-time feed to the home office for underwriting and other product information. This saved the salespeople time and gave them the ability to handle their clients more efficiently and effectively. For example, when a sales associate signed on in the morning, she would see her day's appointments. Current client accounts would be detailed, with the salesperson seeing the same information as the client. The salesperson and her client could even use online instant messaging to communicate, if that was more convenient to the client. Databases enabled the sales staff to research prospects and products, and networking software allowed the sales staff to collaborate. For example, three of the agents worked simultaneously on a complex proposal to provide multiple products to a gynecology office—a proposal that was delivered within a short time frame and which WPG won.

RW Hooking Clients on an Extranet

When Ron was starting out in the business, brokers worked the phones. But financial companies had invested heavily in online producer productivity tools (such as those used by Inez in the preceding example). Ron made sure that NMFC provided all the necessary information to his broker clients via an extranet, including customizable proposals, pricing and commission information, "what-if" scenarios for multiple plan types, and a variety of other useful tools. Ron even convinced the home office to put a couple of sales-skills-building computer games on the site, and he'd noticed that brokers were playing them with other brokers at their firm. In fact, NMFC's was the most-often-used vendor extranet site among the brokers Ron covered.

Key: IG = Inez G., Insurance Group; RW = Ron W., Retirement Wholesaler; BDM = Bonnie-Dee M., Bank District Manager; FA = Frank A., Financial Adviser

BDM   Using the Internet to Drum Up Interest in SAIF

Bonnie-Dee did not initially think the Internet was a useful adjunct to the Silver Assets Investment Focus marketing program, because she thought most seniors did not have online access or made little use of it if they did. But ABC Bank's head of interactive marketing soon set her straight—some 22 percent of seniors nationwide* were busily surfing the Web for a raft of daily activities—and the wealthier the senior, the more likely they were to be online.

Information about SAIF and the calendar of breakfast seminars were immediately put up on ABC's website. Links to co-sponsors were requested and many co-sponsors also added information about the program on their own websites. The bank got in touch with websites visited by seniors in south Florida, both to request links to their sites and, in some cases, to place banner ads on their site. The bank even tested some paid search ads, which were to appear when users in targeted zip codes searched such terms as "interest rates," "investing," and the like. Surveys later showed that some 8 percent of attendees first learned about the SAIF program through the Internet.

FA   Multiple Online Applications

For the first year, Frank used the Internet primarily to gather and disseminate information. He found useful websites that he checked regularly, to keep up with new developments in his field, to check in with wholesalers to see what programs he might participate in, as background for the articles he wrote, and for other items of interest. He regularly communicated with his clients by e-mail, usually on a one-to-one basis. Once he had determined that a client preferred e-mail over the telephone, he used the Internet to remind them of tax deadlines, set up appointments, and keep them apprised of changes that affected their portfolios. He also sent copies of every article he wrote to an e-mail list of clients and prospects, along with a cover message. He found that keeping in touch this way, even if it wasn't fully customized, was a good use of his time. Several prospects called him (or took his call) in response to an article he had sent them.

Frank saw no need to create his own website until he began getting regular requests for copies of his articles. He decided to create a site—nothing fancy—using the free site-building tools and home page space provided by his ISP.

Once he had a site up, Frank decided to make more extensive use of it. He contracted with Google and Yahoo to buy keyword ads for any search containing both the words "529 Plan" and "Pennsylvania." He got permission to link his

---

* Pew Internet and American Life Project survey, February 2004.

site to other websites, listservs, and chat rooms concerned with college funding issues. The articles he put on his site also started getting hits, as they were discovered through searches. Within a very short time, Frank's site was getting more than one hundred hits a day and in the first six months, Frank got some twenty calls from people who had found him online.

Frank started posting an online newsletter and invited site visitors to sign up for an e-mail alert. Now Frank no longer had to print and mail hard copies of his newsletter, saving him nearly a thousand dollars per issue. Within six months, he had 1,200 subscribers and began accepting ads in the newsletter. The revenues were small because Frank only took ads he considered interesting and helpful to his clients. But the ads added interest to the newsletter and covered the salary of the college student he hired to manage it.

Personal Selling in Practice

This section refers to material discussed in chapter 9.

IG Leveraging Financial Resources through Co-Op

Inez G. wanted to increase her marketing spending, but she found it difficult to budget enough to cover all the activities she had planned. While attending a monthly meeting, she learned that the home office was launching a co-op program that would pay for up to two-thirds of her marketing expenses depending on the target market and the anticipated outcome. Inez had identified two local charities her group wanted to support as Platinum-level sponsors. In return she would receive the organization's mailing list, have an opportunity to address attendees during the opening session, and have WPG signage throughout the event. Based on the exposure WPG would receive, the home office agreed to fund 60 percent of the sponsorship event.

RW Producer Changes Benefit Wholesaler

Along with instituting new producer productivity software, the wire houses that Ron worked with were changing the nature of production. Clients were being segmented by asset size, and smaller accounts were being transferred to phone reps. Top producers were expected to handle only accounts with assets of $500,000 or more.

Key: IG = Inez G., Insurance Group; RW = Ron W., Retirement Wholesaler; BDM = Bonnie-Dee M., Bank District Manager; FA = Frank A., Financial Adviser

This change actually benefited Ron, whose target market was only the top producers and only those who handled small-business retirement plans. The fact that the phone reps were now segregated from customers did not matter, since Ron did not do business with them. And by giving up some of their smaller accounts, the top reps had more time to develop the small- and medium-sized business customers that bought Ron's retirement product. Therefore, Ron decided to put even more effort into helping his "A" level brokers increase the size of their own books of business.

BDM   Personal Selling at the SAIF Seminars

Bonnie-Dee worked with her branch managers and their staffs to ensure that each Silver Assets Investment Focus seminar had sufficient coverage. For fifty guests, there needed to be at least five branch sales staff available (including the branch manager and Bonnie-Dee or a member of her staff). One was seated at each table of ten. The responsibilities of the sales staff were to chat with the guests, to provide materials before the presentation began, and to answer any questions raised after the presentation. The salesperson also gave each guest his or her gift—the miniature bank, boxed and hand-wrapped, with a personalized card from the investment specialist. The salesperson was assigned to work with the investment specialist to follow up with each guest. Bonnie-Dee developed sales contests at both the branch and the individual level to further motivate all the branch staff, including the tellers.

FA   Uses of Co-Op Marketing Materials

Frank had been sticking closely to his marketing plan and he was pleased with the results to date. However, he also realized that he was spending much more than he initially planned or budgeted. As a way to offset some of his marketing costs, Frank looked into a co-op program offered to independent advisers by one of the wholesalers he worked with.

Because this company wanted to grow sales by 20 percent over the next twelve months, it would match, on a 50/50 basis, spending to promote its 529 Plan for education funding. All Frank had to do was submit an application and have it approved.

Since Frank already conducted six seminars a year on college funding, the 50 percent match enabled him to either hold twice as many seminars or continue as planned at half the cost.

Key: IG = *Inez G., Insurance Group;* RW = *Ron W., Retirement Wholesaler;* BDM = *Bonnie-Dee M., Bank District Manager;* FA = *Frank A., Financial Adviser*

Trade Shows and Seminars in Practice

This section refers to material discussed in chapter 10.

IG Reaching Decision Makers through Trade Shows

The Women's Planning Group had exhibited at a handful of trade shows over the past five years, with mixed results. But when Inez learned that the National Association of Women Business Owners was going to hold its national meeting in Chicago, she immediately signed up to exhibit. Here was an opportunity to speak directly with her target audience in an environment that was conducive to information sharing. Further, Inez contacted the national NAWBO headquarters to discuss how she could best leverage her exhibit and to determine the availability of attendee lists for mailings prior to the meeting. She asked about speaking opportunities for herself and her team, and explored hosting an on-site reception for local NAWBO attendees.

RW Using Seminars to Help Clients Build Their Business

National Mutual Fund Company offered a number of programs for top brokers who sold large amounts of the company's retirement product. These were designed to reward the brokers and to help them continue to build their business. Twice a year, selected brokers were invited to a resort, where they heard from big-name speakers, participated in business seminars, and were wined and dined by NMFC executives. Ron, of course, participated in these events with his clients. In addition, Ron held his own regional events, at local hotels and restaurants, for those brokers who did not qualify for the national events or who chose not to attend. He also brought in speakers, provided by NMFC, and set up seminars and courses designed to give brokers all the tools they needed to expand their small-business retirement assets.

BDM The SAIF Seminar

Preparations began six weeks before the date of each SAIF breakfast seminar. All branch staff were involved—hand writing invitations, making follow-up calls, making arrangements with the hotel and caterer, coordinating with the co-sponsor. Each branch received a checklist, outlining every step from "day –30" to "day +60," including timing of reminder calls ("day –5") and follow-up calls (by "day +3," "day +30," "day +60").

Key: IG = Inez G., Insurance Group; RW = Ron W., Retirement Wholesaler; BDM = Bonnie-Dee M., Bank District Manager; FA = Frank A., Financial Adviser

Although the breakfast seminars went smoothly for the most part, one last-minute glitch nearly sank the efforts of a Miami branch, which had a synagogue as co-sponsor. Nobody had thought to tell the caterer—who specialized in traditional Southern breakfasts with sausages and bacon—that the group required kosher food. The branch manager saved the day by calling around until she found a kosher restaurant that could accommodate the group at short notice.

Overall, the breakfasts were successful. Not only did sales of investment products soar, but ABC Bank received favorable publicity. Although the bank's contributions to its community co-sponsors totaled in the tens of thousands of dollars, the publicity and goodwill generated were worth millions.

FA   Exhibiting at a Trade Show

While attending a chamber of commerce meeting, Frank learned that in two months the local chapter of the American Bar Association would be holding a two-day conference and expo for its members at a nearby hotel. A limited number of exhibit booths would also be made available to local businesses. Frank immediately considered the possibilities. "This," he thought, "would provide an opportunity to get to know a large number of local attorneys." As a financial planner, Frank was always looking to develop business alliances and get referrals.

As soon as he returned to his office, he called the local chapter of the ABA to reserve a booth and determine where in the exhibit hall it would be located. Frank was pleased with the spot and paid for the exhibit space with his credit card. While he was on the phone, he asked the conference coordinator whether there was an opportunity for outside speakers or seminars. He learned that the speakers would all be ABA members and the ABA had booked all of the hotel's conference rooms for its own use. He did ask for, and was told he would receive, a list of all the attendees approximately three to four weeks before the conference began.

Although disappointed, Frank realized that he would never have been able to work a tradeshow and conduct a seminar at the same time. He saw that he was being overly ambitious. He just didn't have the time or staff to exploit both opportunities. He did decide, however, to print invitations to one of his upcoming seminars and make these available to attendees at the show.

Frank began developing his to-do list, which included:

● Purchase small logoed giveaway items
● Call some attorney friends to discuss the conference and possible opportunities

- Prepare an invitation for attendees to stop by his booth and enter a raffle
- Purchase raffle gift ($150 gift certificate to one of the newest and hottest restaurants)
- Create a special invitation to his next seminar on college funding

Once he completed his list, he considered how he would arrange his booth space. He decided that he wanted his 8' x 10' space to be as inviting as possible, so he would have only one table in the back of the booth with information. He had a tabletop display, highlighting his services, that he would set up on the display table. He also would rent some comfortable chairs so attendees could sit down while Frank spoke with them and so that other attendees could just stop by and take a break. He might even rent a coffee urn and serve coffee all day long, he thought.

Relationship Marketing in Practice

This section refers to material discussed in chapter 11.

IG   Creating Loyalty among the Best Clients

Inez G. knew she needed a process for communicating with her customers and prospects on a regular basis. She asked her team to build a database of prospect names based on attendees at the WPG's monthly seminars, those attending a speaking engagement of a WPG member, responses to the company's advertising, personal introductions, networking activities, and any other activity where information on a qualified lead was available.

The customer database was segmented by value of the account and type of product. Prospects were ranked on a subjective scale of 1 to 10 based on the agent's estimation of the individual's likelihood to buy and amount of prospective business.

Everyone on the database list received a bimonthly newsletter that included reprints of articles featuring the WPG and general financial planning articles of interest. In addition, the top 20 percent of customers and prospects received a phone call at least once a quarter. The next 30 percent were called twice a year. The bottom 50 percent received an annual "financial check-up" letter and a phone call. Inez ultimately hired a marketing person to manage the database and handle the mailings and other activities.

Key: IG = *Inez G., Insurance Group;* RW = *Ron W., Retirement Wholesaler;* BDM = *Bonnie-Dee M., Bank District Manager;* FA = *Frank A., Financial Adviser*

RW Building Relationships with Institutional Clients

Ron W. devoted half his marketing budget to relationship-building—that is, efforts to retain his broker clients, increase the amount of business they did with NMFC, and generate referrals to other brokers. Ron used a number of methods, described earlier, to maintain the relationships, such as his and NMFC's seminar program and extranet site. NMFC also created a quarterly newsletter full of useful selling information, special studies of the small-business market conducted on behalf of their clients, and other information that they continually made available to top brokers. Ron supplemented the home office material with his own online publication, which featured sales successes. For each brokerage firm, he produced a bimonthly e-letter that featured a broker who had made a large or complex sale, outlining the tactics the broker had used to get the business. Other brokers found this information helped them to make their own sales.

The biggest portion of Ron's retention marketing budget went to day-to-day activities, such as inviting client brokers and their clients to a sports event or dinner at a top restaurant. Ron had purchased corporate boxes for local sports teams, and if he wasn't available to meet and greet his guests, he'd pass along the tickets anyway. Ron wrote personal notes for special occasions, such as weddings, birth of children, and holidays. At one time, Ron gave his best clients thoughtful gifts, but compliance rules had become more strict and this was now frowned upon at most firms.

BDM Keeping SAIF Clients Happy

Bringing in so much new investment business with the SAIF breakfasts was a coup for Bonnie-Dee, but she knew that it was only the first step. Now she had to plan ways to keep her new clients happy in order to retain their business, get additional business from them, and get additional referrals.

With her senior managers' approval, Bonnie-Dee contracted with an investment education firm to create a special program for SAIF members. Called SAIF Harbor, the program consisted of several parts:

- A regular monthly late afternoon get-together for all SAIF members at a local yacht club. Each get-together featured an ABC Bank investment specialist speaker along with tea and sandwiches. The cost was low (the yacht club agreed to donate the space in the hopes of generating party business from the SAIF members), and those who attended (about 5–10 percent of members on any given day) were delighted to have an opportunity to meet one another.

Key: IG = *Inez G., Insurance Group;* RW = *Ron W., Retirement Wholesaler;* BDM = *Bonnie-Dee M., Bank District Manager;* FA = *Frank A., Financial Adviser*

- A regular newsletter called *The SAIF Voyager,* distributed quarterly by mail and monthly by e-mail. The newsletters, naturally, were designed with a nautical theme. One regular feature, called "The Captain's Table," offered a summary of the speaker's remarks at the monthly get-togethers, along with photos of those in attendance. Another, "Shipboard Chatter," offered news about members. Merchants were solicited to offer discounts to members, and these were publicized in the "Ship's Gift Shop." There was also information about ABC Bank—news releases, new products, and a regular economic insights column edited from white papers prepared by ABC Bank's chief economist. There was even a bridge column (called, naturally, "On the Bridge"), written on a voluntary basis by two SAIF members.
- Regular follow-up contacts. The investment adviser arranged a regular schedule of follow-ups with clients. Most clients chose a monthly call, which generally lasted between fifteen and thirty minutes. These calls were not only a big hit with SAIF members but resulted in significant new assets transferred to ABC Bank, along with a steady supply of referral business.

FA   Building a Loyal Individual Client Base

At the end of his first year, Frank examined his client base and prospect list, and divided it into two groups:

1   "A" list. These were both clients and prospects who were likely to be worth more than $10,000 a year in fee business.

2   "B" list. Those worth less than $10,000 per year.

Here is what Frank decided he should do for his "A" group:

- Personally handle all questions, returning any messages within twelve hours
- Call them at least once every two months
- Send them articles of interest about specific securities in their portfolio
- Keep a watch for any news of them in the local papers. Send letters, cards, or gifts for important events, such as weddings, birth of children, or deaths.
- Send birthday cards to the client and sometimes also to the client's spouse
- Invite the clients to annual charity golf outing which Frank co-sponsors
- If the clients were not golfers, invite them with their families to an amusement park for a charity outing which he also co-sponsors

For the remaining clients, Frank made sure that he or his assistant returned calls within twenty-four hours and that one of them called the client at least once every three months. In addition, he would:

- on regular calls, while inquiring about any changes/questions, ask the client for referrals to others who might be interested in Frank's services
- immediately send a thank you note after any referral
- if a referral was significant ("A level"), invite both referrer and new client to lunch at the club
- send a newsletter with general articles about college savings and other financial topics of interest to most of his clients
- send reprints of any articles by or about Frank
- send a personalized e-mail or printed card if he learns about a major event in the client's life
- keep an online, up-to-date record of all important client information, including names, ages, and birth dates of spouse and children, who referred them, whether this client has given any referrals, etc.
- send a personalized holiday greeting card (hand-signed by Frank or his assistant)

Conclusion

Using basic marketing principles can improve the efficiency and profitability of every sales effort. The authors look forward to engaging with those in the field through our website, www.fsmhandbook.com, where you will find additional examples, frequently asked questions, and more.

Key: IG = *Inez G., Insurance Group;* RW = *Ron W., Retirement Wholesaler;* BDM = *Bonnie-Dee M., Bank District Manager;* FA = *Frank A., Financial Adviser*

Index

About Bloomberg

Bloomberg L.P., founded in 1981, is a global information services, news, and media company. Headquartered in New York, the company has sales and news operations worldwide.

Bloomberg, serving customers on six continents, holds a unique position within the financial services industry by providing an unparalleled range of features in a single package known as the BLOOMBERG PROFESSIONAL® service. By addressing the demand for investment performance and efficiency through an exceptional combination of information, analytic, electronic trading, and Straight Through Processing tools, Bloomberg has built a worldwide customer base of corporations, issuers, financial intermediaries, and institutional investors.

BLOOMBERG NEWS®, founded in 1990, provides stories and columns on business, general news, politics, and sports to leading newspapers and magazines throughout the world. BLOOMBERG TELEVISION®, a 24-hour business and financial news network, is produced and distributed globally in seven different languages. BLOOMBERG RADIO℠ is an international radio network anchored by flagship station BLOOMBERG® 1130 (WBBR-AM) in New York.

In addition to the BLOOMBERG PRESS® line of books, Bloomberg publishes *BLOOMBERG MARKETS*® and *BLOOMBERG WEALTH MANAGER*®. To learn more about Bloomberg, call a sales representative at:

London:..... +44-20-7330-7500
New York: ... +1-212-318-2000
Tokyo: ...... +81-3-3201-8900

FOR IN-DEPTH MARKET INFORMATION and news, visit the Bloomberg website at **www.bloomberg.com**, which draws from the news and power of the BLOOMBERG PROFESSIONAL® service and Bloomberg's host of media products to provide high-quality news and information in multiple languages on stocks, bonds, currencies, and commodities.

About the Authors

Evelyn Ehrlich, Ph.D., is president of EC Communications, a firm specializing in financial marketing strategy and communications since 1982. Its clients have included Bear Stearns, Deutsche Bank, Dreyfus, J. P. Morgan Chase, Merrill Lynch, New York Life, Prudential, UBS, and many other financial institutions. EC Communications (http://www.eccommunications.com) offers communications planning and support in all media for both business-to-business and consumer markets.

Dr. Ehrlich has a B.A. from Barnard College and a M.S. from Columbia University, and received her Ph.D. from New York University. She has taught at the University of Vermont and the City University of New York, in addition to New York University, where she currently teaches financial services marketing with her co-author. She is active in the Financial Women's Association and the Financial Communications Society and has done pro bono work for the Chamber Music Society of Lincoln Center and the New York City Greenmarkets. Dr. Ehrlich lives in New York City.

Louis "Duke" Fanelli is vice president for local market development at AXA Financial, Inc., New York, a leading, diversified, financial management and advisory group. He is responsible for multicultural marketing and corporate sponsorship and event marketing, as well as overseeing local marketing support to the company's sixty-plus branches throughout the country. Prior to joining AXA Financial in 1998, Duke spent nearly fifteen years at J. P. Morgan Chase. At Chase he had market development responsibilities on both the business and marketing side of the bank's retail operations. This included marketing communications, sales management of its corporate mobile banking services, market segmentation communication and planning, and local marketing.

Earlier in his career, he worked as a public relations account executive and began his career as a journalist with *Advertising Age*. He holds a B.A. in journalism from American University, Washington, D.C.

THE AUTHORS' WEBSITE, **www.fsmhandbook.com**, contains additional resources including a calendar of upcoming events, additional case studies, source documents, and a free online newsletter.